The Best of

PAPER CRAFTS

MAGAZINE ®

LEISURE ARTS
the art of everyday living
www.leisurearts.com

PAPER CRAFTS

Find us on
Facebook

Follow us on
twitter

www.PaperCraftsMag.com

www.PaperCraftsConnection.com

The Best of
Paper Crafts
MAGAZINE®

Editorial

Editor-in-Chief Jennifer Schaerer

Managing Editor Brandy Jesperson

Creative Editor Cath Edvalson

Editors Susan R. Opel, P. Kelly Smith

Design

Art Director Matt Anderson

Graphic Designer Holly Mills

Photography bpd Studios

Offices

Editorial
Paper Crafts magazine
14850 Pony Express Rd., Suite 200
Bluffdale, UT 84065-4801

Phone 801-816-8300

Fax 801-816-8302

E-mail *editor@PaperCraftsMag.com*

Web site *www.PaperCraftsMag.com*

Published by Leisure Arts, Inc., 5701 Ranch Drive, Little Rock, Arkansas
72223-9633. 501-868-8800. *www.leisurearts.com*

Library of Congress Control Number: 2010930705
ISBN-13/EAN: 978-1-60900-077-6

Leisure Arts Staff

Editor-in-Chief Susan White Sullivan
Quilt and Craft Publications Director Cheryl Johnson
Special Projects Director Susan Frantz Wiles
Senior Prepress Director Mark Hawkins
Publishing Systems Administrator Becky Riddle
Publishing Systems Assistant Clint Hanson
Mac Information Technology Specialist Robert Young

President & Chief Executive Officer Rick Barton
Vice President and Chief Operations Officer Tom Siebenmorgen
Director of Finance and Administration Laticia Mull Dittrich
National Accounts Director Martha Adams
Information Technology Director Hermine Linz
Controller Francis Caple
Vice President, Operations Jim Dittrich
Retail Customer Service Manager Stan Raynor
Print Production Manager Fred F. Pruss

Printed in U.S.A.

Posted under Canadian Publication Agreement Number 0551724

Creative Crafts Group, LLC

President and CEO: Stephen J. Kent

VP/Group Publisher: Tina Battock

Chief Financial Officer: Mark F. Arnett

Corporate Controller: Jordan Bohrer

VP/Publishing Director: Joel P. Toner

VP/Director of Events: Paula Kraemer

VP/Production & Technology: Derek W. Corson

Visit our web sites:

www.PaperCraftsMag.com
www.PaperCraftsConnection.com
www.MoxieFabWorld.com

PUBLICATION—*Paper Crafts*™ (ISSN 1548-5706) (USPS 506250) Vol. 33, is published 6 times per year in Jan/Feb, Mar/Apr, May/June, Jul/Aug, Sept/Oct and Nov/Dec, by Creative Crafts Group, LLC, 741 Corporate Circle, Suite A, Golden CO 80401. Periodicals postage paid at Salt Lake City, UT and additional mailing offices.

REPRINT PERMISSION—For information on obtaining reprints and excerpts, please contact Wright's Reprints at 877/652-5295. (Customers outside the U.S. and Canada should call 281/419-5725.)

TRADEMARKED NAMES mentioned in this book may not always be followed with a trademark symbol. The names are used only in an editorial fashion and to the benefit of the trademark owner, with no intention of infringement of the trademark.

PROJECTS—*Paper Crafts* magazine believes these projects are reliable when made, but none are guaranteed. Due to different climatic conditions and variations in materials, *Paper Crafts* disclaims any liability for untoward results in doing the projects represented. Use of the magazine does not guarantee successful results. We provide this information WITHOUT WARRANTY OF ANY KIND, EXPRESSED, IMPLIED, OR STATUTORY; AND WE SPECIFICALLY DISCLAIM ANY IMPLIED WARRANTIES OF MERCHANTABILITY OR FITNESS FOR A PARTICULAR PURPOSE. Also, we urge parents to supervise young children carefully in their participation in any of these projects.

Make a paper crafting connection!

We're celebrating six fun and creative years of *Paper Crafts* magazine, and we're just delighted to bring you this collection of our favorite projects over the years. Our magazine was built around a community – a grassroots community of paper crafting voices and talent at all levels – and you'll see exactly what that means as you stroll through the garden of inspiration in these pages. You'll find everything from trends and techniques to cards, gifts and creative food wraps that are perfect for everyone on your list.

Looking for a particular occasion? We've got that covered too, with a comprehensive index at the back of the book. The next time you need a little something special for a coach or neighbor, a birthday or anniversary, a new baby or recent graduate, or no reason other than you are thinking of someone, you'll find all the ideas you'll need right here.

So go ahead and show those who mean the most to you that a little creativity and paper, crafted with a heartfelt connection, is a gift that means the most.

Jennif

Note: Because these projects are from past issues, some products may not be available. Luckily, the Internet provides a wonderful way to search for similar items so you can still create a beautiful project using these inspiring techniques. So, if you can't find a product, use your creativity to adapt the project or find a replacement.

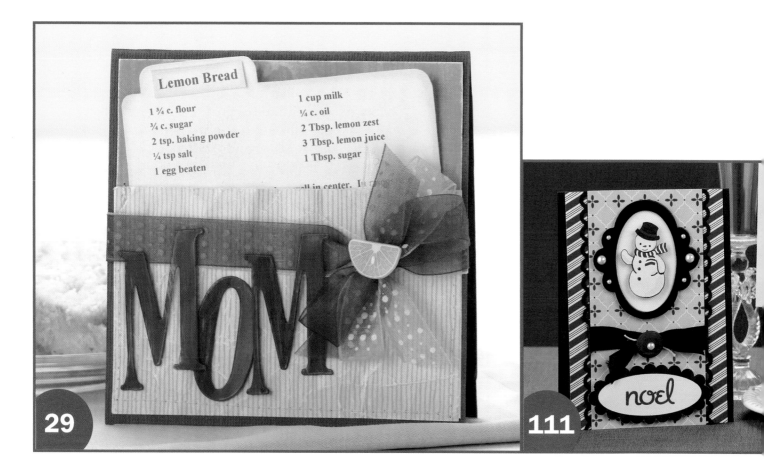

Contents

Gourmet Goodies

Delicious recipes paired with coordinating
paper crafted cards, tags, parties, and gifts.

Pudding Filled Chocolate Cupcakes Stace Hasagawa

This recipe was inspired by my Grandma H., who used to like to hide pudding inside cupcakes as a little surprise for us. She is turning 100 this year!

INGREDIENTS

Cupcakes:

1 pkg. chocolate cake mix

2 tbsp. cherry extract

Vanilla pudding

Approx. 30 frozen pitted cherries

Sugar

Frosting:

1 lb. confectioner's sugar

1 c. butter

1 tsp. cherry extract

1–2 tsp. milk

1 tbsp. meringue powder

2 tbsp. cocoa powder

YIELDS APPROX. 30 CUPCAKES

DIRECTIONS Prepare cake mix, following instructions on package. Add cherry extract. Bake in cupcake papers as directed; cool. Defrost cherries; sweeten with sugar to taste. Cut dime-size circle from top of each cupcake; scoop cake from center and fill with pudding and one cherry. Fill hole with scooped cake.

FOR FROSTING Cream butter; slowly add sugar and meringue powder. Add milk until smooth consistency. Spoon approx. ¼ c. of frosting in piping bag for decorating. Add 2 tbsp. cooking chocolate to remaining frosting. Frost cupcakes. Decorate with frosting in piping bag.

SUPPLIES: *Cardstock:* (Greenbriar, Pinecone, Red, White) Bazzill Basics Paper *Patterned paper:* (Princess Pink Polka Dot/Princess Pink Stripe) Bo-Bunny Press *Paint:* (pink) *Fibers:* (pink polka dot ribbon) Michaels; (brown satin ribbon) My Mind's Eye *Font:* (Freeze) www.abstractfonts.com *Adhesive:* (foam dots) Plaid *Tools:* (tag punch) EK Success; (¼" rectangle punch, paper crimper) Fiskars; (1", ⅛" circle punches) Marvy Uchida *Other:* (gift bag) Nicole Crafts; (wood skewer) **Finished sizes:** invitation 6" square, goody bag 5½" x 9", poke 3½" x 4" (cupcake top)

5 STEPS Cupcake Party Designer: Dee Gallimore-Perry

CUPCAKE 1 Prepare cupcake pieces, following pattern. 2 Adhere frosting to liner. Punch sprinkles from Princess Pink Polka Dot paper and White cardstock; adhere. 3 To make cherry, punch 1" circle from Red cardstock; adhere ⅛" circle punched from White. Cut slit for stem; insert end of stem and adhere in place behind cherry. Adhere cherry.

INVITATION 1 Make card from Pinecone cardstock. 2 Adhere slightly smaller piece of Princess Pink Polka Dot paper. 3 Print "A birthday party!" on White cardstock, trim and adhere. 4 Make and adhere cupcake.

CUPCAKE POKES 1 Cut skewers to desired length. Paint; let dry. 2 Make cupcake and adhere to skewer. Prepare second liner piece, following pattern; adhere behind skewer for reinforcement. 3 Print guest's name on White cardstock; punch into tag and tie to skewer with ribbon.

GOODY BAG 1 Cover bag front with Pinecone cardstock. 2 Adhere slightly smaller piece of Princess Pink Polka Dot paper. 3 Print "Thank you for coming!" repeatedly on White cardstock; trim and adhere to bag. 4 Make and adhere cupcake. 5 Tie ribbon on handle.

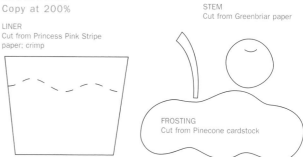

CUPCAKE PATTERN
Copy at 200%

LINER
Cut from Princess Pink Stripe paper; crimp

STEM
Cut from Greenbriar paper

FROSTING
Cut from Pinecone cardstock

Cupcake Box

Designer: Stace Hasegawa

INSTRUCTIONS

1 Cut box lid in half and tape outside rim to box. **2** Cover box with patterned paper (see Figures a–b below). **3** Cut circle from cardstock; cut in half and adhere to each side of lid. **4** Stitch buttons to lid with ribbon, leaving 8" long ribbon tail on one button. Tie tag to tail. Note: Wind tail around buttons to close box. **5** Line inside of box with cardstock (see Figure c). **6** Trim page protector to fit bottom of box; place inside to protect box from grease.

Cupcake Box Diagram

a

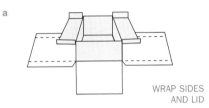

WRAP SIDES
AND LID

b

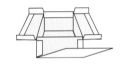

WRAP FRONT AND BACK

c

FOLD CARDSTOCK; LINE BOX

SUPPLIES: *Cardstock:* (red) *Patterned paper:* (Olive Beach Dot from Sun Room collection) Chatterbox *Accents:* (metal-rimmed tag) Jo-Ann Stores; (white buttons) *Fibers:* (white satin ribbon) Offray *Adhesive:* (heavy-duty tape) *Tools:* (circle cutter) *Other:* (paper mache box, page protector) **Finished size: 8½" x 8½" x 4"**

Chocolate Card

Designer: Wendy Sue Anderson

INSTRUCTIONS

1 Make card from Brown cardstock. **2** Adhere piece of patterned paper. **3** Cut piece of Brown; round corners and adhere. **4** Print sentiment on white cardstock. Trim, round corners, and highlight words with yellow pencil. Attach to card with brads. **5** Adhere die cut with foam squares.

SUPPLIES: *Cardstock:* (Brown) Bazzill Basics Paper; (white) *Patterned paper:* (Yellow Plaid) O'Scrap! *Color medium:* (yellow pencil) Faber-Castell *Accents:* (yellow brads) Doodlebug Design; (sun die cut) O'Scrap! *Fonts:* (Arriere Garde) www.stereo-type.net; (An Accidental Kiss) www.abstractfonts.com *Adhesive:* (foam squares) Making Memories *Tools:* (corner rounder punch) EK Success **Finished size: 5½" x 4½"**

Dessert Sushi <small>Stace Hasegawa</small>

Decorate cake pieces to resemble your favorite kind of sushi. Whether your guests are sushi fans or not, they'll love this sweet treat.

INGREDIENTS

Cheesecake or pound cake, cut into rectangles

2 c. strawberries, raspberries, and/or other seasonal fruits

5 tbsp. complementary jam

Fruit roll (optional)

YIELDS 15–25 PIECES

DIRECTIONS Top cake pieces with fruit slices and jam. Wrap with small strip of fruit roll, if desired.

SUPPLIES: *Patterned paper:* (Cherry-Go-Round, Freshly Squeezed from Fruit Stand collection) SEI *Accents:* (fruit tag die cuts) SEI; (black staples, pink fabric-covered brad, white flowers, you're invited label) Making Memories; (pink brad) Heidi Swapp *Rub-ons:* (berry sweet, shower) SEI; (baby, sweet baby) Making Memories; (Outline alphabet, pink dotted line, pink frame) KI Memories; (Bordeaux, Bordeaux Mix alphabets) Heidi Swapp *Stickers:* (cherry, Fruit Stand alphabet, labels, tab) SEI *Fibers:* (light green, light green/pink, strawberry patterned ribbon) SEI; (green polka dot ribbon) May Arts *Font:* (your choice) *Tools:* (⅛" circle punch) *Other:* (baby shoe pattern) www.bydonovan.com; (sandpaper) **Finished sizes: invitation 4" x 9½", napkin ring approx. 3" wide, baby shoe favor 3" x 3" x 5"**

⁵ STEPS Berry Sweet Baby Shower Designer: Nichol Magouirk

INVITATION 1 Cut invitation background piece from pink side of Freshly Squeezed paper; cut two slits in top to create band. **2** Wrap green polka dot ribbon around band; staple in place. **3** Cut invitation from Cherry-Go-Round paper; print "To a" on green side. **4** Decorate with stickers and rub-ons. **5** Punch holes along bottom border. **6** Tuck under band.

NAPKIN RING 1 Apply rub-ons to fruit tag die cut. **2** Thread ribbon through holes and tie behind napkin.

BABY SHOE FAVOR 1 Download and print baby shoe pattern; cut from Cherry-Go-Round paper. **2** Stitch edges of main shoe piece. **3** Assemble shoe as instructed on pattern, with green side of paper facing out. **4** Tie green polka dot ribbon into bow; attach flowers and bow to shoe with pink brad. **5** Attach fabric-covered brad to end of shoe strap. **6** Sand edges of cherry sticker; affix to back of shoe.

BONUS IDEA

Create a shower centerpiece made from square boxes decorated with ribbon and baby motifs. Arrange the boxes to resemble toy blocks.

Asian Tray & Chopsticks Wrap

Designer: Stace Hasegawa

TRAY **1** Cut 5" x 7" piece of vellum. **2** Stamp; let dry. Color with pencil. **3** Fold each side back ¾". **4** Fold corners out diagonally and adhere together to make triangles. **5** To make tray stand, cut top and legs from foam core board. Cover with Parchment Tan paper. **6** Adhere legs under top at slight angle.

CHOPSTICKS WRAP Cut 1" square of Asian Writing paper and wrap around chopsticks pair. Tie in place with ribbon.

SUPPLIES: *Patterned paper:* (Parchment Tan) The Paper Company; (Asian Writing) Hot Off The Press *Vellum:* (white) *Rubber stamp:* (Cherry Blossom) Delta *Solvent ink:* (black) *Color medium:* (pink pencil) *Fibers:* (burgundy) *Other:* (foam core board, chopsticks) **Finished sizes:** tray 3½" x 5½" x ¾", tray stand 3 ¾" x 5" x 1¼"

SUPPLIES: *Cardstock:* (purple, white) *Patterned paper:* (Hip Hop Wide Stripes from Rhythmz Paperz collection) Junkitz *Accents:* (assorted buttons) *Stickers:* (white alphabet) EK Success *Fibers:* (green gingham ribbon) Offray *Font:* (Century Gothic) Microsoft **Finished size:** 3½" x 6¼"

Congratulations Tag

Designer: Wendy Johnson

INSTRUCTIONS **1** Make tag from purple cardstock. **2** Adhere strip of Hip Hop Wide Stripes paper to tag. **3** Adhere strip of white cardstock above patterned paper. **4** Adhere alphabet stickers and buttons. **5** Attach ribbon to top of tag; adhere button. **6** Print "celebrate" on white cardstock, trim and adhere.

BONUS IDEAS

Using this adorable tag to top a beautiful plate of dessert sushi is a great gift for anyone celebrating a promotion at work, the passing of a difficult exam or any number of special occasions.

Chocolate Raspberry Truffle Cake Alisa Bangerter

This recipe was shared with me years ago by Diane Burton. It still remains a very popular treat in my home.

INGREDIENTS

Cake:

1¼ c. semisweet chocolate chips

½ c. butter or margarine

¾ c. brown sugar

2 eggs

2 tbsp. water

½ tsp. baking powder

¾ c. flour

Truffle Topping:

1 c. semisweet chocolate chips (melted and cooled)

1 (8 oz.) pkg. cream cheese, softened

¼ c. powdered sugar

⅓ c. seedless red raspberry jam

Glaze:

¼ c. semisweet chocolate chips

1 tsp. shortening

YIELDS 9 SERVINGS

DIRECTIONS Melt chocolate with margarine. Cool. Beat eggs and sugar. Add chocolate and water; mix. Stir in flour and baking powder. Bake in well-greased and floured 8" square or 9" round or heart-shaped cake pan at 350 degrees for 30–35 minutes.

FOR TRUFFLE TOPPING Beat cream cheese and powdered sugar; add jam and beat. Beat in melted chocolate chips. Spread over cooled brownies.

FOR GLAZE Melt chocolate chips with shortening. Drizzle over cream cheese layer.

Chill at least 2 hours before serving. Garnish with fresh raspberries, if in season.

SUPPLIES: *Cardstock:* (Chocolate) Prism; (white) *Patterned paper:* (Pink With White Stitches, Pink/Orange Small Flowers) The Paper Studio *Accents:* (pewter photo hangers, brads, label holder) Stampin' Up!; (chipboard blocks) Bazzill Basics Paper; (pink flowers) Doodlebug Design; (pink patterned brads) Queen & Co. *Fibers:* (red gingham ribbon, pink rickrack) Making Memories *Fonts:* (Futura) www.linotype.com; (Georgia) Microsoft *Adhesive:* (foam dots) Stampin' Up! *Tools:* (⅛" circle punch) *Other:* (metal pail, sandpaper) **Finished sizes: invitation 4" square, place card 3" x 2", treat pail 3½" diameter x 3" height**

Girl Talk Party
Designer: Nichole Heady

INVITATION 1 To make covers, adhere Chocolate cardstock to front of two chipboard blocks; sand edges. **2** For front cover, adhere piece of Pink/Orange Small Flowers paper and rickrack to one block. Sand edges. **3** Print "You're invited to an afternoon of girl talk" and party date on white cardstock. Trim and adhere label holder over date. Adhere piece to front cover with foam dots. Attach flowers together with brad; adhere. **4** Cover inside of covers with Pink With White Stitches paper. Adhere strip of Pink/Orange Small Flowers. **5** Print party details on white; trim and adhere. **6** Attach two photo hangers to edge of each cover with brads. Tie covers together with ribbon.

PLACE CARD 1 Make place card from Chocolate cardstock. **2** Adhere strip of Pink/Orange Small Flowers paper and rickrack. **3** Print guest's name on white cardstock; trim and adhere with foam dots. **4** Attach flowers together with brad; adhere. **5** Punch hole in corner and tie with ribbon.

TREAT PAIL 1 Cut Pink/Orange Small Flowers paper in hexagonal shape to fit front of pail; mat with Chocolate cardstock. Adhere. **2** Print "Girl talk" and party date on white cardstock; trim and adhere with foam dots. **3** Tie ribbon on handles. **4** Fill with party favors.

SUPPLIES: *Cardstock:* (Green Tea) Bazzill Basics Paper; (dark pink) *Patterned paper:* (Fun Dots, Stripes from Chocolate collection) EK Success *Accents:* (tinsel trim) Hollywood Ribbon Industries *Fonts:* (Bodoni MT Black, Century Gothic) www.myfonts.com *Other:* (party horn, cone hat) Amscan; (staples) **Finished sizes:** invitation 6" x 8", party horn 1¾" diameter x 9"height, cone hat 7" diameter x 14" height

5 STEPS New Year's Party Designer: Julie Medeiros

INVITATION 1 Make invitation from Green Tea cardstock. Cut edge of front flap into curve. **2** Adhere piece of Stripes paper to inside of back flap. **3** Adhere Fun Dots paper to front flap. **4** Print "Out with the old in with the new" on Green Tea; trim and mat with dark pink cardstock. Adhere to invitation. **5** Adhere trim to edge of front flap. **6** Print party details on Green Tea. Trim, mat with dark pink, and adhere inside card.

PARTY HORN 1 Wrap Stripes paper around party horn; adhere. **2** Adhere trim around both ends.

CONE HAT 1 Take apart hat; lie flat and cover outside of hat with Fun Dots paper. **2** Staple trim along bottom edge of hat. **3** Reassemble hat. Add more adhesive, if necessary. **4** Insert one end of several lengths of trim into top hole of hat. Adhere or staple in place.

BONUS IDEA

Wear shimmering top hats to welcome the New Year. Just spray them with gold paint and trim with patterned paper.

Great Grandma Jessie's Sour Cream Pound Cake Valerie Pingree

As a child, my brother, Doug, would request this cake for his birthday. Sadly, he passed away in a car accident years ago. My mom still makes this cake each year to commemorate his birthday.

INGREDIENTS

1 c. unsalted butter

3 c. sugar

6 eggs separated; at room temperature

¼ tsp. cream of tartar

3 c. sifted cake flour

¼ tsp. baking soda

¼ tsp. salt

1 tsp. vanilla extract

1 c. sour cream

6 cup mini fluted mold, Wilton Excelle Elite series

YIELDS APPROX. 12 SERVINGS

DIRECTIONS Separate eggs; beat and peak egg whites and cream of tartar. Set aside. Cream butter and sugar; add vanilla extract. Beat in egg yolks one at a time. Lightly sift together soda, salt, and flour with wire whisk. Alternately add flour mixture and sour cream to butter mixture in small parts. Fold in egg whites. Pour into greased and floured tube pan. Bake at 300 degrees for 70-90 minutes. Remove from oven. Rest pan on bottle to cool. Flip onto cooling rack after 15 minutes.

SUPPLIES: *Cardstock:* (Blue, Evening Surf, Guacamole) Bazzill Basics Paper *Patterned paper:* (Baby Shower Flowers, Baby Boy Dots, Baby Boy Stripes) Sandylion; (Kiwi Sherbet Dotz) Me & My Big Ideas *Stickers:* (baby motifs, baby letters, border strips, shower words) Sandylion *Fibers:* (green grosgrain ribbon) American Crafts *Adhesive:* (foam dots) *Other:* (gift bag) DMD, Inc.; (wood flower) Provo Craft; (sandpaper) **Finished sizes:** invitation 6" x 4", flower approx. 3¼" diameter, bag 5½" x 8¾"

5 STEPS Pastel Baby Shower Designer: Sara Horton

INVITATION 1 Make card from Evening Surf cardstock. **2** Adhere strip of Baby Boy Dots to bottom. **3** Affix baby, shower, and flower border stickers. **4** Cut flower from Baby Shower Flowers paper; adhere to card with foam dot.

FLOWER 1 Trace wood flower on patterned paper; trim and adhere. **2** Sand edges. **3** Affix baby motif sticker.

GIFT BAG 1 Cover bag front with Guacamole cardstock. **2** Adhere slightly smaller piece of Kiwi Sherbet Dotz paper. **3** Affix congratulations sticker to Blue cardstock; adhere. **4** Affix striped border strip sticker. **5** Cut flower from Baby Shower Flowers paper; adhere to bag with foam dot. **6** Thread ribbon through tag sticker; tie to bag handle. Affix sticker to bag.

DESIGNER TIPS

• Decorate several flowers to sprinkle on the table or place in a clear vase as a shower decoration.

• Use the flower as a baby gift tag.

• Attach the flower to a card, album cover, or picture frame.

BONUS IDEA

Decorate the cover of a baby album for the mom-to-be.

Apple Crisp <small>Heather D. White</small>

This recipe is divine—and extra yummy when served with vanilla ice cream on top.

INGREDIENTS

4 c. apples (peeled and sliced)

½ c. water

1 tsp. cinnamon

1 c. sugar

¾ c. flour

7 tbsp. butter

YIELDS 10 SERVINGS

DIRECTIONS Coat 9" x 13" pan with cooking spray. Add apples; pour water and cinnamon over apples. Combine sugar, flour, and butter with fingers until crumbly; spread over apples. Bake uncovered at 400 degrees for 30–45 minutes.

Teachers deserve much gratitude.

Thank you!

Teacher Gratitude Card

Designer: Amber Crosby

INSTRUCTIONS 1 Make card from Green Tea cardstock. **2** Print sentiment on White cardstock. Trim, round corners, and attach to card with brads. **3** Cut rectangle from each patterned paper; round corners and adhere.
4 Adhere flower and coin.

SUPPLIES: *Cardstock:* (Green Tea, White) Bazzill Basics Paper *Patterned paper:* (Multi Diamonds on White, Small Multi Flower Whimsy from Festivale collection) Scenic Route Paper Co. *Accents:* (red leather flower, thank you enamel coin) Making Memories; (green brads) Die Cuts With a View *Fonts:* (Century Gothic) www.myfonts.com; (Cezanne) www.p22.com *Tools:* (corner rounder punch) Carl Manufacturing **Finished size: 5¼" x 6½"**

A Recipe for a
Warm Welcome...

Warm Welcome Card

Designer: Michelle Tardie

INSTRUCTIONS 1 Make card from cardstock, ink edges. **2** Adhere pieces of Red Floral, Red Gingham, and Orange Stripes paper to card. **3** Apply rub-on stitching. **4** Print "A recipe for a warm welcome . . ." on School Paper; trim and adhere to card. **5** Attach brad. **6** Adhere pie sticker with foam tape. Affix rolling pin sticker.

SUPPLIES: *Cardstock:* (Ciliega) Prism *Patterned paper:* (Red Gingham, School Paper from Wisdom Way collection; Red Floral from Sun Drenched Square collection; Orange Stripes from Courage Corner collection) Homespun Harvest *Pigment ink:* (Black) Clearsnap *Accents:* (antique copper decorative brad) Making Memories *Rub-ons:* (black stitching) Die Cuts With a View *Stickers:* (rolling pin, pie) Provo Craft *Fonts:* (Courier) Microsoft *Adhesive:* (foam tape) **Finished size: 5" square**

Coconut Goddess Cake

Ana Cabrera

This recipe is an adaptation of English trifle (cake, pudding, cream, and fruit). I wanted to have a cake that featured the tropical flavors that I love from the Philippines, my home country. The challenge was coming up with something easy enough for everyday—and this is it. As for the name, Coconut Goddess is my nickname, so this is my signature cake.

INGREDIENTS

1 pkg. yellow cake mix
1 can crushed pineapple
1 c. sugar
2 small boxes instant French vanilla pudding
1 tub whipped topping
1½ c. shredded coconut

DIRECTIONS

Prepare cake following package directions for 13" x 9" cake. While cake is baking, pour pineapple, including juice, into small saucepan. Add sugar. Heat over medium heat until sugar dissolves completely. Bring to a boil, then immediately remove from heat. When cake is done, remove from oven. Using a fork, poke holes in cake about ½" apart. Slather cake with pineapple and juices. Let cool completely.

Make pudding following directions. Let set up in fridge. Spread coconut onto a baking sheet and toast in oven at 325 degrees. *Note: Be sure to stir the coconut often.* Allow coconut to get a light brown, with some bits still white.

Once the cake is completely cool, spread pudding over pineapple layer. Then, spread whipped topping over the top of the pudding and sprinkle with coconut. Chill for one hour.

INVITATION 1 Open 3½" x 7" project in software. Drop in flourishes, draw border. Type sentiments and print on cardstock. Make card from printed piece. **2** Cut cardstock to finished size. Adhere slightly smaller patterned paper piece. **3** Adhere ends of felt scroll, butterfly die cut, and flat marbles. Slide card under scroll.

BUCKET 1 Adhere patterned paper strips to bucket. **2** Adhere felt scrolls and butterfly die cuts. **3** Adhere flat marbles.

WASHCLOTH WRAP 1 Insert photo in bracelet. **2** Roll towel. Wrap bracelet around towel. **3** Adhere felt scrolls and flat marbles to butterfly die cut. **4** Insert completed butterfly behind bracelet.

YOU'RE INVITED

SUPPLIES: *Cardstock:* (teal, cream) Die Cuts With a View *Patterned paper:* (Word Fresco from Mira collection) K&Company *Accents:* (red, orange, green, blue, purple, brown, white epoxy flat marbles) The Robin's Nest; (butterfly die cuts) K&Company; (blue felt scrolls) Queen & Co. *Digital elements:* (flourishes from Rhonna Swirls kit) www.twopeasinabucket.com *Fonts:* (Scriptina) www.dafont.com; (Algerian Condensed) www.myfonts.com *Software:* (photo editing) *Other:* (red photo bracelet) Making Memories; (metal bucket, teal washcloth, photo) **Finished sizes: invitation 4" x 9¾", bucket 6¾" diameter x 5¾" height, washcloth wrap 5¾" x 4¾"**

Sunday Pie Brenda Peterson

Sunday Pie has been a family tradition for as long as I can remember. It is easy to make and is also very versatile. I have made it for Sunday dinner dessert, as well as dressed it up with chocolate shavings and put fresh berries on top for a dinner party.

INGREDIENTS

1 c. flour
1 cube butter
1 tbsp. sugar
1 tbsp. vanilla flavoring
1 pkg. (8 oz.) cream cheese
1 c. Cool Whip topping
1 c. powdered sugar
1 small box chocolate instant pudding
1 small box vanilla instant pudding
2½ c. cold milk

DIRECTIONS Mix flour, butter, sugar, and vanilla flavoring together with pastry blender. Sprinkle into 9" x 13" baking pan and press. Bake at 350 degrees for 20 minutes. Cool.

In medium bowl, mix cream cheese, Cool Whip topping, and powdered sugar together. Spread over cooled crust.

In large bowl, mix chocolate pudding, vanilla pudding, and milk together until pudding is thick. Spread over cream cheese/Cool Whip topping layer. Refrigerate 1 to 2 hours before serving.

Serving suggestions: Top with Cool Whip topping, chocolate shavings, and/or fresh berries.

YIELDS APPROX. 16-24 SERVINGS.

Father's Day Card & Photo Cube Designer: Jessica Witty

CARD 1 Make card from cardstock. **2** Adhere patterned paper. **3** Cut strips of patterned paper; staple together. Sand edges and adhere. **4** Stamp It's Good To Be King on cardstock. Trim, mat with patterned paper, sand edges, and adhere. **5** Tie ribbon on clip. Attach clip to card. **6** Write "Happy Father's Day" with marker.

PHOTO BLOCK 1 In software, crop and resize five photos to 3½" square. Print photos on specialty paper. Trim, sand edges, and adhere to block. **2** Cut square of patterned paper. Sand edges and adhere to block. **3** Embellish as desired with stickers, ribbon, and patterned paper strips. **4** Write sentiment and names using marker.

SUPPLIES: *Cardstock:* (Whisper White, kraft) Stampin' Up! *Patterned paper:* (Grey Grid on White, Worn Lined from Background collection) Scenic Route; (Organized One Word from Choices I collection) KI Memories; (Fresh Linens Green Plaid from Front Porch collection) My Mind's Eye *Specialty paper:* (photo) *Rubber stamps:* (It's Good to be King) Inkadinkado *Dye ink:* (Bashful Blue, Chocolate Chip) Stampin' Up! *Color medium:* (brown marker) *Accents:* (paper clip, silver staples) *Stickers:* (kraft words) Making Memories *Fibers:* (green/white striped ribbon) May Arts *Software:* (photo editing) *Adhesive:* (decoupage) Plaid *Other:* (block)
Finished sizes: card 5½" x 4¼", photo block 3½" cube

Mint Chocolate Frozen Dessert Wendy Gallamore

This is a variation of a dessert recipe that I had at a book group meeting.

INGREDIENTS

½ gallon chocolate chip mint ice cream
1 pkg. Oreo cookies
⅓ c. sugar
½ c. melted butter or margarine
1 jar (16 oz.) hot fudge
1 tub (8 oz.) Cool Whip topping

DIRECTIONS Set ice cream out to soften. Crush cookies; mix with melted butter or margarine and sugar. Spread in 9" x 13" pan and freeze 20 minutes, reserving 1 c. of mixture. Spread hot fudge over crust (let stand in hot water 10 minutes to soften). Freeze 20 minutes. Spread ice cream over hot fudge; freeze 20 minutes. Spread Cool Whip on top. Drizzle hot fudge and sprinkle remaining crumb mixture over the top. Freeze until ready to serve.

1 Fold cardstock in half; cut circle card. **2** Cut 6¼" and slightly smaller circles from patterned paper; layer and adhere. **3** Cut patterned paper strips; adhere. **4** Punch circles from cardstock to make bear. Assemble and adhere. Cut patterned paper pieces to make hat. Adhere. **5** Spell sentiment with rub-ons and stickers.

DESIGNER TIPS

Transform the polar bear into a lion by changing the color and adding a paper strip mane.

Change the word "cool" to "wild" and change the colors of the card to match your favorite wild dessert.

SUPPLIES: *Cardstock:* (Pear, Lily White, Ebony) Bazzill Basics Paper *Patterned paper:* (In Love from Crush collection, Claire from Sweet Pea collection) Fancy Pants Designs; (Corteza from Madera Island collection) SEI *Rub-on:* (Simply Sweet alphabet) Doodlebug Design *Stickers:* (Newsprint alphabet) Heidi Swapp *Tools:* (circle cutter; ⅛", 1 ½" circle punches) **Finished size: 6¼" diameter**

Yummy Sandwich Cookies
Brenda Peterson

I can't eat just one. My daughter and I love to make these cookies, which is so easy to do. Plus, these cookies are great for pot lucks and bake sales!

COOKIE INGREDIENTS

2 pkgs. Devil's Food cake mix
1 c. vegetable oil
4 large eggs

ICING INGREDIENTS

½ c. margarine
1 pkg. (8 oz.) cream cheese
2 tsp. vanilla
3-4 c. icing sugar

DIRECTIONS Mix cookie ingredients together. Roll mix into small balls and place on cookie sheet. Bake 10 to 12 minutes at 350 degrees. Cool until chilled.

For icing: Combine ingredients.

Assemble: Cover each cookie with icing and place another cookie on top of it to make the cookie sandwich. Chill until cookies are firm.

TREAT CAN 1 Cut 2½" x 6" window in container using craft knife. Cover container and lid with patterned paper. *Note: Cut window from patterned paper to match container window.* **2** Adhere transparency piece behind window. **3** Adhere cardstock strips. **4** Attach brads and adhere ribbon.

TAG 1 Make tag from cardstock. **2** Affix sticker and apply rub-on. **3** Punch circle from patterned paper; adhere to tag. Punch hole. **4** Tie on ribbon.

SUPPLIES: *Cardstock:* (lime green) Die Cuts With a View *Patterned paper:* (Roxie Bands from Love, Elsie collection) KI Memories *Transparency sheet:* Hammermill *Accents:* (black brads) Doodlebug Design *Rub-on:* (sentiment) American Crafts *Sticker:* (piano) EK Success *Fibers:* (lime green grosgrain ribbon) *Tool:* (¾" circle punch) *Other:* (potato chip container) **Finished sizes: treat can 3" diameter x 9¼" height, tag 2¾" x 5"**

Pain de Citron (Lemon Bread) Heather Ence

A friend introduced me to this zesty lemon bread on my first Thanksgiving away from home while I was in France. Now every time I make this lemon bread I think of my days in France, good friends, and the bonheur that this bread brought me on a rainy Thanksgiving day. Mangez-vous bien!

INGREDIENTS

1¾ c. flour

¾ c. sugar

2 tsp. baking powder

¼ tsp. salt

1 egg, beaten

1 c. milk

¼ c. vegetable oil

2 tbsp. shredded lemon peel (1 lemon)

3 tbsp. lemon juice

1 tbsp. sugar

YIELDS 8 SERVINGS

DIRECTIONS Mix dry ingredients and make well in center. In separate bowl mix egg, milk, oil, and 1 tbsp. lemon juice. Pour wet mixture into well in center of dry and mix until moist (stir as little as possible—may be lumpy). Fold in lemon peel. Bake at 350 degrees for 50 minutes in loaf pan lined with parchment paper. Mix lemon juice with sugar. Brush on bread while warm.

Mom Recipe Card

Designer: Alisa Bangerter

INSTRUCTIONS 1 Make card from Walnut cardstock. **2** Cut Anuenue Slices paper slightly smaller than card; adhere. **3** Cut Bumblebee Stripe paper and crumple. Smooth and sand lightly. Adhere to card. **4** Sew three sides of Bumblebee Stripe to create pocket. **5** Print recipe on white cardstock. Cut card into tab shape and chalk edges. **6** Tie brown and yellow ribbons around card front. Adhere button to card. **7** Paint back of acrylic letters. When dry, adhere to card.

SUPPLIES: *Cardstock:* (Walnut) Bazzill Basics Paper; (white) *Patterned paper:* (Anuenue Slices from Aloha collection) Rusty Pickle; (Bumblebee Stripe from Fundamentals collection) Doodlebug Design *Color medium:* (yellow chalk) *Paint:* (Mississippi Mud) DecoArt *Accents:* (Clear Rhyme Uppercase acrylic alphabet) Heidi Swapp; (lemon button) *Fibers:* (sheer brown, yellow polka dot ribbon) *Font:* (Times New Roman) Microsoft **Finished size: 5" square**

Thinking of You Card & Wrap

Designer: Susan Neal

CARD Ink all edges with Mustard Seed and Tea Stain. **1** Make card from white cardstock. **2** Adhere Skylar cardstock to card. **3** Cut Sunflower Stripe paper slightly smaller than card; adhere. **4** Die-cut 4" circle from Lemon Drop cardstock. Stamp sentiment around edge with Blue Lagoon. **5** Die-cut 3" circle from white. Stamp Lemons with Mustard Seed. Stamp sentiment with Blue Lagoon. **6** Adhere smaller circle to larger. Attach photo anchor and adhere piece to card.

WRAP Ink all edges with Mustard Seed and Tea Stain. **1** Make wrap from Sunflower Stripe paper. **2** Cut square and 5" x 1⅝" strip of Lemon Drop cardstock. **3** Adhere wrap to Lemon Drop strip. **4** Die-cut 3" circle from white cardstock. Stamp Lemons with Mustard Seed. Stamp sentiment with Blue Lagoon. **5** Adhere circle to wrap and attach photo anchors. **6** Adhere Lemon Drop square to wrap with foam squares.

SUPPLIES: *Cardstock:* (Lemon Drop, Skylar) Bazzill Basics Paper; (white) *Patterned paper:* (Sunflower Stripe) Bo-Bunny Press *Rubber stamps:* (Neapolitan Card Sentiments) Inkadinkado; (Lemons) Impression Obsession *Dye ink:* (Mustard Seed, Tea Stain) Ranger Industries; (Blue Lagoon) Tsukineko *Accents:* (photo anchors) *Adhesive:* (foam squares) *Dies:* (3", 4" circles) *Tools:* (die cut machine) **Finished sizes: card 5" square, wrap 12" x 1½"**

Piña Colada Bread Alisa Bangerter

This bread contains the flavors of the tropics: coconut, pineapple, and different extract combinations. It's perfect for a luncheon, shower, or even a mocktail party!

INGREDIENTS

4 eggs

1¼ c. vegetable oil

2 c. sugar

1 tsp. coconut extract

1 tsp. vanilla extract

1 tsp. orange extract

20 oz. can crushed pineapple, drained

¼ c. pineapple juice (from crushed pineapple)

½ tsp. orange zest

3 c. flour

1 tsp. salt

1 tsp. baking soda

1 tsp. cinnamon

½ c. flaked coconut

½ c. chopped maraschino cherries

½ c. chopped macadamia or other nuts (optional)

YIELDS 12 SERVINGS

DIRECTIONS Beat eggs slightly. Stir in oil and sugar. Add extracts, pineapple juice, and orange zest.

In separate bowl, sift together flour, salt, soda, and cinnamon. Add to egg mixture and mix just until ingredients are moistened. Gently stir in crushed pineapple, coconut, maraschino cherries, and nuts. Do not over-stir or bread will be very heavy.

Pour batter into greased and floured medium loaf pans (approx. 7" x 4"). Bake at 350 degrees for 45–50 minutes or until inserted toothpick comes out clean. Allow to cool in pan for 10 minutes and then remove.

Good Food ❀ Good Friends
Good Times

Join us for dinner and mocktails
with a Caribbean flair
as we celebrate our 13ᵗʰ anniversary

Saturday, September 16, 2006
7:00 p.m.

Lance & Jennifer Miller
1234 Main Street

RSVP: (123) 456-7890

SUPPLIES: *Patterned paper:* (Create, Wonder, Celebrate, Explore, Grow, Laugh, Learn from Color Me Silly collection) BasicGrey *Paint:* (Leaf Green) Plaid *Accents:* (rhinestones, jump rings, ear hoops) *Font:* (CK Toehead) Creating Keepsakes *Adhesive:* (decoupage) Plaid; (pop-up dots) *Dies:* (flower, circle tag) QuicKutz *Tools:* (die cut machine) QuicKutz; (corner rounder punch, circle cutter) *Other:* (round wood box, chipboard) **Finished sizes: invitation 5" x 6¾", box 4½" diameter x 1½" height, coaster 3¼" diameter, charms 1½" diameter**

⁙5⁙ Mocktail Party Designer: Jennifer Miller

INVITATION 1 Make invitation from Create paper. **2** Print party details on paper. **3** Trim two strips of Wonder paper and adhere to card. **4** Trim Celebrate paper and adhere between Wonder strips. **5** Round corners.

COASTER BOX 1 Paint wood box. **2** Decoupage Explore paper around box. **3** Use circle cutter to trim Laugh paper to fit inside lid; adhere. **4** Mat circle of Learn paper with Grow paper; adhere to box. **5** Die-cut flower from Grow and adhere using pop-up dot. Adhere rhinestone to flower. **6** Adhere strips of Explore to outside of lid.

COASTERS 1 Cut four circles from chipboard. **2** Cut one circle each from Create, Wonder, Grow, and Laugh paper. Decoupage circles to chipboard. **3** Die-cut flower and small ring from each paper and adhere to coaster. **4** Coat coaster with layer of decoupage adhesive.

DRINK CHARMS 1 Die-cut four circle tags and flowers from Create, Wonder, Grow, and Laugh paper. Adhere flowers to tags. **2** Coat tags with layer of decoupage adhesive. **3** Adhere rhinestones to tags. **4** Attach tags to jump rings and place on ear hoops.

BONUS IDEA

Wrap matching paper around a can for a fun matching drink stir holder.

Cinnamon Rolls DeAnn Clark

INGREDIENTS

Rolls:

2 yeast cakes

⅔ c. warm water

2 tbsp. sugar

⅔ c. milk

I cube margarine or butter

⅔ c. sugar

I½ tsp. salt

4½ c. flour

3 eggs, well beaten

Cinnamon

Glaze:

2 c. powdered sugar

3 tbsp. butter

1 tsp. vanilla

YIELDS 24 SERVINGS

I made these delicious rolls every fall for my children when they lived at home. Although they take a bit of time and effort to prepare, the end result is well worth it.

DIRECTIONS Dissolve yeast cakes and 2 tbsp. sugar in warm water. Scald milk and then add margarine or butter; cool. Add ⅔ cup sugar, salt, flour, and eggs. Add yeast mixture and mix. Let rise for one hour and roll out. Spread with melted margarine. Sprinkle with cinnamon and sugar. Simmer raisins in small amount of water until plump. Spread over dough mixture. Roll and cut. Let rise until double in size and bake for 20 minutes at 375 degrees.

Mix glaze ingredients together and heat until smooth. Spread over warm rolls.

Sweeten Your Day
Card Designer: Melanie King

INSTRUCTIONS 1 Make card from Desert Wind cardstock. **2** Cut Tweed cardstock slightly smaller than card front; zigzag-stitch to card. **3** Cut square of Sassy Hex paper; attach photo corners and adhere to card. **4** Add sentiment with stickers and rub-ons. Note: Leave space for "Sweeten". **5** Cut strip of Sassy Hex, spell "Sweeten" with stickers, and stitch line. Adhere to card.

SUPPLIES: *Cardstock:* (Tweed, Desert Wind) Bazzill Basics Paper *Patterned paper:* (Sassy Hex) All My Memories *Accents:* (photo corners) Heidi Swapp *Rub-ons:* (white alphabet) All My Memories *Stickers:* (Tiny alphabet) Making Memories **Finished size: 5" square**

Let's Crop! Card
Designer: Julie Medeiros

INSTRUCTIONS 1 Make invitation from Striped paper. **2** Cut Richmond Circle Clover paper to cover invitation. Cut partial circle from top right edge. **3** Stitch Richmond Circle Clover to invitation. Cut top edge with decorative-edge scissors. **4** Print party details on dark pink cardstock. Cut out and adhere to invitation. **5** Cut Multi Flowers paper into stars; layer with acrylic stars and attach with brads.

SUPPLIES: *Cardstock:* (dark pink) *Patterned paper:* (Richmond Circle Clover from Charlotte collection) Scenic Route Paper Co.; (Striped from Happy Birthday collection) EK Success; (Multi Flowers from Grace collection) Treehouse Memories *Accents:* (acrylic stars, blue brads) *Fonts:* (Prissy Frat Boy, Elise) www.searchfreefonts.com *Tools:* (decorative-edge scissors) **Finished size: 4¼" x 6"**

Grandma Betty's Pull-Aparts Tanja Rigby

This has become a family favorite in our home. It's perfect for holiday mornings or when you have guests visiting overnight. The smell will wake up anyone from a long winter's nap.

INGREDIENTS

18 Rhodes dinner rolls (frozen)

1 pkg. Jell-O Cook 'n Serve butterscotch pudding mix

½ c. butter

¾ c. packed brown sugar

½ c. chopped pecans

1 tbsp. cinnamon

YIELDS 18 SERVINGS

DIRECTIONS Grease bottom and sides of bundt cake pan and sprinkle layer of pecans along bottom. Arrange frozen rolls around bottom of pan. Sprinkle dry pudding mix on top.

Mix butter, cinnamon, and brown sugar over heat, mixing well. Pour over top of rolls. Cover and let rolls rise overnight in cold oven. In morning, take out of oven and heat oven to 350 degrees. Bake rolls for 25–30 minutes. Invert over plate.

SUPPLIES: *Cardstock:* (tan) *Patterned paper:* (Lil' Princess Brown Polka Dot, Girly Girl Flower from Frou-Frou collection) Fancy Pants Designs *Dye ink:* (Jet Black) Ranger Industries *Paint:* (metallic silver) *Accents:* (chipboard letters, silver bookplate, silver brads, silver photo corners) *Stickers:* (family, Collage alphabet) Li'l Davis Designs *Font:* (Century Gothic) Microsoft *Other:* (wood frame, black journaling pocket envelope, small journal, family photo) **Finished sizes: invitation 4¼" x 5¼", journal 5" x 4½", frame 8" square**

5 STEPS Our Family Reunion Ensemble Designer: Teri Anderson

INVITATION 1 Seal envelope and slit top, bottom, and right side so it opens like a card. **2** Adhere Girly Girl Flower paper to front. Adhere Lil' Princess Brown Polka Dot to invitation. Sand edges. **3** Print "It's family reunion time!" on tan cardstock. Trim and adhere to invitation. **4** Cut two flowers from Girly Girl Flower and adhere to invitation. **5** Adhere family photo. Adhere photo corners around photo. **6** Adhere Girly Girl Flower to inside. Trim Lil' Princess Brown Polka Dot and sand. Adhere to inside. **7** Print text on tan. Trim and adhere to inside of card.

MEMORY JOURNAL 1 Remove covers from journal. **2** Adhere Girly Girl Flower paper to covers and sand edges. **3** Place covers back on journal. **4** Adhere strip of Lil' Princess Brown Polka Dot paper to cover. **5** Paint chipboard letter; let dry. Adhere letter to journal. **6** Print "Favorite family" on tan cardstock. Trim and adhere to cover. **7** Spell "Memories" with letter stickers.

FRAME 1 Cut Lil' Princess Brown Polka Dot paper to fit over frame; sand edges. **2** Adhere family sticker to paper. **3** Print date on tan cardstock. Trim and adhere to paper. **4** Adhere bookplate and brads to paper. **5** Cut four flowers from Girly Girl Flower paper and adhere to paper. **6** Adhere paper to frame. Sand.

BONUS IDEA

Stamp napkins with a simple monogram for a great touch at meals. Try also stamping paper plates and bowls.

INSIDE

Vanilla Chex Mix Heather D. White

This snack makes an easy and popular holiday treat for neighbors and coworkers. It's way too tasty to eat only during the holiday season—enjoy this simple recipe at gatherings throughout the year.

INGREDIENTS

1 bag semisweet chocolate chips

3 c. Corn Chex cereal

3 c. Rice Chex cereal

3 c. Wheat Chex cereal

2 c. salted dry-roasted nuts (peanuts, cashews, or almonds)

2 c. small pretzel twists

2 c. miniature marshmallows

1 (20 oz.) pkg. vanilla-flavored candy coating (almond bark/ambrosia)

YIELDS 20 SERVINGS

DIRECTIONS Place chocolate chips in freezer to chill. Mix cereals, peanuts, pretzels, and marshmallows in large bowl; set aside. Microwave candy coating in large uncovered microwavable bowl on high for 1 min. 30 sec. Stir, breaking up large chunks. Microwave about 30 seconds more or until coating can be stirred smooth. Gently and quickly pour coating onto cereal mixture and fold in until evenly coated. Stir in chilled chocolate chips. Spread on waxed paper; cool completely. Break into chunks. Store in airtight container in refrigerator.

SUPPLIES: *Cardstock:* (white) *Patterned paper:* (Maison Button Dots Flat, Maison Gold Stars Flat) K&Company *Accents:* (antique buttons) *Fibers:* (gold trim) Model Crafts *Adhesive:* (packaging tape) *Other:* (take-out box) **Finished sizes: cone 11½", box 3¾" x 3⅜" x 2⅞"**

5 STEPS Treat Mix Box & Cone Designer: Heather D. White

BOX 1 Cover box with both patterned papers. **2** Adhere trim around top of box. **3** Adhere three buttons.

CONE 1 Cut 9" square of cardstock; roll into cone shape and tape to secure. **2** Cover cone with Maison Button Dots Flat paper. **3** Cut 2" wide strip of Maison Gold Stars Flat paper; adhere around top of cone. Adhere trim over strip. **4** Line inside top of cone with Maison Gold Stars Flat. **5** Adhere two buttons.

Death by Chocolate Fondue Pattie Donham

Just the thought of liquid chocolate makes my mouth water. I like to use both milk chocolate and semi-sweet chocolate bits so that everyone's chocolate preference is satiated. And, when you add the whipping cream and liqueur, the texture is so silky it will make you swoon!

INGREDIENTS

1 pkg. (11 oz.) Ghirardelli semi-sweet chocolate bits
1 pkg. (11 oz.) Ghirardelli milk chocolate bits
½ pint whipping cream
½ c. Kahlua liqueur

DIRECTIONS Place chocolate bits in a large bowl, and pour cream and liqueur over chocolate, stirring it in. Melt slowly in a microwave, stirring frequently with a wood spoon until melted. Pour into a fondue pot, and light the flame underneath the pot to keep it warm.

Serve with marshmallows, crushed graham crackers, strawberries, crushed nuts, pineapple and apple chunks, and/ or shredded coconut.

⟨5 STEPS⟩ Do You Fondue? Party
Designer: Kim Kesti

INVITATION 1 Make card from cardstock. **2** Cut patterned paper slightly smaller than card front. Adhere paper trim; adhere piece. **3** Print sentiment on cardstock. Trim and adhere. **4** Attach brad to paper flower; adhere.

PARTY MEMORIES BOOKLET

Prepare Cut rectangle of cardstock. Tri-fold to create booklet.

Cover 1 Cut patterned paper slightly smaller than booklet front; adhere. **2** Print title on cardstock. Trim and adhere. **3** Attach brad to paper flower. Adhere.

Inside 1 Print questions on cardstock. Trim and adhere. **2** Cut cardstock slightly smaller than booklet section. Adhere. **3** Adhere paper trim to backside of two patterned paper strips. Adhere. **4** Print booklet section titles on cardstock. Trim and adhere.

PLACE HOLDER 1 Cut cardstock to finished size. **2** Cut patterned paper slightly smaller; adhere. **3** Print guest name on cardstock. Trim and mat with paper trim. Adhere. **4** Adhere smiley face patch with foam tape.

SUPPLIES: *Cardstock:* (Lily White, Lilac, Lemon Drop) Bazzill Basics Paper *Patterned paper:* (Summer Scallop from Summer Crush collection) Glitz Design *Accents:* (pink corduroy brads) Imaginisce; (pink paper flowers) Prima; (purple paper trim) Doodlebug Design *Fonts:* (Bell Bottom Laser) www.dafont.com; (your choice) *Adhesive:* (foam tape) *Other:* (smiley face patch) **Finished sizes: invitation 4½" x 5½", party memories booklet 11" x 6", place holder 4¾" x 4¾"**

Annie's Fruit Salsa & Cinnamon Chips

Courtesy of AllRecipes.com

This delicious salsa, made with fresh kiwis, apples, and berries, is a sweet treat when served on homemade cinnamon tortilla chips. Enjoy it as a summer appetizer or an easy dessert.

INGREDIENTS

2 kiwis, peeled and diced
2 Golden Delicious apples, peeled, cored, and diced
8 oz. raspberries
1 lb. strawberries
2 tbsp. white sugar
1 tbsp. brown sugar
3 tbsp. fruit preserves, any flavor
10 (10") flour tortillas
Butter-flavored cooking spray
2 c. cinnamon sugar

DIRECTIONS In a large bowl, thoroughly mix kiwis, apples, raspberries, strawberries, white sugar, brown sugar, and fruit preserves. Cover and chill in refrigerator at least 15 minutes. Preheat oven to 350 degrees. Coat one side of each tortilla with cooking spray. Cut tortillas into wedges and arrange in a single layer on large baking sheet. Sprinkle with cinnamon sugar. Spray again with cooking spray. Bake 8 to 10 minutes. Allow to cool 15 minutes. Serve with chilled fruit salsa.

⁙5⁙ Just Because Set Designer: Julia Stainton

BAG TOPPER 1 Stamp French Script backgrounder, branch, and sentiment on cardstock; trim and ink edges. **2** Die-cut scalloped rectangle from cardstock; ink edges. Adhere stamped block to rectangle, stitch, and attach brad. **3** Make topper from patterned paper. Adhere patterned paper strip. **4** Punch holes through front and back of topper. Set eyelets in front. **5** Place topper over bag; poke holes in bag through eyelets. Thread ribbon through eyelets and tie.

JAR BAND 1 Cut patterned paper to fit around jar. Adhere patterned paper strip, zigzag-stitch edge, and ink edges. **2** Stamp French Script background and strawberry on cardstock; trim and ink edges. **3** Die-cut scalloped rectangle from patterned paper; adhere stamped block. Stitch edges. **4** Tie ribbon through button; adhere flower and button. **5** Adhere rectangle to band; adhere band around jar.

SUPPLIES: *Cardstock:* (Blush Red Light, Natural Smooth) Prism *Patterned paper:* (Girl Floral, Love Stripes from Party collection) My Mind's Eye *Rubber stamps:* (sentiment, branch from Nature's Silhouettes set; French Script Backgrounder; strawberry from Sweet Thang set) Cornish Heritage Farms *Dye ink:* (Antique Linen, Juniper) Ranger Industries; (white) *Specialty ink:* (Noir hybrid) Stewart Superior Corp. *Color medium:* (Rose Red, Old Olive markers) Stampin' Up! *Accents:* (green button) Autumn Leaves; (copper brad) Making Memories; (white velvet flower) Maya Road; (white eyelets) *Fibers:* (pink gingham ribbon) Stampin' Up! *Die:* (scalloped rectangle) Spellbinders *Tools:* (die cut machine) Provo Craft; (⅛" circle punch) **Finished sizes: bag topper 5" x 3", jar band 12" x 2¾"**

Creamy Marshmallow Fruit Dip   Alisa Bangerter

This dip is quick to make, and it looks so pretty displayed with colorful fruit on skewers. You can also easily change the flavor to suit your taste or party theme.

INGREDIENTS

1 (8 oz.) pkg. cream cheese

1 (7 oz.) jar marshmallow creme

1 tbsp. orange juice

1 tsp. grated orange zest

Dash of ground ginger (optional)

YIELDS 8–10 SERVINGS

DIRECTIONS Mix all ingredients together. Serve with berries and fruit, or fruit on skewers.

TIPS

Try using strawberry cream cheese for more fruit flavor, or try adding lemons and lemon juice. Add dry flavored gelatin to create different colors and flavors.

SUPPLIES: *Cardstock:* (Blue, Arctic) Bazzill Basics Paper; (white, red) *Patterned paper:* (Sew American Stripe, Ladybug Picnic) Doodlebug Design *Accents:* (July 4th gel label) Doodlebug Design *Rub-ons:* (All Mixed Up alphabet) Doodlebug Design *Tools:* (1¼" circle punch, large star) McGill *Other:* (white cloth-wrapped wire, wood skewers, candy roll package) **Finished sizes: invitation 4¼" x 7¼", dip sign 3" x 8", fruit pick 1¼" x 6½", firecracker favor 6"**

Fourth of July Party Designer: Alisa Bangerter

INVITATION 1 Make invitation from Arctic cardstock. Cover bottom half of front with Sew American Stripe paper. **2** Cut strip of red cardstock; apply rub-ons to spell "Party!" **3** Punch five stars from various cardstock. Curl five wire lengths; adhere stars to tops. **4** Adhere wire lengths behind red strip; adhere to card. **5** Add gel label.

FIRECRACKER FAVOR 1 Remove paper wrapper from candy roll, leaving foil lining. **2** Cover bottom several inches with Sew American Stripe paper. Cover top with red cardstock. **3** Cut strip of Blue to fit around candy roll; apply rub-ons to spell guest's name. Adhere. **4** Punch three sets of stars from various cardstock. Curl three wire lengths. Adhere each set of stars together, sandwiching wire length between. **5** Poke wires into top of candy roll.

DIP SIGN & FRUIT PICK 1 Cut red cardstock to 3" x 2¼". Cover bottom of sign with Sew American Stripe paper. **2** Cut strip of Blue cardstock; apply rub-ons to spell "Fruit dip". **3** Punch three stars from various cardstock. Curl three wire lengths; adhere stars to tops. **4** Adhere wire lengths behind Blue strip; adhere to sign. **5** Adhere skewer to back of sign. **6** Punch two circles and two stars from various cardstock and Ladybug Picnic paper; adhere contrasting stars to circles. **7** Adhere circles back-to-back, sandwiching skewer in between.

Scrumptious Candy Apple Dip Valerie Pingree

This dip is easy to make and oh, so good. It's a hit with kids and adults at any kind of party.

INGREDIENTS

1 (8 oz.) pkg. cream cheese, softened

½ c. brown sugar

¼ c. powdered sugar

1 tsp. vanilla

½–⅔ c. toffee bits

YIELDS 12–15 SERVINGS

DIRECTIONS Mix together with hand mixer. Chill. Serve with apple slices or assorted fruit.

TIP

If you can't find toffee bits (usually near the chocolate chips at the grocery store), then buy toffee candy bars and chop them up.

SUPPLIES: *Cardstock:* (White) Prism; (Deep Luscious Lime) WorldWin *Specialty paper:* (photo) *Color medium:* (green chalk) Pebbles Inc. *Accents:* (nickel eyelet brad) Pebbles Inc.
Fibers: (light blue rickrack) Wrights; (jute, tan striped ribbon) Wrights *Fonts:* (T-Rex, Brontosaurus, Triceratops) www.letteringdelights.com; (Century Gothic) Microsoft *Tools:* (corner rounder
punch) Creative Memories *Other:* (T-Rex, Brontosaurus, Triceratops clip art) www.letteringdelights.com; (dinosaurs, fruit snacks, cellophane bag) **Finished sizes: invitation 6⅜" x 5¾",**
bookmark favor 3" x 6", treat bag topper 5¾" x 2½"

⁵⁄ₛₜₑₚₛ Dino-Mite Birthday Party Designer: Valerie Pingree

INVITATION 1 Insert Brontosaurus image in word processing
program. **2** Insert text box with party details. **3** Print on photo
paper; round edges. **4** Zigzag-cut piece of White cardstock;
chalk edges. Fold around invitation and adhere together in back.
5 Print "Breaking news for (child's name)!" on Deep Luscious
Lime cardstock; trim into tag. Tie to envelope with twine.

BOOKMARK FAVOR 1 Insert Triceratops image in word processing program. **2** Insert text box with poem. **3** Print on photo
paper; cut out. **4** Attach eyelet brad; tie on ribbon. **5** Adhere
rickrack to bottom.

TREAT BAG TOPPER 1 Insert T-Rex image in word processing program. **2** Insert text box with sentiment. **3** Print on photo
paper; cut out. **4** Cut rectangle of White cardstock; fold over top
of cellophane bag. Adhere T-Rex image to front. **5** Fill bag with
dinosaurs and fruit snacks. Attach topper.

BONUS IDEA

Create a dinosaur card game using the same rules as Go Fish.

INSIDE

Cowboy Caviar Sande Krieger

Any time we're invited to a neighborhood or family party, we're always asked to bring this dish—it's a guaranteed party favorite.

INGREDIENTS

6 tbsp. red wine vinegar

1 tbsp. vegetable oil

2 tbsp. hot sauce

2 tsp. chopped garlic

¼ tsp. pepper

1 avocado, chopped

1 can corn, drained and rinsed

1 can black eyed peas, drained and rinsed

½ c. green onions, chopped

6–8 Roma tomatoes, chopped

¼ c. cilantro, chopped

YIELDS 8–10 SERVINGS

DIRECTIONS In large bowl, combine the following: vinegar, oil, hot sauce, garlic, and pepper. Add avocado, corn, and black eyed peas. Stir, then add onions, tomatoes, and cilantro. Stir everything together well and serve with chips or on warm pita bread.

SUPPLIES: *Cardstock:* (brown) *Patterned paper:* (Extreme Skinny Stripe) KI Memories; (Chiffon from Urban Couture collection) BasicGrey *Chalk ink:* (brown) Clearsnap *Color medium:* (brown pen) *Accents:* (brown fringe) Jo-Ann Stores; (antique eyelet, large tag) *Fibers:* (brown cord) *Font:* (Bernard MT Condensed) Microsoft *Tools:* (star punch) Marvy Uchida *Other:* (photo) **Finished size: 3" x 6½"**

SUPPLIES: *Cardstock:* (kraft, brown) *Patterned paper:* (Cowgirl Solo, Western Stripe from Wild West collection) Flair Designs *Rubber stamps:* (Typewriter Lower Case alphabet) PSX; (Printer's Type Uppercase alphabet) Hero Arts *Dye ink:* (Van Dyke Brown) Ranger Industries *Accents:* (antique copper, decorative brads) Making Memories *Fibers:* (jute) *Font:* (Good Dog Plain) www.scrapvillage.com *Tools:* (¾" circle punch) **Finished size: 2¾" x 5½"**

Back in the Saddle Tag Designer: Sande Krieger

INSTRUCTIONS 1 Adhere Extreme Skinny Stripe and Chiffon paper to tag. **2** Punch star from Chiffon; draw line around edges with pen. **3** Adhere star to tag; attach eyelet and tie on cord. **4** Trim and adhere photo to tag. **5** Print sentiments on cardstock; trim into strips and draw decorative borders with pen. Adhere to tag. **6** Adhere fringe, and ink edges of tag.

Howdy, Neighbor Tag Designer: Julie Medeiros

INSTRUCTIONS 1 Print sentiment on kraft cardstock; cut into tag shape. **2** Stamp "Howdy neighbor" at top of tag. **3** Cut cowgirl from Cowgirl Solo paper; adhere to tag. **4** Cut strips of brown cardstock; fringe edge of one strip. Stitch both to tag. **5** Cut strip of Western Stripe paper; ink edges and attach with brads. **6** Punch circle from brown cardstock; adhere to tag top and punch hole in center. **7** Attach jute and decorative brad to tag top.

Bacon Wrapped Water Chestnuts Tammy Olsen

This appetizer is great for family reunions and Christmas parties. Not only is it quick and easy to make, but it also fills the house with the delicious aroma of barbecue sauce and mouth-watering bacon.

INGREDIENTS

2 cans whole water chestnuts
1 pkg. bacon slices, cut into thirds
Barbecue sauce

DIRECTIONS Wrap chestnuts with bacon and secure with toothpicks. Bake in 9" x 13" pan at 350 degrees for 25 minutes. Drain grease. Cover chestnuts with barbecue sauce and bake an additional 20 minutes.

As a chapter closes
in your life
And a new one
starts for you
May your years
be filled
With all the things
You're looking forward to!

Enjoy your
retirement!

We invite you to join
us in celebrating the
retirement of

James Grimm

*after 45 years of service
to the United States
Government*

Saturday, January 31, 2009
8:00 p.m. until midnight

The Knolls Country Club
2201 Old Cheney Rd.
Lincoln, Nebraska

retirement
memories

SUPPLIES: *Specialty paper:* (photo) *Digital elements:* (black medallion, red patterned paper, circle frame, black rickrack from Story Time kit; flourishes from On the Edge Flourishes No. 01 kit) www.designerdigitals.com; (silver brads from The Simple Florist kit, corded bookplate from Urban Bohemian kit) www.jenwilsondesigns.com; (wax seal from Wax Seal Alpha kit) www.storeide.se/gunhild/index.htm *Stickers:* (striped tape) 7gypsies *Fonts:* (Verdana, Georgia) www.myfonts.com *Software:* (photo editing) Adobe *Other:* (album, digital photos) **Finished sizes: invitation 4" x 6", card 8" square, album 9¾" x 8¾, layout 8" x 8"**

Retirement Party Designer: Stefanie Hamilton

INVITATION 1 Create finished size project in software; open digital elements. **2** Drag patterned paper onto project. Cut and paste patterned paper rectangle; add drop shadow. **3** Create new 3" x 5" project, drag onto project, and add drop shadow. **4** Type invitation text. **5** Drop in flourish; copy, invert, and drop in place. **6** Drop in wax seal. Print on photo paper and trim.

CARD 1 Create finished size project in software; open digital elements. **2** Drag patterned paper onto project; color edges black. **3** Create new project, change color to cream, and drag onto project. Cut and paste patterned paper rectangle. **4** Drop in circle frame; fill with cream and type sentiment. **5** Print on photo paper; trim. **6** Cut cardstock to 11" x 8"; score left edge at 3" and fold. Adhere printed piece to flap to form card.

ALBUM COVER 1 Create 6" x 8" project in software; open digital elements. **2** Cut and paste patterned paper. Drop in rickrack. **3** Drop in corded bookplate; type title. **4** Print on photo paper; trim. **5** Affix tape along album edge. Adhere printed piece and affix tape to seam.

LAYOUT 1 Create finished size project in software; open digital elements. **2** Change project color to black. Cut and paste patterned paper. **3** Create 4" x 5¾" project, change color to black, and drop in photos. Drag onto project. **4** Create text, drag onto project. **5** Drop in brads; resize as desired. **6** Print on photo paper, trim, and insert in album.

Still the same, at age 18, 44, 50, and 63 - just less hair!

Southern Pepper Jelly Ashley Butler

This recipe is special to me because it is made by my Mawmaw. Everyone loves her pepper jelly, but as a child I thought the name sounded disgusting. So, I didn't try it until I was an adult. But once I tried it, I discovered it has an unusually pleasing taste—a mix of sweet and peppery.

INGREDIENTS

¾ – 1 c. jalapeno peppers, seeded and finely chopped
1⅓ c. bell pepper, chopped
6½ c. sugar
1½ c. wine vinegar
6 oz. liquid pectin
Red food coloring, as desired

DIRECTIONS Combine peppers, sugar, and vinegar in large pot. Boil 1 minute. Reduce heat; cook 5 minutes, stirring constantly. Remove pot from heat. Add liquid pectin and food coloring; gently stir mixture. Pour into jars immediately. Wipe jar tops with wet towel before sealing.

YIELDS 8 JARS (8 OZ. EACH) *NOTE: COOKED JELLIES MAY BE STORED ON THE SHELF UNOPENED FOR 1 YEAR.*

SERVING SUGGESTIONS

Serve the jelly over cream cheese and with crackers.

Baste grilled meats.

Mix with cream cheese until smooth and serve over ice cream.

DESIGNER TIPS

Wear gloves when working with jalapeno peppers, or use a food processor to avoid potential eye irritation from the pepper juice.

For best results, use Certo liquid pectin.

Do not double the recipe, as it may not set.

Use sterilized jars, lids, and utensils when preparing cooked jellies. Wash items in hot, soapy water and rinse. Place them in boiling water for 10 minutes and keep them in hot water until you're ready to use them.

TAG 1 Make tag from cardstock. **2** Cut flames, from cardstock; layer and adhere to tag. **3** Apply chalk to flames. **4** Print "Happy birthday" and "Stuff!" on cardstock; trim. Apply chalk; adhere to tag. **5** Spell "Hot" with stickers. Punch hole in tag; attach chain.

JAR WRAP 1 Wrap jar with cardstock. **3** Cut flames, from cardstock; layer, chalk, and adhere to jar.

SUPPLIES: *Cardstock:* (Bazzill Red, Apricot, Bazzill Yellow) Bazzill Basics Paper; (white, black) Provo Craft *Color medium:* (black chalk) Pebbles Inc. *Accents:* (silver bead chain) Making Memories *Stickers:* (Cheeky Shimmer alphabet) Making Memories *Font:* (CK Jolly Elf) Creating Keepsakes *Other:* (jar) Cost Plus World Market
Finished sizes: tag 3¾" x 4¼", jar 2¼" x 4" x 1¾"

June's Broccoli Cheese Soup June Schaefer

This creamy soup is a great way to warm up after a long day. It is delicious when served in a big bowl with lots of cheese.

INGREDIENTS

4–5 c. potatoes, cubed

2 c. sliced carrots

1–2 c. chopped celery

1 c. chopped onion

6 cubes chicken bouillon

2½ c. water

10 oz. frozen or fresh broccoli, chopped

½ c. butter

¼ c. flour

1½ tsp. salt

1 tbsp. dry mustard

½ tsp. black pepper

2 c. milk

1 block Velveeta cheese, cubed

YIELDS 12-15 SERVINGS

DIRECTIONS Combine potatoes, carrots, celery, onion, bouillon, and water in pot. Boil about 20 minutes, until vegetables are tender. Add broccoli; cook about 7 more minutes. In a separate pan, melt butter. Add flour, salt, mustard, pepper, and milk. Cook until thickened, stirring constantly. Add cheese and stir until melted. Add cheese mixture to vegetables; cook 10 more minutes.

SUPPLIES: *Cardstock:* (White, Brick) Bazzill Basics Paper *Patterned paper:* (Chill Out Blizzard, Chill Out Journaling) KI Memories *Accents:* (white metal-rimmed tag) Avery; (snowflake epoxy circle) KI Memories *Stickers:* (Roosevelt alphabet) American Crafts *Fibers:* (snowflake, blue printed ribbon) KI Memories; (white floss) *Font:* (Peanut Butter) www.twopeasinabucket.com *Adhesive:* (pop-up dots) Plaid *Tools:* (¾" circle punch) *Other:* (white gift bag) Nicole **Finished sizes: invitation 4½" x 8", gift bag 5½" x 8¾", place card 4" x 3"**

⁵ Sledding Party Dee Gallimore-Perry

INVITATION 1 Make card from Brick cardstock. **2** Cut Chill Out Blizzard paper slightly smaller than card front; adhere. **3** Cut rectangle of Chill Out Journaling paper; adhere. **4** Print party details on rectangle of White cardstock; adhere to card. **5** Punch several snowflakes from Chill Out Blizzard; adhere to card with pop-up dots. **6** Cut slit in card fold; attach ribbon and knot in front.

GIFT BAG 1 Cut Brick cardstock to finished size. **2** Cut Chill Out Blizzard paper slightly smaller than Brick piece; adhere. **3** Cut rectangle of Chill Out Journaling paper; adhere. **4** Print sentiment on rectangle of White cardstock; adhere.

5 Punch several snowflakes from Chill Out Blizzard paper; adhere to piece with pop-up dots. Adhere entire piece to bag front. **6** Adhere epoxy circle to tag; attach to handle with floss. Knot ribbons on handle.

PLACE CARD 1 Make card from Brick cardstock. **2** Cut Chill Out Journaling paper slightly smaller than card front; adhere. **3** Cut rectangle of White cardstock; apply stickers to spell guest's name. Adhere to card. **4** Punch snowflakes from Chill Out Blizzard paper; adhere to card with pop-up dots. **5** Knot ribbon around card.

Chicken Noodle Soup Brenda Peterson

This soup is a winter tradition that makes me feel warm and cozy inside. Its aroma reminds me of playing outside in the snow and the excitement of coming home to a steamy bowl of soup.

INGREDIENTS

3 boneless, skinless chicken breasts

1 chopped small onion

1 chopped carrot

2 stalks chopped celery

2 tbsp. butter or margarine

1 (12–16 oz.) bag egg noodles

1 tbsp. granulated chicken bouillon

Salt, pepper to taste

YIELDS 6 SERVINGS

DIRECTIONS In 5 qt. Dutch oven, sauté vegetables in butter till tender. Boil all ingredients except noodles, adding enough water to cover ingredients an inch or two. When chicken is cooked through, cut chicken into bite-size pieces. Return to soup and add noodles. Add salt and pepper to taste. Boil for 10 more minutes.

Homemade Soup Tag

Michelle Tardie

INSTRUCTIONS 1 Make tag from reverse side of Rooster paper. **2** Cut Stripe paper slightly smaller than tag; adhere. Ink edges of tag. **3** Cut rectangle of beige mesh; ink and adhere. **4** Cut strips of Vignes and Fleur paper; ink edges and adhere. **5** Print "Homemade soup" on reverse side of Fleur paper; trim into strip, ink edges, and adhere. **6** Ink canvas tag; adhere sticker with pop-up dot. Adhere to tag. **7** Adhere metal mesh to tag; add staple. **8** Punch hole at top of tag; knot twine. Print "Chicken noodle" on mini tag; emboss. Ink edges, and attach to twine with safety pin.

SUPPLIES: *Patterned paper:* (Fleur, Stripe, Rooster, Vignes from French Market collection) Daisy D's *Chalk ink:* (Chestnut Roan) Clearsnap *Walnut ink:* (Tea Stain) Fiber Scraps *Embossing powder:* (clear) *Accents:* (mini tag) Daisy D's; (circle metal-rimmed canvas tag, red metal mesh) Creative Imaginations; (staples) Swingline; (beige mesh) Magic Mesh; (white safety pin) Making Memories *Sticker:* (chicken) Provo Craft *Fibers:* (twine) *Font:* (Pine Lint Germ) www.acidfonts.com *Adhesive:* (pop-up dots) **Finished size:** 2½" x 5"

Made with Love Gift Basket
Michelle Tardie

CARD 1 Make card from Cafe Curtains paper. **2** Cut strips of Cafe Curtains, Sunnyside, and Apron paper; adhere to card. *Note: Adhere Cafe Curtains and Apron strips reverse side up.* **3** Apply rub-ons. **4** Adhere chipboard tag with pop-up dots.

TAG 1 Make tag from reverse side of Apron paper. **2** Cut rectangle of Cafe Curtains paper; trim top corners and adhere to tag. **3** Cut strips of Cafe Curtains and Sunnyside paper; adhere to tag, leaving space in between strips. *Note: Adhere Cafe Curtains strip reverse side up.* **4** Apply rub-ons. **5** Spell "Soup" with chipboard letter and stickers; outline with marker. **6** Punch hole in tag; adhere chipboard tag and knot ribbon through.

GIFT BASKET 1 Cut strip of Sunnyside paper to fit around basket rim; adhere. *Note: Thread through basket weaving if possible.* **2** Thread chipboard tag with twill ribbon; attach to basket. Adhere button. **3** Tie ribbon around handles. **4** Embellish tissues, chocolates, crackers, and wooden spoons as desired with chipboard tags, raffia, twill ribbon, safety pin, rub-on stitching, and patterned paper.

SUPPLIES: *Patterned paper:* (Sunnyside, Cafe Curtains, Apron from Kitchen collection) We R Memory Keepers *Color medium:* (black fine-tip marker) *Accents:* (chipboard letters, tags) We R Memory Keepers; (brown button, gold safety pin) *Rub-ons:* (stitching) Die Cuts With a View *Stickers:* (alphabet) Polar Bear Press *Fibers:* (olive, rust, brown, light brown twill ribbon) Creative Impressions; (raffia) *Adhesive:* (pop-up dots) *Other:* (wicker basket) Target; (chocolates, crackers, facial tissues, wooden spoons) **Finished sizes:** card 6" x 4", tag 2⅜" x 4½", gift basket 9" diameter x 7" height

Chicken Enchilada Soup Judy Ezola

My family and friends love this soup! Even my son, who is a very picky eater, loves it and asks for it as soon as it gets cold outside.

DID YOU KNOW?

Masa harina is the dried and ground form of masa, which is the dough used for making corn tortillas. You can find masa harina in most grocery stores today, often in the specialty food aisles.

INGREDIENTS

2 c. chicken, cooked and shredded

4 c. chicken broth

1 c. masa harina

3 c. water

1 c. enchilada sauce

16 oz. Velveeta cheese

1 tsp. salt

1 tsp. chili powder

YIELDS 8-10 SERVINGS

DIRECTIONS Heat chicken broth in large pan. Combine masa harina with 2 c. water in medium bowl; whisk until blended. Add masa mixture to pot of broth. Add remaining water, enchilada sauce, cheese, and spices and bring to boil. Add shredded chicken. Reduce heat and simmer for 30–40 minutes or until thick. Serve soup with shredded cheese, crumbled tortilla chips, and pico de gallo.

SUPPLIES: *Patterned paper:* (Create, Play, Grow, Learn, Explore, Inspire, Believe from Color Me Silly collection) BasicGrey *Rubber stamps:* (Small Formal alphabet) Karen Foster Design *Dye ink:* (Black from Primary set) Karen Foster Design; (Fired Brick, Mustard Seed, Peeled Paint) Ranger Industries *Accents:* (chipboard letters) Heidi Swapp; (colored tags) BasicGrey; (green, yellow looping brads) Karen Foster Design *Stickers:* (alphabet) BasicGrey *Fibers:* (green fringed cord) Kate's Paperie *Font:* (Red Dog) www.twopeasinabucket.com *Other:* (green, orange takeout boxes) Westrim Crafts; (green gift shred) Target; (cellophane bags) Wilton; (green, orange, yellow jelly beans) Jelly Belly **Finished sizes: invitation 5¼" x 7½", garland size as desired, takeout favors 2" x 2½" x 2"**

5 STEPS South of the Border Party Designer: Alice Golden

INVITATION 1 Make invitation base from Explore paper; ink edges with Fired Brick. **2** Print party details on Create paper, leaving room for stickers. Tear edges with ruler; ink with Mustard Seed and cut fringe on bottom edge. Adhere top of printed piece to base. **3** Spell "Fiesta" with stickers on invitation. **4** Cut strip of Inspire paper; ink edges with Fired Brick and adhere to invitation. **5** Attach brads at top; string cord between brads.

TAKEOUT FAVORS 1 Cut chili pepper from patterned paper; ink edges of pepper with Fired Brick and stem with Peeled Paint. **2** Stamp "Gracias" on pepper with Black ink. **3** Fill cellophane bag with jelly beans; tie closed with cord and attach pepper. **4** Place in takeout box filled with gift shred.

GARLAND 1 Cut chili peppers from patterned paper; ink edges of peppers with Fired Brick and stems with Peeled Paint. **2** Cover chipboard letters with patterned paper as desired. Spell "Fiesta" with chipboard letters on tags. **3** Attach chili peppers and letters to cord with brads.

DESIGNER TIPS

- If you're using a font that doesn't have special characters, draw the tildes over the n's with a black marker.
- Find clever ways to word your invitations by looking online. This invitation uses wording from www.verseit.com.
- Don't be put off by the price of specialty trims, like the fringed cord in this project. Often, a little can go a long way, and the unique look can really add spice to your creations!

Louisiana Gumbo Melanie Douthit

I was led to believe gumbo was something complicated to make, and as I learned to make it, I realized that wasn't true. I usually make this at least twice a month and my family loves it. It's inexpensive to make and, according to my husband, better than what you can get in a restaurant.

INGREDIENTS

1 lb. deboned chicken breasts
1 lb. smoked sausage
¼ - ⅓ c. vegetable oil
1 medium onion, chopped
½ bell pepper, chopped
3 stalks celery, chopped
1 can (6 oz.) okra and tomatoes mix
½ c. chopped green onions
Tony Chachere's Creole Seasonings to taste
Salt and pepper to taste
½ tsp. crushed red pepper
¼ c. all purpose flour
Stock from chicken
Gumbo filé (optional)

DIRECTIONS Boil chicken breasts on low heat until cooked through. Reserve stock. When cooled, chop chicken into bite size pieces; set aside. Slice smoked sausage and place in cooking pan with 1 tsp. vegetable oil. Cook until browned, stirring frequently. Drain on paper towels. Place chicken in same pan used for sausage. Cook chicken for 1 to 2 minutes, stirring frequently. Remove. In large dutch oven, add onion, green pepper, and celery along with approx. 1 tbsp. oil; sauté until tender. Remove from pan. To make roux, add remaining oil to pan. Add flour. Cook over medium heat stirring constantly until mixture is caramel colored, but do not burn.

Add onion, green pepper, and celery to roux. Add chicken broth (approx. 4 c.); stir frequently. Add sausage, chicken, and seasonings. Bring to boil. Reduce heat and simmer. In small blender, blend ½ of the canned okra tomatoes mix. Add to gumbo. Continue to cook for 1½ to 2 hours on low heat. Do not use a lid. Add more water to pot if gumbo seems too thick. Add chopped green onions the last 10 to 15 minutes of cooking. Add file right before serving. Serve over hot cooked rice.

You're Invited
to a
**Mardi Gras
Masquerade**
on
Saturday, February 2nd
7pm at the home of
Jeff and Melanie

R.S.V.P. 555-5151

SUPPLIES: *Cardstock:* (black) *Patterned paper:* (Lovely Lace from First Blush collection) Paper Salon *Rubber stamps:* (frame from Monogram Builder II set; for you from Wedding Essentials set) Paper Salon *Watermark ink:* Ranger Industries *Embossing powder:* (gold) Ranger Industries *Accents:* (black safety pin) Making Memories; (black feathers) *Fibers:* (black organza ribbon) Offray; (black sequin trim) *Font:* (Freehand 521) www.myfonts.com *Adhesive:* (foam tape) *Template:* (pillow box) C&T Publishing *Die:* (photo corner) Provo Craft *Tool:* (die cut machine) Provo Craft *Other:* (black decorative netting; gold, green, purple bead necklaces, gold coins) **Finished sizes: card 4½" x 5¾", gift box 5¾" x 3¼" x 1", mask 8¾" x 3"**

⁙5⁙ Mardi Gras Party Designer: Melanie Douthit

CARD 1 Make card from cardstock. **2** Adhere decorative netting to patterned paper piece. Adhere trim; tie with ribbon. Adhere to card. **3** Print invitation on patterned paper; trim and mat with cardstock. **4** Die-cut photo corners from cardstock; emboss and adhere. **5** Adhere with foam tape.

GIFT BOX 1 Trace pillow box template onto patterned paper; cut out and assemble. **2** Adhere decorative netting. Adhere trim; tie with ribbon. **3** Stamp frame and for you on cardstock; emboss and trim. **4** Attach to ribbon with safety pin. **5** Fill with necklaces and coins.

MASK 1 Cut mask from patterned paper and cardstock.
2 Adhere trim and feathers to patterned paper mask.
3 Mount on cardstock mask.

Machaca Beef Kim Kesti

This is a yummy Mexican-style dish that cooks up in the crockpot with very little supervision. That leaves me with more time for paper crafting!

INGREDIENTS

1½ lbs. boneless beef roast
1 large onion, sliced
1 can (4 oz.) chopped green chiles
1 tbsp. minced garlic
1 can (28 oz.) chopped tomatoes
1 tsp. salt
½ tsp. cumin
1 tsp. fresh ground pepper

DIRECTIONS Place all ingredients in crockpot, cook on low for 8 to 10 hours. Remove beef from crockpot, set cooking liquid aside. Shred beef, using two forks. Chop remaining ingredients, if necessary, and mix back in with shredded beef.

Use beef for a variety of main dishes: burritos, tacos, enchiladas, chimichangas. Mostly, we like to roll the meat in a warmed tortilla with a dollop of sour cream and enjoy!

Knit 1 Ball of Yarn
Purl 2 Knitting Needles
Chain Stitch 4 Special Friends

SUPPLIES: *Cardstock:* (white) *Patterned paper:* (Gold Die Cut from Lucky collection) Creative Café; (Ring Around The Rosie from Play collection) American Crafts *Accents:* (white library pocket) Bazzill Basics Paper; (felt flowers) Creative Café; (orange brad) Heidi Swapp *Stickers:* (Sweater alphabet) American Crafts *Fibers:* (green striped ribbon) Scrapworks; (orange twine) *Font:* (Attic Antique) www.oldfonts.com *Other:* (yarn skein, knitting needles) **Finished sizes: invitation wrap 4" x 6", favor pocket 3½" x 5"**

:5: Knitting Party   Designer: Kim Kesti

INVITATION 1 Trim patterned paper to finished size. **2** Print invitation on cardstock, trim, and adhere. **3** Wrap invitation around yarn skein. Attach felt flower with brad.

FAVOR POCKET 1 Adhere patterned paper inside library pocket. **2** Adhere patterned paper to pocket front. **3** Affix stickers. Adhere ribbon. **4** Tie felt flower with twine; adhere. Insert knitting needles.

Sticky Chicken Cindy Schow

A friend shared this recipe with me a few months back and it has quickly become one of our family favorites. It's quick and easy to put together with very few ingredients and the best part is that it tastes really good! We like to serve it over rice and have a green salad on the side.

INGREDIENTS

½ c. Kraft Russian salad dressing
½ c. apricot jam
½ envelope Lipton onion soup mix
1 tsp. curry powder
10 - 12 boneless skinless chicken thighs

DIRECTIONS

Arrange chicken pieces in a roaster pan. Mix first four ingredients well and pour over chicken pieces. Cover and bake at 350 degrees for approx. 1½ hours, until tender. Pull chicken apart into small bite-size pieces and mix into sauce. Serve over rice.

SUPPLIES: *Patterned paper:* (Bright Floral, Bright Polka Dot from C'est la Vie collection) My Mind's Eye; (Non-fat Yogurt from Two Scoops collection) BasicGrey *Dye ink:* (Old Paper) Ranger Industries *Accents:* (white, clear buttons) Melissa Frances; (blue felt, cream paper flowers) Making Memories; (red plaid fabric) *Rub-ons:* (Ginger alphabet) American Crafts *Fibers:* (tan twill ribbon) Wrights; (red floss) Martha Stewart Crafts; (aqua grosgrain ribbon) *Font:* (Times New Roman) Microsoft *Die:* (heart bookplate) Provo Craft *Tools:* (decorative-edge scissors, die cut machine) Provo Craft *Other:* (album) Junkitz **Finished size: 9" x 6"**

Family Reunion Recipes Book Designer: Melissa Phillips

BOOKPLATE 1 Die-cut 4" bookplate from patterned paper; sand edges. **2** Adhere fabric behind bookplate; stitch opening edge with floss. **3** Spell "Family recipes" with rub-ons. **4** Stitch buttons to bookplate with floss.

COVER 1 Cut patterned paper to fit cover. Adhere patterned paper strip; ink edges. **2** Trim patterned paper strip with decorative-edge scissors; punch edge. Ink edges and adhere. **3** Stitch edges, tie with ribbon, and adhere. **4** Adhere bookplate. Stitch flowers and button with floss; adhere.

INSIDE 1 Trim patterned paper strips with decorative-edge scissors; punch edges and adhere to patterned paper pieces. **2** Ink edges of patterned paper pieces; adhere. *Note: Tie ribbon around one piece before adhering.* **3** Print recipe on patterned paper; trim. Ink edges and adhere. **4** Stitch flowers and buttons with floss; adhere.

DESIGNER TIP

Collect family favorite recipes from attendees in advance and include them in each family's copy of this recipe book.

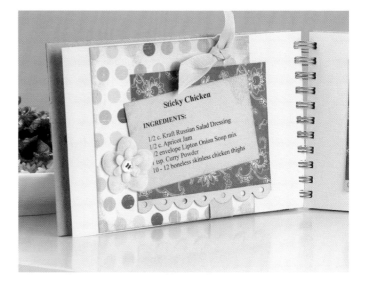

Banana Slush Julie Wilson

This bubbly slush is just the right combination of cool sweetness, and has been a family favorite for years.

INGREDIENTS

6 ripe bananas

1 can frozen orange juice, thawed

1 can frozen pineapple juice, thawed

1 can frozen lemonade, thawed

3 c. sugar

6 c. water

1 liter Sprite

YIELDS 25 SERVINGS

DIRECTIONS Bring water and sugar to boil; let cool. Mix bananas and juices together in blender. Mix into sugar mixture; freeze overnight. To serve, break up frozen mixture with potato masher or large spoon, add Sprite, and mix to create slush.

SUPPLIES: *Cardstock:* (Pineapple) Paper Salon *Patterned paper:* (Beach Towel, Rattan, Swaying Leaves, Stripes from Cabana collection) Paper Salon *Accents:* (trapezoid, flower die cuts) Paper Salon *Rub-ons:* (Heidi alphabet) Making Memories *Stickers:* (green alphabet) EK Success; (Cabana alphabet) Paper Salon *Fibers:* (raffia) *Adhesive:* (foam squares) *Other:* (gift bag) **Finished sizes: invitation 4¼" x 5½", place card 4¾" x 3", gift bag 5½" x 8½"**

 It's a Luau Party Designer: Melanie Douthit

INVITATION 1 Make invitation from Pineapple cardstock. **2** Cut rectangle of Rattan paper slightly smaller than invitation front; adhere. **3** Cut rectangle of Swaying Leaves paper and mat with Beach Towel paper. **4** Apply rub-ons and green alphabet stickers to trapezoid die cut; adhere to Swaying Leaves. **5** Tie raffia around piece and adhere to invitation with foam squares.

PLACE CARD 1 Make card from Pineapple cardstock. **2** Cut rectangle of Rattan paper slightly smaller than card front; adhere. **3** Cut rectangle of Beach Towel paper, apply Cabana alphabet, and adhere to card. **4** Punch holes on corners of Beach Towel; tie raffia.

GIFT BAG 1 Cut rectangle of Rattan paper slightly smaller than bag front; adhere. **2** Cut rectangle of Swaying Leaves paper, mat with Beach Towel paper, and adhere. **3** Cut strip of Stripes paper; adhere. **4** Apply flower die cut with foam square and tie raffia to handle.

Raspberry Sherbet Punch Wendy Gallamore

This pretty pink punch is foamy and light. While simple to prepare, it adds a fancy touch to any festivity.

INGREDIENTS

1 can (12 oz.) raspberry lemonade concentrate
2 cans cold water
½ gal. raspberry sherbet
2 bottles (2 ltr.) lemon-lime soda, chilled

DIRECTIONS

In large punch bowl, combine lemonade concentrate and water. Scoop sherbet into bowl. Pour soda on top just before serving.

YIELDS 25 SERVINGS

5 STEP Pretty in Pink Baby Shower — Designer: Betsy Veldman

BABY FEET CHARMS 1 Stamp baby feet on cardstock; punch. **2** Punch hole in top.

INVITATION 1 Make invitation from patterned paper. Adhere square of patterned paper; stitch edges. **2** Die-cut scalloped square from patterned paper; adhere. **3** Adhere label die cut. Adhere patterned paper strip; stitch. **4** Adhere printed ribbon. Apply rub-on. **5** Emboss flower circle on patterned paper. Punch with scallop circle. Tie baby feet charm with floss, and attach scalloped circle, flower, and charm with brad. Adhere to invitation.

FAVOR 1 Emboss flower circle on patterned paper. Punch with scallop circle. **2** Adhere patterned paper strip. Wrap around chocolate and adhere ends. **3** Tie ribbon around chocolate and knot through scalloped circle, flower, and baby feet charm.

BLOCK 1 Cut patterned paper to fit block sides; stitch edges. **2** Die-cut scalloped squares from patterned paper; adhere to squares; stitch. Adhere to block. **3** Stamp precious baby sentiment on block top. Adhere photos to sides. **4** Embellish as desired.

SUPPLIES: *Cardstock:* (pink) Bazzill Basics Paper *Patterned paper:* (Audrey Pink Floral from Noteworthy collection) Making Memories; (Pink Quilt, Pink Gingham, Adorable Girl Stripe from Adorable Girl collection) Creative Imaginations; (It's a Girl News) KI Memories *Clear stamps:* (baby feet, precious baby sentiment from Baby Sentiments set) My Sentiments Exactly! *Accents:* (pink glitter brads) Creative Imaginations; (white embossed flowers) Prima; (pink felt flowers, scalloped border) Fancy Pants Designs; (label die cut) Making Memories; (pink glitter glue, pink rhinestones) *Rub-on:* (you're invited) Die Cuts With a View *Stickers:* (Adorable Girl alphabet) Creative Imaginations *Fibers:* (white printed ribbon) Creative Imaginations; (pink twill ribbon) Jo-Ann Stores; (pink floss) *Template:* (flower circle embossing) Provo Craft *Die:* (scalloped square) Provo Craft *Tools:* (die cut, embossing machine) Provo Craft; (scallop circle punch, ½" circle punch) EK Success; (⅛" circle punch) *Other:* (wood block) K&Company; (pink wrapped chocolates) Ghirardelli Chocolate; (photos) **Finished sizes: invitation 4½" square, favor 3" x 2", block 4" cube**

Cameron's Orange Smoothie Brenda Peterson

My son, Cameron, started creating smoothies when he was in seventh grade. Now he's the official smoothie maker when our family plays board games. The creamy orange flavor always reminds me of him tossing the ice cubes in the blender for us all to enjoy.

INGREDIENTS

4 oz. frozen orange juice concentrate
¾ c. milk
1 tsp. vanilla
¼ c. sugar
10-12 ice cubes

DIRECTIONS Combine all ingredients in blender. Blend until smooth. *Note: More milk can be added to achieve desired consistency.* Pour into glasses and serve.

YIELDS 2-3 SERVINGS

INVITATION 1 Make card from patterned paper. *Note: Align tail on fold. Ink edges.* **2** Cut large fins and tail from patterned paper. Ink edges; adhere. Cover tail with patterned paper. **3** Affix sticker. Adhere cording and rickrack. **4** Print party information on paper. Trim to fit inside card; adhere.

HAT CHARM 1 Cut small fish and fins from patterned paper. Cover tail with patterned paper. **2** Ink edges and adhere. **3** Attach brad; adhere cording and rickrack. **4** Repeat for additional charms.

HAT 1 Unfold party hat to use as pattern. Trace on patterned paper and cut out. Assemble. **2** Adhere cording. **3** Attach hat charm with cording. **4** Knot ends of ribbon together. Thread through hat; adhere.

STRAW CHARMS 1 Cut small fish and fins from patterned paper. Cover tail with patterned paper. **2** Cut patterned paper to cover back. Adhere ends only to form sleeve. Slide onto straw.

GAME SIGN & CARDS 1 Paint skewer. **2** Cut rectangle from patterned paper. **3** Print game title on paper; trim and adhere. **4** Adhere rickrack. **5** Adhere game sign and hat charm to skewer. Place in fishbowl filled with fish crackers. **6** Print game cards on paper.

We're *reelin'* in a ton of fun as we celebrate **Matthew's birthday!**

We'd love for you to make a *splash* and join us on Saturday, July 18th at 1:00 p.m. at Caldwell Park

Inside

Little Fishy, Little Fishy, Guess how many!

Little Fishy, Little Fishy
Name _____
Guess _____

SUPPLIES: *Paper:* (white) *Patterned paper:* (Stripe/Dot, Confetti/Green from Party Time Boy collection) Pebbles Inc. *Dye ink:* (Citrus Leaf, Sunflower) Close To My Heart *Paint:* (Honeydew) Making Memories *Accents:* (black brads) American Crafts *Sticker:* (dimensional black dot) Pebbles Inc. *Fibers:* (white rickrack) Wrights; (green ribbon) American Crafts; (blue, yellow polka dot ribbon) Michaels; (orange ribbon) Adornit-Carolee's Creations; (white cording) *Font:* (Huxtable) www.1001fonts.com *Other:* (glass fishbowl, straw, party hat, wood skewer, fish crackers) **Finished sizes: invitation 5½" x 6", hat charm 2" x 1¾", hat 4" diameter x 6" height, straw charms 4¼" x 3½", game sign 4¼" x 2¾", game cards 4¼" x 3½"**

Warm Christmas Punch Valerie Pingree

This warm Christmas Punch heats you up from the inside out and is a great addition to a red and green holiday party!

INGREDIENTS

1 (64 oz.) bottle cranberry juice

1 (32 oz.) can pineapple juice

½ c. red-hot candies

1 cinnamon stick

YIELDS 2 QUARTS

DIRECTIONS In slow cooker, combine juices, red-hots, and cinnamon stick. Cook on low for 2–5 hours. Remove cinnamon stick before serving.

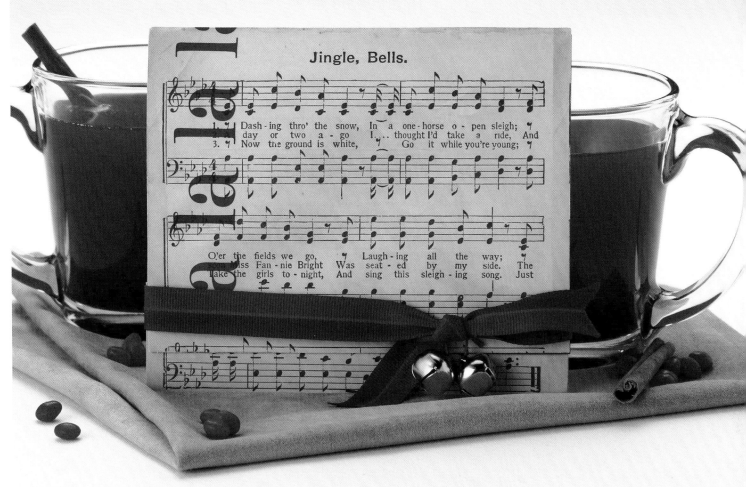

SUPPLIES: *Cardstock:* (red, cream) *Patterned paper:* (Jingle Bells Music) Flair Designs *Dye ink:* (Tea Dye) Ranger Industries *Accents:* (silver jingle bells) *Rub-ons:* (Eddie alphabet, red snowflakes) American Crafts *Fibers:* (red ribbon, red floss) *Fonts:* (TXT Santafont) www.scrapnfonts.com *Other:* (chipboard, music CD) **Finished size: 6¼" x 5¼"**

Christmas Caroling Invite Designer: Valerie Pingree

INSTRUCTIONS 1 Cut chipboard to 6¼" x 11½", then score at 4¾" and 10" to create invitation. **2** Fold flaps and staple bottom for CD pocket. **3** Cover outside of invitation and inside flap with Jingle Bells Music paper. Cover inside with red cardstock. **4** Wrap ribbon around flap, thread bells with floss, and tie. **5** Print party details on cream cardstock, ink edges, and adhere to inside invitation. **6** Cover CD with patterned paper, apply rub-ons, and insert in flap. **7** Apply rub-ons to outside of invitation.

BONUS IDEA

To add warmth and light to your party, wrap candles in matching paper. Complete the look with red ribbon and silver bells.

Creamy Hot Cocoa Orpha Boyden

This chocolate cream can be made the day before an event and easily stored in the fridge. But keep your eye on it—it might disappear early!

INGREDIENTS

4 squares semi-sweet chocolate

1 c. milk

1½ c. sugar

2 dashes salt

1 pint whipping cream, whipped

Hot milk

YIELDS 12–16 SERVINGS

DIRECTIONS Heat chocolate, milk, sugar, and salt in pan, stirring constantly. Boil 4 minutes. Let cool. Fold in whipping cream. To serve, put spoonful in bottom of mug and pour in hot milk. Mix and enjoy!

SUPPLIES: *Patterned paper:* (Velvet Floral, Candy Stripe, Candy Hearts from Ooh La La collection) Bo-Bunny Press *Foam stamps:* (diamonds from Halloween collection) Making Memories *Dye ink:* (black) Stampin' Up! *Paint:* (black) *Rub-ons:* (Jane) American Crafts *Fibers:* (sheer black organza) *Font:* (CK Heritage) Creating Keepsakes *Tools:* (½", 1" circle punch) McGill **Finished size: 3¼" x 6"**

Hot & Steamy Valentine Tag Designer: Valerie Pingree

INSTRUCTIONS **1** Make tag from Velvet Floral paper, and punch hole at top. **2** Punch ½" circle from Candy Stripe, adhere over hole, and tie on ribbon. **3** Stamp diamonds with paint on reverse side of Candy Hearts paper. Cut into strip, ink edges, and adhere to tag. **4** Create sentiment pocket from Candy Stripe paper. Punch half-circle at top. **5** Apply rub-ons, ink edges, and adhere to tag. **6** Print "Wishing you a hot and steamy Valentines Day" on Candy Hearts paper. Trim, ink edges, and slip into pocket.

Christmas Creations

Festive holiday cards, décor, wraps, and more that are sure to inspire and uplift.

The Heart of Christmas

The holiday season is inevitably filled with fresh-baked goodies and sweet confections. Give loved ones a treat to wish them well, and deliver it in one of these smile-inducing gift bags, canisters, or wraps.

SUPPLIES: *Patterned paper:* (Sugar Cookies from Good Cheer collection) October Afternoon *Accents:* (pink button) Autumn Leaves; (white paper snowflake) Making Memories; (clear rhinestones) American Crafts *Stickers:* (scalloped frame) American Crafts; (Shin-Dig alphabet) Doodlebug Design *Fibers:* (white string) *Font:* (Segoe UI) www.ascenderfonts.com *Tool:* (border punch) Fiskars *Other:* (white gift bag) **Finished size: 4¾" x 6½"**

SUPPLIES: *Cardstock:* (pink) *Patterned paper:* (Candy Stripes, Sweet Sprinkles from Be Merry collection) My Mind's Eye *Accents:* (red button) Blumenthal Lansing; (joy tag) My Mind's Eye *Fibers:* (light blue ribbon, pink rickrack) Wrights; (white floss) DMC *Template:* (stocking box) Papertrey Ink **Finished size: 4¾" x 6" x 2¾"**

Snowballs Gift Bag

Designer: Wendy Sue Anderson

❶ Cut rectangle of patterned paper; punch border and adhere.

❷ Print recipe on patterned paper; cut out, adhere to scalloped frame, and adhere frame to bag.

❸ Spell "Snow balls" with stickers.

❹ Adhere rhinestones and snowflake. Thread button with string; tie bow and adhere.

Stocking Stuffer Treat Box

Designer: Wendy Johnson

❶ Cut stockings and box from patterned paper, using template; stitch border on front stocking. Wrap ribbon around piece; tie bow. Assemble and adhere box pieces.

❷ Cut heel and toe pieces from cardstock, using template; stitch borders and adhere.

❸ Cut stocking top from patterned paper, using template. Adhere rickrack and adhere to box.

❹ Thread button with floss; tie to bow. Adhere tag.

SUPPLIES: *Patterned paper:* (Poinsettia Stripe from Fa La La collection) Making Memories *Accents:* (red flower) Prima; (holly leaves, gold brad) Making Memories; (white tag, paper bag) DMD, Inc.; (green button, silver staple) *Stickers:* (Fa La La Tiny Alpha alphabet; Merry Christmas, holiday cheer tags) Making Memories **Finished size:** 4½" x 12"

SUPPLIES: *Patterned paper:* (Red Cabbage Flower from Red & Black collection) Jenni Bowlin Studio *Chalk ink:* (Chestnut Roan) Clearsnap *Accent:* (bird tag) Cavallini Papers & Co. *Sticker:* (believe) Cavallini Papers & Co. *Fibers:* (green ribbon) Offray *Other:* (round tin canister, scrap paper) **Finished size:** 4½" diameter x 6" height

Merry Christmas Bread Wrap

Designer: Susan Neal

❶ Cut strip of patterned paper 4½" wide.

❷ Adhere Merry Christmas tag to white tag; staple and place in bag.

❸ Spell "Recipe" with stickers on tag; adhere bag to strip.

❹ Affix holiday cheer tag; adhere holly leaves.

❺ Attach brad to flower; adhere flower to button. Adhere button.

Believe Canister

Designer: Sherry Wright

❶ Cut patterned paper to fit around canister; ink edges and adhere.

❷ Affix sticker to scrap paper; cut out and adhere to canister, leaving edges unadhered.

❸ Wrap ribbon around canister; tie bow.

❹ Cut bird and branch from tag; adhere.

BONUS IDEA

Wrap this festive accent around a freshly-baked loaf of your favorite holiday bread. Include the recipe so the recipient can re-create your specialty whenever they wish.

SUPPLIES: *Cardstock:* (kraft) Papertrey Ink *Patterned paper:* (Yuletide, Merry & Bright from Oh Joy collection) Cosmo Cricket *Accent:* (red glitter star) Prima *Tool:* (star punch) Stampin' Up! *Other:* (candy) **Finished size: 4" triangle**

SUPPLIES: *Cardstock:* (Classic Red) Prism; (Ripe Avocado, Vintage Cream) Papertrey Ink *Patterned paper:* (tan floral with black flock, black dot, cream print from La Crème collection) Die Cuts With a View; (Winding Vine from Admire collection) My Mind's Eye *Clear stamps:* (teapot, tea time from Tea for Two set) Papertrey Ink; (holiday from Holiday Whimsy set) Tinkering Ink *Chalk ink:* (Creamy Brown) Clearsnap *Specialty ink:* (True Black, Pure Poppy hybrid) Papertrey Ink *Accents:* (clear rhinestones) Kaisercraft *Fibers:* (black ribbon) Papertrey Ink *Template:* (printable recipe holder) Papertrey Ink *Tool:* (border punch) Fiskars **Finished size: 3½" x 4" x ¾"**

Holiday Tree Gift Box

Designer: Maren Benedict

❶ Cut 10¾" x 1½" strip of cardstock; score at 3⅝", 6⅞", and 10½".

❷ Fold strip into triangle; adhere ¼" end over top.

❸ Trace triangle on cardstock, adding slightly larger flaps on each side; cut out and adhere as box bottom.

❹ Cut 11" x 1" strip of patterned paper; adhere around triangle box. *Note: Adhere overlapping edges at bottom of triangle.* Fill box with candy.

❺ Punch star from patterned paper; adhere glitter star.

❻ Attach star to top of box.

Holiday Tea Sampler

Designer: Betsy Veldman

TEA HOLDER

❶ Make holder from cardstock, using template.

❷ Cut strip of cardstock to fit around holder; adhere.

❸ Cut rectangle of patterned paper; ink edges and adhere.

❹ Wrap ribbon around holder; tie bow.

FRONT EMBELLISHMENT

❶ Cut rectangle of patterned paper; mat with cardstock.

❷ Cut strip of patterned paper; punch border on bottom edge and adhere to matted piece. Zigzag-stitch edges.

❸ Cut strip of patterned paper; adhere.

❹ Stamp teapot; cut out, ink edges, and adhere to piece with foam tape. Adhere rhinestones.

❺ Stamp sentiment and adhere entire piece to holder with foam tape.

SUPPLIES: *Accents:* (mini bingo card) Jenni Bowlin Studio; (green holly leaves, white button, red rhinestones, sentiment tag) *Fibers:* (red polka dot ribbon, red floss) *Other:* (clear frosted gift bag, white gift shred, candy) **Finished size: 3" x 5½" x 2"**

SUPPLIES: *Cardstock:* (Crimson) Bazzill Basics Paper; (brown, white) *Patterned paper:* (Peppermint Sticks from Good Cheer collection) October Afternoon *Dye ink:* (black) *Accents:* (red brads) American Crafts; (brown button) Blumenthal Lansing Co. *Fibers:* (red plaid ribbon) Offray; (twine) *Font:* (Minya Nouvelle) www.1001fonts.com *Die:* (3" box) Provo Craft *Tool:* (border punch) *Other:* (paper candy stick) **Finished size: 3" x 3" x 2¼"**

Christmas Wishes Treat Bag

Designer: Melissa Phillips

1 Adhere sentiment tag and rhinestones to bag.
2 Fill bag with gift shred and candy. Fold bingo card over bag top; punch hole, thread ribbon through, and tie knot.
3 Adhere holly leaves.
4 Thread button with floss and adhere.

Muffin for Christmas Caddy

Designer: Wendy Johnson

1 Die-cut box from patterned paper; cut off top flaps, ink top edge, and assemble.
2 Cut strip of cardstock; punch border and adhere inside box.
3 Adhere ribbon around box.
4 Cut heart from cardstock; sand edges, attach brads, and adhere with foam tape.
5 Print sentiment on cardstock; cut out, mat with cardstock, and adhere to candy stick.
6 Thread button with twine; adhere to candy stick.

BONUS IDEA

This cute container is perfect for home-baked muffins, cupcakes, or cookies at a holiday party. You can even send guests home with "one more for the road" in this caddy they can keep.

SUPPLIES: *Cardstock:* (Mocha Divine, Harvest) Bazzill Basics Paper *Patterned paper:* (Mr. Campy Flannel, Nature Walk from Mr. Campy collection) Cosmo Cricket *Sticker:* (car with tree) EK Success *Font:* (Segoe Print) www.fontstock.net *Tool:* (border punch) *Other:* (thermos) **Finished size: 3¼" diameter x 7" height**

SUPPLIES: *Cardstock:* (kraft) *Rubber stamp:* (hot chocolate sign from Winter Vintage Signage set) Cornish Heritage Farms *Dye ink:* (Espresso) Ranger Industries *Pigment ink:* (Sand) Tsukineko *Color media:* (white pen) Ranger Industries; (brown marker) *Accent:* (gold eyelet) *Fibers:* (jute) *Other:* (cream fabric sack) **Finished size: 6½" x 9"**

Tree-Cutting Treat Thermos

Designer: Kim Kesti

1 Cut patterned paper to fit thermos; adhere.

2 Cut wide strip of cardstock; punch borders and adhere.

3 Cut strips of patterned paper; adhere.

4 Affix sticker.

5 Print sentiment on cardstock; cut out and adhere.

BONUS IDEA

Make a thermos for each family member and fill it with steamy hot cocoa. Then surprise them on the ride out to get your tree!

Hot Chocolate Gift Sack

Designer: Joanne Allison

1 Stamp sack randomly.

2 Stamp sign on cardstock; cut out and color.

3 Set eyelet; tie around bag with jute.

DESIGNER TIPS

Place scrap paper inside the sack when stamping both sides to prevent the ink from bleeding through the sack.

Let the stamped image go off the edges of the sack for a more natural look.

SUPPLIES: *Patterned paper:* (Love Shack from Love Shack collection) BoBunny Press *Accent:* (red rhinestones, pink rhinestone flourish) Zva Creative *Fibers:* (red ribbon) Beaux Regards *Other:* (plastic takeout box, scrap cardstock) **Finished size: 4" x 3" x 3"**

SUPPLIES: *Cardstock:* (white) WorldWin *Patterned paper:* (striped, retro diamonds from Glitter Christmas stack) Die Cuts With a View *Accents:* (pink, red rhinestones) Kaisercraft *Fibers:* (black ribbon) May Arts *Font:* (CK Holiday Spirit) Creating Keepsakes *Tools:* (corner rounder, circle punches) *Other:* (can of nuts) **Finished sizes: can 4" diameter x 3¾" height, tag 3¾" x 6½"**

Bejeweled Takeout Box

Designer: Kim Hughes

❶ Remove handle and open box; trace each panel on cardstock.

❷ Cut panels from patterned paper, using cardstock pattern; adhere pieces to box. Reassemble box and attach handle.

❸ Tie ribbon bows around handle.

❹ Cut holly leaves from patterned paper; bend slightly and adhere.

❺ Adhere rhinestones and flourish.

Nutty Gift Set

Designer: Teri Anderson

CAN

❶ Cut patterned paper to fit around can; adhere.

❷ Cut strip of patterned paper to fit around can; adhere.

❸ Adhere rhinestones.

❹ Wrap ribbon around can and tie bow at top.

TAG

❶ Print sentiment on cardstock; trim to finished size.

❷ Adhere strips of patterned paper; round tag corners.

❸ Punch hole; thread ribbon through and knot.

SUPPLIES: *Cardstock:* (red) Bazzill Basics Paper; (brown) *Patterned paper:* (plaid, snow scene from Alpine Frost Tag stack) SEI *Clear stamps:* (foliage, sentiment, icon from Alpine Frost set) SEI *Dye ink:* (black) Stewart Superior Corp. *Accents:* (iridescent glitter) Ranger Industries; (chipboard frame) Tattered Angels; (black buttons) Papertrey Ink *Fibers:* (black gingham ribbon) Papertrey Ink; (black twill, white string) *Die:* (circle) Spellbinders *Other:* (tin canister) **Finished size: card 3" x 3½", canister 2½" diameter x 6" height**

SUPPLIES: *Cardstock:* (kraft) Papertrey Ink *Patterned paper:* (Number from Fa La La collection) Making Memories; (Chopped Tomatoes from Minestrone collection) Jillibean Soup *Chalk ink:* (Dark Brown) Clearsnap *Stickers:* (Tiny Alpha alphabet) Making Memories; (She alphabet) Heidi Swapp *Fibers:* (brown gingham ribbon) Michaels; (red twine) Martha Stewart Crafts *Tools:* (slit, slot punches) Stampin' Up! *Other:* (kraft cookie box) **Finished size: 3½" diameter x 7½" height**

Happy Holidays Gift Canister

Designer: Kimberly Crawford

CARD

❶ Make card from patterned paper; distress edges and adhere glitter.

❷ Cut strip of patterned paper; adhere.

❸ Cut patterned paper to fit behind chipboard frame; adhere to frame.

❹ Punch hole through frame and card; thread ribbon through and tie bow.

❺ Thread button with string; attach to bow.

❻ Adhere ribbon to back of card, leaving 1½" above top of card.

CANISTER

❶ Adhere patterned paper around canister.

❷ Cut cardstock to fit around canister; stamp foliage and adhere.

❸ Cut cardstock strip to fit around canister; stamp sentiment and icon, adhere glitter, and adhere.

❹ Adhere buttons.

❺ Apply glitter glue around edge of lid.

❻ Die-cut circle from cardstock; stamp foliage. Adhere ribbon on card to lid; adhere die-cut circle.

12 Days of Christmas Cookie Box

Designer: Jessica Witty

❶ Adhere patterned paper to cookie box. *Note: Adhere circle of patterned paper to box top.*

❷ Trim strip of patterned paper; adhere.

❸ Cut tag from cardstock, punch slot, and affix stickers to spell "Days of Christmas."

❹ Trim patterned rectangle from patterned paper, affix stickers, and adhere piece to tag with foam tape.

❺ Trim edge of patterned paper strip with slit punch; adhere to tag.

❻ Tie ribbon bow around lid and tie on tag with twine.

GIFT TRIOS:
SPECIAL
A Bag, a Tag, & a Card

CAN'T KEEP YOURSELF FROM BUYING
YOUR FAVORITE PAPER BY THE DOZEN?
HERE ARE SOME IDEAS
THAT WILL HELP YOU GET THE MOST OUT OF YOUR
FAVORITE SUPPLIES AND CREATE A BEAUTIFUL
BAG, TAG, AND CARD IN THE PROCESS!

SUPPLIES: *Cardstock:* (Watermelon) Bazzill Basics Paper; (kraft) Stampin' Up! *Patterned paper:* (Christmas Words) Heidi Grace Designs *Paint:* (Tompte Red, white) Delta *Accents:* (clear rhinestones) Kaisercraft; (chipboard snowflakes) Bazzill Basics Paper *Fibers:* (silver ribbon) *Tools:* (circle, scalloped circle punches) Stampin' Up!; (large circle punch) Marvy Uchida; (border punch) *Other:* (kraft gift bag) Jo-Ann Stores **Finished sizes: bag 4" x 5¼" x 4", tag 3" diameter, card 3¾" square,**

Merry & Bright Trio

Designer: Tanis Giesbrecht

BAG

❶ Cut rectangle of cardstock slightly smaller than bag front and adhere.

❷ Cut cardstock rectangle; punch borders and adhere.

❸ Cut rectangle from patterned paper and mat with cardstock. Adhere.

❹ Paint snowflake; let dry. Adhere rhinestones. Adhere to bag.

TAG

❶ Punch large circle from cardstock and mat with scalloped circle punched from cardstock.

❷ Paint snowflake; let dry. Adhere rhinestones.

❸ Punch word from patterned paper; double-mat with cardstock.

❹ Adhere matted piece to snowflake; adhere snowflake to tag.

❺ Punch hole in tag; tie on ribbon.

CARD

❶ Make card from cardstock.

❷ Cut square of cardstock; mat with cardstock and adhere.

❸ Paint snowflake; let dry. Adhere rhinestones and adhere to card.

❹ Trim sentiment from patterned paper and mat with cardstock. Adhere with foam tape.

SUPPLIES: *Cardstock:* (Vintage Cream, Dark Chocolate) Papertrey Ink *Patterned paper:* (Spice Tea, Cranberry Sauce, Snow Dust from Wassail collection) BasicGrey *Rubber stamps:* (Santa's Coat, Ho! Ho! Ho!) A Muse Artstamps *Dye ink:* (black) Ranger Industries *Color media:* (white gel, gold pens) *Accent:* (copper brad) American Crafts *Fibers:* (red ribbon) May Arts *Dies:* (circle, tag) Spellbinders *Tools:* (corner rounder punch) Creative Memories; (½" circle punch) Stampin' Up!; (⅛" circle punch) McGill; (border punch) **Finished sizes: bag 3" x 5", tag 2⅝" x 2", card 4¼" x 5½"**

Ho! Ho! Ho! Trio

Designer: Maren Benedict

TAG

❶ Make tag from patterned paper and round corners.

❷ Die-cut tag and stamp sentiment.

❸ Attach tag and ribbon with brad.

BAG

❶ Cut 6½" x 11" rectangle of cardstock.

❷ Score at 1", 4", 6", and 9" on long edge. Score at 5" on short edge.

❸ Cut up on two sets of the 1" edges to make box bottom.

❹ Fold along scores and adhere to make box shape. Adhere.

❺ Punch two circles along bag top and tie ribbon through.

❻ Punch border on strip of patterned paper. Adhere.

CARD

❶ Make card from cardstock. Round bottom corners.

❷ Cut rectangle of patterned paper slightly smaller than card front; round corners and adhere.

❸ Cut slit at top of card. Pull ribbon through and tie bow.

❹ Punch circle from patterned paper; mat with cardstock. Stamp coat.

❺ Stamp coat on patterned paper; cut out, color with pens, and adhere with foam tape.

SUPPLIES: *Cardstock:* (Ocean Tides, kraft) Papertrey Ink *Patterned paper:* (Candywrapper from Festive collection) My Mind's Eye *Rubber stamp:* (Joyous Snowfall) Unity Stamp Co. *Dye ink:* (Ruby Red, Sage Shadow) Stampin' Up!; (Antique Linen) Ranger Industries *Fibers:* (blue ribbon) Papertrey Ink; (white string) *Tools:* (decorative-edge scissors, circle punches) Stampin' Up! **Finished sizes: card 4¼" x 5½", tag 3" x 4", bag 8" x 10½"**

Joy Trio

Designer: Maren Benedict

CARD

❶ Make card from cardstock.

❷ Cut rectangle of patterned paper slightly smaller than card front. Mat with cardstock and stitch edges.

❸ Tie ribbon around front flap.

❹ Stamp Joyous Snowfall on cardstock. Trim and adhere with foam tape.

TAG

❶ Cut tag from cardstock.

❷ Cut tag top from patterned paper; trim with decorative-edge scissors. Stitch and bend decorative edge. Punch hole at top and adhere.

❸ Punch circle frame from cardstock, adhere, and attach ribbon. Tie ribbon with string.

❹ Stamp decorative border.

Note: Mask sentiment on stamp.

BAG

❶ Adhere patterned paper to cardstock, zigzag-stitch edges, and adhere.

❷ Tie ribbon in bow and adhere.

SUPPLIES: *Cardstock:* (Vintage Cream, gold) Papertrey Ink *Clear stamps:* (windows from Home for the Holidays set, sentiments from Believe set) Papertrey Ink *Dye ink:* (Antique Linen) Ranger Industries *Accents:* (cream buttons) Papertrey Ink; (white glitter) *Fibers:* (cream ribbon) Papertrey Ink; (gold trim) *Template:* (embossing swirl) Provo Craft *Tool:* (corner rounder punch) EK Success **Finished sizes:** card 4¼" x 5½", tag 2¾" x 2½", box 2⅝" x 5¼" x 2⅝"

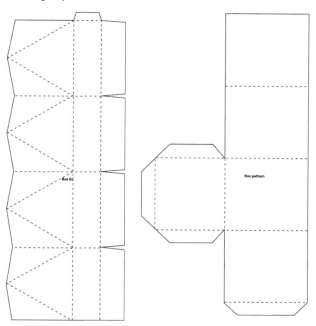

Christmas Wishes Trio

Designer: Claire Brennan

CARD
❶ Make card from cardstock.
❷ Stamp windows and ink edges.
❸ Tie ribbon around card front.

TAG
❶ Stamp sentiment on cardstock; trim and round corners. Ink edges.
❷ Thread buttons with gold trim; adhere
to sentiment.

BOX BASE
❶ Cut box, following pattern.
❷ Stamp windows and ink edges.
❸ Fold box and adhere.

BOX TOP
❶ Cut roof, following pattern; emboss.
❷ Fold and adhere roof with lines on inside.
❸ Adhere glitter.
❹ Stamp sentiment; trim and round corners.
Ink edges.
❺ Thread buttons with gold trim; adhere to sentiment. Adhere other end to inside of roof.

BOX PATTERN
Enlarge by 300%.

Box lid

Box pattern

SUPPLIES: Cardstock: (pink, red, blue) Bazzill Basics Paper Patterned paper: (Snow Dust from Wassail collection) BasicGrey; (Snow Soiree, Tinsel to the Top, Jingle Baubles from Snowy Jo collection) Imaginisce Dye ink: (red, green) Clearsnap Color medium: (red marker) Accents: (red, white glitter glue) Ranger Industries Fibers: (green rickrack) Making Memories; (green ribbon) Dies: (Moxie, Bright alphabets) Quickutz Tools: (decorative-edge scissors, circle punch) EK Success Other: (white gift bag) **Finished sizes: tag 2⅓" x 3¾", bag 4" x 5¼", card 5" x 3¾"**

Be Merry Trio

Designer: Kalyn Kepner

TAG

❶ Make tag from cardstock; ink edges.

❷ Adhere patterned paper rectangle. Trim patterned paper with decorative-edge scissors, ink, and adhere.

❸ Cut circles from patterned paper and adhere. *Note: Adhere center circle with foam tape.*

❹ Draw stitching and apply glitter glue.

❺ Punch hole in top; tie rickrack through hole.

BAG

❶ Cut cardstock to cover bag front; adhere.

❷ Cut paper pieces and adhere.

❸ Punch circles from patterned paper and cardstock; adhere. Draw stitching on center circle.

❹ Cut circles from patterned paper. Adhere.

❺ Apply glitter glue.

CARD

❶ Make card from cardstock; cover front with patterned paper.

❷ Die-cut sentiment from cardstock. Apply glitter glue.

❸ Mat cardstock strip with patterned paper. Trim top edges with decorative-edge scissors and adhere with foam tape.

❹ Draw stitching, apply glitter glue to mat, and adhere letters to spell "Be merry."

❺ Cut circles from patterned paper; adhere. *Note: Adhere ornament circle with foam tape.*

SUPPLIES: *Cardstock:* (cream) Bazzill Basics Paper *Patterned paper:* (Polar Express, 34th Street, Nutcracker, Paislee Postcards from Tinsel Town collection) Pink Paislee *Dye ink:* (brown) *Accents:* (white chipboard star) Melissa Frances; (clear rhinestones) Michaels *Fibers:* (dotted white ribbon) May Arts; (cream trim) Webster's Pages *Tools:* (corner rounder punch) EK Success; (decorative-edge scissors) Fiskars *Other:* (gift bag with clear window) Emma's Paperie *Finished sizes:* card 4¼" x 5½", tag 3" diameter, bag 4¾" x 9½"

Pink & Green Christmas Trio

Designer: Anabelle O'Malley

CARD

❶ Make card from cardstock.

❷ Cut rectangle of patterned paper; stitch edges and adhere. Round corners and ink edges.

❸ Cut sentiment and flourishes from patterned paper; adhere.

❹ Adhere ribbon, trim, and star. Adhere rhinestones.

TAG

❶ Cut tag, tree, and words from patterned paper.

❷ Adhere words and tree to tag. Adhere rhinestone.

❸ Punch hole and tie ribbon through.

BAG

❶ Cut patterned paper to fit bag front; adhere.

❷ Cut rectangle of patterned paper; cut window, trim with decorative-edge scissors, and adhere.

❸ Adhere trim and rhinestones.

❹ Cut trees and flourish from patterned paper; adhere. *Note: Adhere flourish with foam tape.*

❺ Adhere star and rhinestones.

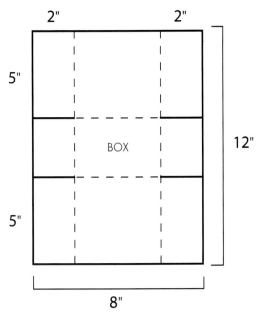

SUPPLIES: Cardstock: (white) Patterned paper: (Flocked Floral, Varnished Vine from Greenhouse Paperie collection; green bracket from Paperie notebook) Making Memories Dye ink: (Close to Cocoa) Stampin' Up! Accents: (red flowers, clear rhinestone brads) Fibers: (cream ribbon) Michaels Fonts: (Notnorval Hmk Bold) Hallmark; (Century Gothic) Microsoft **Finished sizes: box 4" x 5" x 2", tag 6" x 3¾", card 5¾" x 4¾"**

Poinsettia Trio

Designer: Wendy Johnson

BOX

❶ Cut box, following pattern.
❷ Cut lid, following pattern.
❸ Print sentiment on cardstock and trim.
❹ Attach sentiment and flower to box with brad.
❺ Tie box with ribbon.

TAG

❶ Cut triangle from patterned paper.
❷ Cut rectangle from cardstock; ink and adhere.
❸ Print sentiment on cardstock and trim. Attach sentiment and flower with brad.
❹ Punch hole and tie ribbon through.

CARD

❶ Remove page from notebook and trim. Print sentiment, adhere to cardstock, and trim to make base.
❷ Cut slit in fold and tie ribbon bow through. Attach flower with brad.

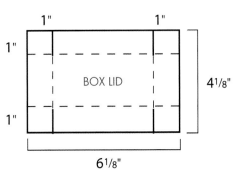

BOX DIAGRAM

Symbols of the Season

THIS HOLIDAY SEASON, GIVE YOUR
FAMILY AND FRIENDS A CARD THEY WILL BE
DELIGHTED TO RECEIVE AND PROUD TO DISPLAY.
These projects include familiar symbols of the holiday season
that will bring the spirit of the holidays to all who see them.

Jingle All the Way Card

Designer: Rae Barthel

Distress all edges.

❶ Make card from cardstock.

❷ Cut rectangles of patterned paper; ink edges and adhere.

❸ Tie on rickrack and twine.

❹ Stamp snowflake on cardstock; cut out. Apply glitter and adhere with foam tape.

❺ Tie on bells with twine.

❻ Adhere journaling tag with foam tape.

SUPPLIES: *Cardstock:* (kraft) DMD, Inc. *Patterned paper:* (Sleigh Bells, Gingerbread from Good Cheer collection) October Afternoon *Foam stamp:* (snowflake) Pebbles Inc. *Chalk ink:* (Charcoal) Clearsnap *Accents:* (brown journaling tag) Cosmo Cricket; (iridescent glitter) Sulyn Industries; (copper bells) *Fibers:* (white rickrack, jute twine) **Finished size: 5½" square**

Snowflake Greetings Card

Designer: Ivanka Lentle

❶ Make card from cardstock; adhere ribbon.

❷ Adhere snowflake and rhinestone.

❸ Apply rub-on.

SUPPLIES: *Cardstock:* (white) Bazzill Basics Paper *Accents:* (red rhinestone) Kaisercraft; (white glitter snowflake) *Rub-on:* (season's greetings) Deja Views *Fibers:* (red ribbon) **Finished size: 5" x 5½"**

5 STEPS · *Merry Christmas Tree Card*

Designer: Sherry Wright

❶ Make card from cardstock; trim into tree shape.

❷ Adhere cardstock triangles to front; ink edges.

❸ Punch photos and cardstock, adhere together, and adhere to card with foam tape.

❹ Stamp and emboss sentiment.

❺ Adhere rhinestones.

5 STEPS · *Peace, Joy, & Love*

Designer: Stefanie Hamilton

❶ Create 3½" x 6½" project in software. Import candy cane clip art and drop onto project.

❷ Open photos and resize to fit on candy cane. Print on photo paper, fold into card, and trim.

❸ Open paper and sentiment in software. Layer sentiment over paper, print on cardstock, and trim into tag shape.

❹ Punch hole in tag and tie to card with ribbon.

SUPPLIES: *Cardstock:* (medium green, light green, red) Bazzill Basics Paper *Rubber stamp:* (merry from Mini Christmas set, Christmas from Holiday Spotlight set) Inque Boutique *Watermark ink:* Ranger Industries *Chalk ink:* (green) Clearsnap *Embossing powder:* (white) Ranger Industries *Accents:* (red, clear, green rhinestones) Creative Crystal *Adhesive:* (foam tape) *Tools:* (1", 1¼" circle punches) McGill *Other:* (photos) **Finished size: 6" x 6¼"**

SUPPLIES: *Cardstock:* (white) *Specialty paper:* (photo) *Digital elements:* (red patterned paper, sentiment from Primary Christmas kit) Creative Memories; (candy cane) www.christmas-graphics-plus.com *Fibers:* (gold ribbon) Offray *Software:* (photo editing) Adobe *Other:* (digital photos) **Finished size: 3¼" x 6½"**

Winter Tin

Designer: Lisa Nichols

❶ Adhere patterned paper to tin.

❷ Apply rub-on.

❸ Punch decorative circles from cardstock; embellish with paper piercer and pen.

❹ Adhere punched circles; punch circle from center. Adhere to lid.

❺ Adhere flat pearl.

❻ Adhere ribbon to lip of lid.

SUPPLIES: All supplies from Stampin' Up! unless otherwise noted. *Cardstock:* (Whisper White, Garden Green, Bravo Burgundy) *Patterned paper:* (Festive from Figgy Pudding collection) BasicGrey *Color medium:* (white pen) *Accent:* (flat pearl) *Rub-on:* (winter snowflake) *Fibers:* (burgundy ribbon) *Tools:* (decorative circle, 1¼" circle punch); (decorative circle punches) Marvy Uchida *Other:* (white tin) Target **Finished size:** 3¾" diameter x 1¼" height

Our House to Yours Box

Designer: Susan Neal

❶ Cover box with patterned paper; cover front of slider with cardstock.

❷ Attach brad to circle sticker; affix to red brad and adhere to slider drawer.

❸ Wrap ribbons around box; adhere.

❹ Print sentiment on cardstock; trim and mat with cardstock. Adhere.

❺ Attach brads to stickers; affix.

SUPPLIES: *Cardstock:* (Spice, Nathan, white) Bazzill Basics Paper *Patterned paper:* (Peppermint Stick from Holly Lane collection) SEI *Accents:* (gold brads) Making Memories; (red brad) SEI *Stickers:* (circle, flower epoxy stickers) SEI *Fibers:* (red, green ribbon) SEI *Font:* (Academia SSi) www.fonts101.com *Other:* (white slider box) **Finished size:** 4½" x 6½" x 2¼"

Christmas Present Topiary

Designer: Kathleen George, courtesy of The Dow Chemical Co.

❶ Cut pairs of squares in various sizes from foam; adhere together to form blocks. ❷ Wrap blocks with patterned paper and wrapping paper. *Note: Use cellophane tape and craft pins to secure.* ❸ Adhere wrapped blocks together. ❹ Slice ½" from each side of foam cube. Cut off angled pieces from sides to create topiary base. ❺ Cover base with cardstock. Cut strip of cardstock with decorative-edge scissors; adhere. ❻ Cover dowel with cardstock. ❼ Insert and adhere dowel into present stack and base. ❽ Adhere and tie on ribbon lengths. Adhere glass balls.

Designer Tip
Cut through polystyrene foam easily with a serrated knife. For even smoother cuts, run the knife along a bar of soap or candle first.

Bonus Idea
This unique topiary can work for many occasions and makes an especially cute party decoration. Try romantic paper for fun shower décor, or bright shapes and geometric patterns for a darling birthday party accent. Mix and match patterned paper and wrapping paper for unique combinations.

SUPPLIES: *Cardstock:* (red, hot pink, tan, green) Bazzill Basics Paper *Patterned paper:* (assorted Christmas prints) *Accents:* (lavender glass balls) *Fibers:* (olive wired, sage sheer ribbon) Offray *Adhesive:* (cellophane tape) *Tool:* (decorative-edge scissors) *Other:* (polystyrene foam pieces: 1" x 12" x 18" sheet; 5" cube) The Dow Chemical Co.; (⅝" wood dowel, craft pins, Christmas wrapping paper) **Finished size: 7" x 16" x 7"**

BONUS IDEA

Create a pail for each season of the year.

Warmth of Christmas Gift Bag

Designer: Jodi Sanford, Courtesy of Fancy Pants Designs

STAR PIECE

❶ Apply paint to star. Let dry.

❷ Apply rub-ons. Tie on ribbon.

BAG FRONT

Ink all paper edges.

❶ Cut patterned paper slightly smaller than bag front. Adhere.

❷ Cut rectangle of patterned paper; tear one end.

❸ Cut strip of patterned paper.

❹ Print sentiment on cardstock. Trim with decorative-edge scissors.

❺ Trim quote from patterned paper. Adhere to patterned paper strip.

❻ Attach scalloped border with staples. Adhere buttons and star piece.

❼ Layer strips and sentiment piece. Attach to bag with clip.

Christmas Tree Pail

Designer: Courtney Kelley

❶ Cut Christmas tree, from patterned paper. Ink edges; adhere.

❷ Adhere buttons.

❸ Knot ribbon around handle as desired.

SUPPLIES: *Cardstock:* (white) *Patterned paper:* (Tree Lot, Candy Cane, Happy Holidays Cards from Happy Holidays collection) Fancy Pants Designs *Pigment ink:* (brown) Tsukineko *Paint:* (pink) *Accents:* (acrylic star; red, brown, green buttons; teal felt scalloped border) Fancy Pants Designs; (red clip) *Rub-ons:* (heart, black alphabet) Fancy Pants Designs *Fibers:* (red/white striped ribbon) Fancy Pants Designs *Font:* (Old Type) www.twopeasinabucket.com *Tool:* (decorative-edge scissors) *Other:* (staples) **Finished size: 8¼" x 11¼"**

SUPPLIES: *Patterned paper:* (Rockville Park from Roxbury collection) Scenic Route *Pigment ink:* (Graphite Black) Tsukineko *Accents:* (pink, red, blue, green buttons) Autumn Leaves *Fibers:* (green, olive, blue stitched, red stitched, blue polka dot ribbon) *Other:* (red pail) Michaels **Finished size: 5" diameter x 4½" height**

5 STEPS — Boxing Day Box

Designer: Stefanie Hamilton

❶ Cover box and lid with patterned paper. ❷ Tie ribbon around box. ❸ To make tag, double-mat sticker with cardstock and patterned paper. ❹ Open new document in word processing program. Create text box and type sentiment. Fill box with red. Change font color to gold. Print on cardstock, trim, and adhere to tag. ❺ Tie twine through button; adhere to tag. Adhere.

5 STEPS — Celebrate Hanukkah Gift Bag

Designer: Lisa Johnson

❶ Stamp and emboss "Hanukkah" on gift bag. ❷ Cut two triangles from cardstock; adhere together to form star. ❸ Stamp celebrate circle on cardstock; punch out. Adhere to larger circle punched from cardstock. Attach snap and adhere to star. ❹ Adhere star to end of cardstock strip; adhere end to bag front. Adhere opposite end to back of bag.

SUPPLIES: *Cardstock:* (red, white) *Patterned paper:* (Holiday Scroll Red, Winterberry from Christmas collection) Flair Designs *Accent:* (tan button) Autumn Leaves *Sticker:* (tag) EK Success *Fibers:* (hemp twine) Michaels; (cream organdy ribbon) *Font:* (Santa's Sleigh) www.dafont.com *Software:* (word processing) **Finished size:** 6¼" x 5¼" x 2¾"

SUPPLIES: *Cardstock:* (Blue Steel, Cryogen White, Gold Ore) Prism *Clear stamps:* (Adrienne's alphabet, celebrate circle from Celebration set) My Sentiments Exactly! *Dye ink:* (Vivid Ultramarine) Clearsnap *Embossing ink:* (clear) Clearsnap *Embossing powder:* (silver) Clearsnap *Accent:* (yellow rhinestone snap) We R Memory Keepers *Tools:* (1½", 1" circle punches) Marvy Uchida *Other:* (white gift bag) DMD, Inc. **Finished size:** 5½" x 8½"

5 STEPS Ribbon Tree

Designer: Laura Stoller

❶ Fold tape strips in half; cut into 3" strips. Fold each piece into loop; pin in rows on foam cone, overlapping each row. ❷ Cut slit through coaster circle; adhere to top of tree. ❸ Adhere two coaster stars together; affix rhinestone star. Fold leftover strip of coaster and insert between coaster stars. Insert inside slit cut through coaster circle.

SUPPLIES: *Accents:* (assorted decorative tape, coaster star, coaster circle) Imagination Project *Sticker:* (rhinestone star) Me & My Big Ideas *Other:* (foam cone) Hobby Lobby; (stick pins) **Finished size: 4" diameter x 9" height**

5 STEPS Noel Wall Hanging

Designer: Emily Montenaro

❶ Trim patterned paper to fit inside frame. ❷ Stamp "Noel" and Loopy Flake on cardstock; mat with cardstock. Embellish with fibers and eyelet; adhere to patterned paper. ❸ Punch snowflake from cardstock; adhere. ❹ Insert piece into frame.

SUPPLIES: *Cardstock:* (black, white) Stampin' Up! *Patterned paper:* (Snowflakes from Joy collection) Autumn Leaves *Rubber stamps:* (Polka Dot alphabet, Loopy Flake) A Muse Artstamps *Specialty ink:* (L'Amour Red hybrid) Stewart Superior Corp. *Accent:* (black eyelet) Doodlebug Design *Fibers:* (black crochet thread) Coats & Clark; (sheer polka dot ribbon) May Arts; (black gingham ribbon) Offray *Tool:* (snowflake punch) Martha Stewart Crafts *Other:* (black frame) **Finished size: 14½" x 7½"**

Joy Wreath

Design: Courtesy of Close To My Heart

1. Stamp sentiments on cardstock; ink edges. Cut out; adhere to tags. Tie ribbon through tag; adhere tags to wreath. 2. Thread buttons and adhere to form holly. Stamp leaves on cardstock; trim and adhere to wreath. 3. Ink edges of cardstock letters. Adhere to wreath to spell "Joy". 4. Tie ribbon to top of wreath to create hanger.

Birdie Box

Designer: Lisa Zappa

1. Paint; let dry. 2. Trim and adhere patterned paper. Apply finish; let dry. 3. Tie ribbon around box. 4. Mat bird image with cardstock; ink and distress edges. Adhere to ribbon.

SUPPLIES: All supplies from Close To My Heart unless otherwise noted. *Cardstock:* (Colonial White, New England Ivy) *Clear stamps:* (leaf from O Christmas Tree, sentiments from Christmas Greeting set) *Dye ink:* (Chocolate, Cranberry, New England Ivy) *Accents:* (silver brad, metal-rimmed circle tags, red buttons, chipboard letters) *Fibers:* (Cranberry, New England Ivy ribbon) *Other:* (grapevine wreath) no source **Finished size: 9" diameter**

SUPPLIES: *Cardstock:* (Real Red, True Thyme) Stampin' Up! *Patterned paper:* (Red Floral, Green Flowers Earthy, Beige Classic, Birds from Heartwarming Vintage collection) Crafty Secrets *Dye ink:* (Vintage Photo) Ranger Industries *Paint:* (Cranberry) Making Memories *Fibers:* (red gingham ribbon) May Arts *Finish:* (sealer) Delta *Other:* (wood box) Michaels **Finished size: 6¾" x 4½" x 4½"**

DESIGNER TIPS

Fill the cellophane bags with ribbon, tag blanks, brads, sparkly flowers, and other coordinating embellishments.

Use the basket as a functional decoration. Fill it with scissors, tape, and pens for people to use throughout the evening.

It's a Wrap Party

Designer: Kim Kesti

INVITATION

❶ Make gate-fold invitation from cardstock. Adhere slightly smaller piece of patterned paper. ❷ Adhere ribbon. ❸ Stamp scalloped oval on cardstock, write "It's a wrap" with marker, trim, and adhere with foam squares.

FAVOR

❶ Make bag topper from patterned paper. ❷ Stamp scalloped oval on cardstock, write "Tag kit" with marker, trim, and adhere.
❸ Fill bag with tag kit supplies; adhere topper to cellophane bag.

BASKET

❶ Tie ribbon around top. ❷ Stamp dotted gift on cardstock; apply glitter glue. Trim into tag shape, punch hole and attach to ribbon with safety pin.

SUPPLIES: *Cardstock:* (Cherry Splash, Lace) Bazzill Basics Paper *Patterned paper:* (Candy Cane from Winter Wonderland collection) Sassafras Lass *Rubber stamp:* (scalloped oval) 7gypsies *Clear stamps:* (snowflake, dotted gift from Winter Wonders set) Autumn Leaves *Dye ink:* (black) *Chalk ink:* (Lipstick Red) Clearsnap *Color medium:* (black marker) Sakura *Accents:* (red glitter glue) Ranger Industries; (red safety pin) *Fibers:* (red grosgrain ribbon) May Arts *Adhesive:* (foam squares) *Other:* (cellophane bag, wicker basket, tag kit supplies) **Finished sizes: invitation 4" square, favor 5" x 7", basket 5½" x 4" x 3"**

⁵⁵ₛₜₑₚₛ *Christmas Organizer*

Designer: Maria Burke

❶ Affix stickers to spell "Christmas". ❷ Apply rub-ons.
❸ Tie and adhere rickrack and button to front flap.
❹ Print "Organizer" on cardstock; ink edges and adhere.

Designer Tip
Give these handy organizers to your family after
Thanksgiving dinner as a fun way to kick off the
holiday season.

Gingerbread Man Coupon Book

Designer: Alisa Bangerter

❶ Fold cardstock in half twice. ❷ Draw gingerbread man on
folded card stock, lining up edges of arms and legs on folds;
trim. ❸ Adhere two sets of gingerbread men together with
cardstock strips behind arms and legs. ❹ Create perforations
along arm and leg folds with paper piercer. ❺ Chalk all edges
and cheeks. ❻ Punch two red hearts and adhere to cheeks.
Draw mouth and attach brads to form eyes. ❼ Thread buttons;
adhere. ❽ Adhere rickrack to arms and legs. Tie bow; adhere.
❾ Print sentiment and coupons on cardstock. Trim, ink
edges, and mat with cardstock; adhere.

SUPPLIES: *Cardstock:* (white) SEI *Pigment ink:* (green) *Accents:* (clear button)
Autumn Leaves *Rub-ons:* (trees, snowflakes, border) SEI *Stickers:* (Doodley-Doo
Holiday alphabet) SEI *Fibers:* (green rickrack) SEI *Font:* (Acoustic Light) www.mom-
scorner4kids.com *Other:* (accordion notes file) Target **Finished size: 6½" x 4¼"**

SUPPLIES: *Cardstock:* (cream, red, light brown) *Color media:* (pink, brown chalk)
Craf-T Products; (black pen) *Accents:* (red buttons) American Crafts; (black brads)
Making Memories *Fibers:* (brown polka dot ribbon) May Arts; (white rickrack) Wrights;
(white string) *Fonts:* (CK Darling, CK Sassy) Creating Keepsakes *Tool:* (small heart
punch) Fiskars **Finished size: 2¾" x 4"**

INSIDE

BONUS IDEA

Create a fold-out scrapbook or accordion album using the same paper and accents to put inside the tin.

GOOD THINGS COME IN SMALL PACKAGES

SUPPLIES: *Patterned paper:* (First Gift, Sleigh Ride, Holly & Berries, Strip Tease, Holiday Cheer, Journaling Cards from Wonderland collection) Cosmo Cricket *Dye ink:* (Vintage Photo) Ranger Industries *Accents:* (silver jump ring) Darice; (glitter) Stampin' Up! *Fibers:* (burgundy stitched ribbon) Offray; (burgundy velvet ribbon) BasicGrey *Adhesive:* (foam squares) *Tool:* (decorative-edge scissors) Fiskars *Other:* (tin) KI Memories **Finished size: 5" x 7" x ½"**

Good Things Tin

Designer: Lisa Falduto

TIN

❶ Trace front and back of tin on patterned paper. Trim, ink edges, and adhere. ❷ Cut strip of patterned paper to fit around lip of lid. Ink edges and adhere. ❸ Cut strip of patterned paper. Trim one edge with decorative-edge scissors. Ink edges. ❹ Adhere ribbon and sentiment to strip; adhere.

EMBELLISHMENTS

❶ Cut snowflake from patterned paper. Apply glitter; let dry. ❷ Punch hole and attach jump ring. ❸ Cut rectangle, oval, and Santa from patterned paper. ❹ Punch hole in rectangle; attach jump ring and snowflake. ❺ Tie ribbon bow; adhere to embellishment. ❻ Adhere pieces together with foam squares; adhere to tin.

Merry Christmas Thanks Card Set

Designer: Jessica Witty

CARDS & ENVELOPES

❶ Cut strips of patterned paper. Round one corner; adhere. ❷ Stamp sentiment on card and ink edges. ❸ Repeat steps 1–2, using different patterned paper. ❹ Stamp border on bottom of envelopes.

TAG

❶ Cut tag shape from cardstock; ink left edge. ❷ Cut strip of patterned paper; adhere. ❸ Stamp sentiments; round edges. ❹ Punch hole and thread floss through tag. ❺ Tie ribbon around cards and envelopes; attach tag.

SUPPLIES: *Cardstock:* (Whisper White) Stampin' Up! *Patterned paper:* (King's Daughter, The Well, Golden Ball from Frog Prince collection) Piggy Tales *Clear stamps:* (just a little note from Thank You set, border from Celebrate set) Fiskars; (to, from, Merry Christmas from Carolers set) Rubber Soul *Chalk ink:* (Olive Pastel) Clearsnap *Fibers:* (blue dotted grosgrain ribbon) Offray; (white floss) *Tool:* (corner rounder punch) EK Success *Other:* (cards, envelopes) MPR Paperbilities **Finished sizes: cards 4¾" square, tag 3½" x 2¾"**

Tic Tac Snow Game

Designer: Mandy Douglass, courtesy of American Crafts

COVER

❶ Cut two squares of patterned paper; round edges. ❷ Trim sheet protector to fit bottom half of one square. Stitch to reverse side to form pocket. ❸ Adhere ribbon to cover. ❹ Adhere squares, patterned sides together. ❺ Affix stickers to spell "Tic tac snow". ❻ Adhere snowflakes to front; fill pocket with snowflakes. ❼ Insert cover into CD case.

GAME BOARD

❶ Cut chipboard square. ❷ Cover with patterned paper; round edges and sand. ❸ Cut four strips of patterned paper. Adhere reverse side up. ❹ Insert into CD case.

SUPPLIES: All supplies from American Crafts unless otherwise noted. *Patterned paper:* (Peanut, Lil' Man from The Goods collection) *Accents:* (chipboard snowflakes) *Stickers:* (Sweater alphabet) *Fibers:* (snowflake ribbon) *Tool:* (corner rounder punch) EK Success *Other:* (chipboard, sheet protector, CD case) no source **Finished size: 5½" square**

Sugar Cookies
3/4 Cup Shortening (part butter)
1 Cup Sugar
2 eggs
1/2 Tsp. Vanilla
2 1/2 Cups Flour
1 Tsp. baking soda
1 Tsp. Salt
Mix first four ingredients Thoroughly. Blend in Flour, Baking powder and Salt. Chill at Least one hour. Roll Dough 1/8" Thick, Cut with Cookie cutter, Bake at 400 degrees for 6-8 minutes

Have a Wonderful Holiday "With Sprinkles on Top" With This Cookie Decorating Kit Love, The Kesti's

Cookies for You Decorating Party

Designer: Kim Kesti

RECIPE CARD & SIFTER WRAP

❶ Print cookie recipe on cardstock; round corners. Mat with cardstock. ❷ Paint dots on cardstock, adhere rickrack border, and mat with cardstock. Adhere. ❸ Repeat step 2 for sifter wrap.

COOKIE CUTTER INSERT

❶ Cut cardstock to fit inside cookie cutter. ❷ Print text on cardstock, trim slightly smaller than cardstock base; adhere. ❸ Adhere rickrack border and paint dots. ❹ Adhere insert sides to inside of cookie cutter.

JAR WRAPS

❶ Adhere borders to cardstock. Trim and adhere to jars. ❷ Punch circles from patterned paper. Adhere to lids.

Bonus Ideas

- Give this kit to neighbors or family friends for an interactive approach to the holidays.
- Fill the spice jars with sprinkles and other treats for cookie decorating, and include some fun icing to help your recipients really dress up their sugary creations.

SUPPLIES: *Cardstock:* (Dark Grassy Green) WorldWin; (Cardinal, Lily) Bazzill Basics Paper *Patterned paper:* (Orange with Aqua Dots) American Crafts; (Seabreeze Polka Dots) Doodlebug Design; (Shabby Princess Dot) Bo-Bunny Press; (Green Dots) Sassafras Lass *Paint:* (Key Lime, School Bus, Waterslide, Red Wagon) Making Memories *Accents:* (green scalloped, yellow scalloped, red rickrack, blue rickrack borders) Doodlebug Design *Font:* (Snoopy Snails) www.myfonts.com *Tools:* (corner rounder punch, 1½" circle punch) *Other:* (cookie cutter, sifter, spice jars) **Finished size: recipe card 3½" x 7", sifter wrap 12" x 2½", cookie cutter insert 3" x 4", jar wraps 6" x 1"**

Be Jolly Treat Bag

Designer: Cheryl Kanenwisher, courtesy of One Heart One Mind

❶ Remove perforated piece from patterned paper. Trace bag shape on reverse side of paper, using template. *Note: Position torn edge at top of bag.* Cut out. ❷ Cut round window in bag front. Cut circle from transparency sheet and adhere behind window. Apply rub-on. ❸ Assemble. ❹ Adhere paper strip for handle. ❺ Attach brads.

SUPPLIES: *Patterned paper:* (Coverall from Merry Merry Too collection) One Heart One Mind *Transparency sheet:* Hammermill *Accents:* (polka dot brads, striped border strip) One Heart One Mind *Rub-on:* (be jolly) One Heart One Mind *Templates:* (circle) Provo Craft; (Jack O'Lantern Treat Bag) www.dltk-holidays.com **Finished size:** 2½" x 4½" x 1¾"

Season's Eatings Box

Designer: Meera D'Souza

❶ Adhere lace around box. ❷ Adhere patterned paper and rick-rack. ❸ Stitch button to flower; adhere. ❹ Spell "Season's eatings" with rub-ons and chipboard letters. ❺ Tie ribbon on handle.

SUPPLIES: *Patterned paper:* (Rudolph from The Goods collection) American Crafts *Accents:* (red button) Autumn Leaves; (white flower) Imaginisce; (chipboard alphabet) Heidi Swapp *Rub-ons:* (Heidi alphabet) Making Memories *Fibers:* (assorted ribbon) Michaels; (white rickrack) May Arts; (white lace) Jo-Ann Stores *Other:* (green take-out box) Westrim Crafts **Finished size:** 4" x 4" x 4"

DESIGNER TIP

For an alternative look, accent boxes with photos or stamped images.

Photo Ornaments

Designer: Sherry Wright

❶ Adhere reverse side of patterned paper to ornaments. ❷ Using ornaments as templates, trim patterned paper to fit front. Punch out circles; adhere, leaving open on one side to insert photos. ❸ Adhere stickers with foam tape. ❹ Punch hole through each ornament top; tie on ribbon to create hanger.

Joy Tree

Designer: Julia Sandvoss

❶ Paint wood tree; let dry. ❷ Trim patterned paper to fit around tree. Ink and doodle edges; adhere to tree. ❸ Trace shape of tree openings; trim patterned paper to fit inside each opening. Embellish with stickers, rub-ons, and rhinestones; adhere inside tree. ❹ Cut stars from patterned paper; embellish with glitter, button, and pen; adhere to top of tree.

SUPPLIES: *Patterned paper:* (Starburst, Blizzard, Pear Flourish from Dazzle collection) Paper Salon *Stickers:* (sentiments) Making Memories *Fibers:* (red sheer ribbon) Offray *Adhesive:* (foam tape) *Tool:* (1¼" circle punch) Marvy Uchida *Other:* (chipboard ornaments) Creative Imaginations; (photos) **Finished sizes: tree 3½" x 5", star 5" x 5", ornament 3½" x 5¼"**

SUPPLIES: *Patterned paper:* (Garland, Candy Stripe, Blizzard, Starburst from Dazzle collection) Paper Salon *Chalk ink:* (blue) Clearsnap *Color medium:* (black pen) American Crafts *Paint:* (blue, white) *Accents:* (acrylic snowflakes) Heidi Swapp; (clear rhinestones, glitter, red button) *Rub-ons:* (Dazzle alphabet) Paper Salon *Stickers:* (trees, stocking, ornament) EK Success; (silver snowflakes) EK Success *Tool:* (decorative-edge scissors) Fiskars *Other:* (wood tree) Hobby Lobby **Finished size: 11" x 12"**

DESIGNER TIP

Make a photo album for grandma or grandpa using photos from your child's school program or church's holiday play.

Christmas Snapshots Album

Designer: Debbie Olson

❶ Cover album cover with patterned paper. Die-cut patterned paper and adhere.

❷ Mat photo with cardstock; ink edges and adhere.

❸ Stamp Christmas and "Snapshots" on patterned paper, round corners, and sand edges. Mat with cardstock, round corners, stitch edges, and adhere.

❹ Adhere patterned paper to star, sand edges, and adhere. Tie string through button and adhere.

❺ Tie ribbon bow.

❻ Decorate inside pages as desired, attach together with book ring.

INSIDE

SUPPLIES: *Cardstock:* (New Leaf) Papertrey Ink *Patterned paper:* (Merry & Bright, Mitten Mitten from Oh Joy collection) Cosmo Cricket *Clear stamps:* (Christmas from Holiday Wishes set, Fresh Alphabet) Papertrey Ink *Dye ink:* (Red Riding Hood) Stampin' Up!; (Antique Linen) Ranger Industries *Accents:* (yellow button) Autumn Leaves; (chipboard star) Cosmo Cricket *Fibers:* (green ribbon) Papertrey Ink; (white string) *Die:* (bracket) Stampin' Up! *Tool:* (corner rounder punch) *Other:* (chipboard album, silver book ring) Cosmo Cricket; (photo) **Finished size: 6" x 3¾"**

New Dad Keychain

Designer: Kim Kesti

① Apply rub-on and adhere rhinestones to tag.

② Trim photo and adhere. Adhere patterned paper.

③ Knot ribbon and adhere. Attach ring.

For You Gift Card Holder

Designer: Teri Anderson

① Trim patterned paper into triangle.

② Trim slightly smaller piece of patterned paper; stitch edges with crochet thread. Adhere two sides of triangle, creating pocket.

③ Punch tag from cardstock, write "For you", and tie on with twine.

④ Thread button with crochet thread and adhere.

⑤ Insert gift card into pocket.

SUPPLIES: *Patterned paper:* (Smarty Pants from Let's Pretend collection) Imaginisce *Accents:* (orange rhinestones) Heidi Swapp *Rub-on:* (antique frame) Hambly Screen Prints *Fibers:* (black houndstooth ribbon) Scrapworks *Other:* (acrylic tag, silver book ring) Scrapworks; (photo) **Finished size: 5" x 3"**

SUPPLIES: *Cardstock:* (white) *Patterned paper:* (Greetings, Tree Lot from Wassail collection) BasicGrey *Color medium:* (black pen) *Accent:* (red button) Oriental Trading Co. *Fibers:* (white crochet thread) DMC; (jute twine) *Tool:* (tag punch) Martha Stewart Crafts *Other:* (gift card) **Finished size: 4½" x 5¼"**

INSIDE

Frosty Nights Card
Designer: Kimberly Crawford

ACCENT

1. Die-cut scalloped oval from cardstock; paint edges.
2. Die-cut and emboss two ovals from cardstock. Cut one oval in half with curve. Layer ovals on scalloped oval; apply glitter glue.
3. Stamp snowman on cardstock; color and cut out. Stamp snowman clothing on patterned paper; cut out and adhere to snowman. Adhere to oval piece with foam tape.

CARD

1. Make card from cardstock; distress edges.
2. Stamp polka dots on card; apply glitter glue.
3. Mat patterned paper strip with cardstock; distress edges and adhere.
4. Stamp sentiment on card.
5. Adhere accent to card with foam tape.
6. Paint snowflake and heart; adhere. Thread button with twine; tie and adhere.

To You from Me Card
Designer: Cathy List

Ink all edges.

OUTSIDE

1. Accordion-fold cardstock; paint edges.
2. Stitch and distress edges of patterned paper; adhere.
3. Stamp sentiment on cardstock; stitch and distress edges. Mat with cardstock and adhere.
4. Stamp tree and bird on cardstock; trim, color, and apply glitter. Wrap tree with string. Adhere bird and tree with foam tape.
5. Color star; adhere rhinestones.

INSIDE

1. Adhere center folds together. Stamp snowflake on cardstock and adhere. Die-cut center section.
2. Adhere patterned paper.
3. Stamp definition on cardstock. Adhere patterned paper strips; stitch.
4. Adhere definition panel; trim.

SUPPLIES: *Cardstock:* (Pure Poppy, Aqua Mist, kraft, white) Papertrey Ink *Patterned paper:* (Stripes from Snowed In collection) My Mind's Eye *Clear stamps:* (polka dots from Polka Dot Basics set; sentiment, snowman from Made of Snow set) Papertrey Ink *Dye ink:* (Tuxedo Black) Tsukineko *Watermark ink:* Tsukineko *Color medium:* (orange, blue markers) Copic *Paint:* (white, red) Making Memories *Accents:* (iridescent glitter glue) Ranger Industries; (blue button) Autumn Leaves; (chipboard heart) Maya Road; (chipboard snowflake) Making Memories *Fibers:* (natural twine) May Arts *Adhesive:* (foam tape) *Dies:* (oval, scalloped oval) Spellbinders **Finished size: 5" square**

SUPPLIES: *Cardstock:* (kraft) Paper Reflections; (Real Red, Whisper White) Stampin' Up! *Patterned paper:* (blue snowflakes from Ski Slope collection; green brocade from Bella Rose collection) Stampin' Up! *Rubber stamps:* (tree from Three Trees set; bird from Decorative Birds set) Hero Arts; (to you sentiment from Best Yet set; because definition from Define Your Life set; snowflake from Winter Post set) Stampin' Up! *Dye ink:* (Kiwi Kiss, Baja Breeze, Real Red) Stampin' Up!; (black) Stewart Superior Corp. *Watermark ink:* Tsukineko *Color medium:* (Real Red, Chocolate Chip markers) Stampin' Up! *Paint:* (white) *Accents:* (red glitter) Stampin' Up!; (blue, star rhinestones) Hero Arts *Fibers:* (white string) *Adhesive:* (foam tape) Stampin' Up! *Die:* (bracket) Ellison **Finished size: 3" x 4¼"**

Pretty Paper Tags
Designer: Kristen Swain

LOVE
1. Cut patterned paper to finished size, using decorative-edge scissors.
2. Cut rectangle of patterned paper; mat with patterned paper and adhere.
3. Cut square of patterned paper; adhere.
4. Cut triangles and strips of patterned paper; adhere to create trees. *Note: Adhere one tree with foam tape.*
5. Adhere buttons; tie twine bow and adhere.
6. Cut rectangle of patterned paper; attach brad and spell "Love" with stickers. Adhere.
7. Set eyelets; knot ribbon ends through eyelets to create hanger.

NOEL
1. Cut patterned paper to finished size, using decorative-edge scissors.
2. Cut rectangle of patterned paper; mat with patterned paper and adhere.
3. Cut rectangle of patterned paper; adhere.
4. Cut rectangle of patterned paper; attach brad and spell "Noel" with stickers. Adhere.
5. Die-cut snowflakes from patterned paper; adhere. *Note: Adhere one snowflake with foam tape.*
6. Thread button with twine; tie bow and adhere.
7. Set eyelets; knot ribbon ends through eyelets to create hanger.

JOY
1. Cut patterned paper to finished size, using decorative-edge scissors.
2. Cut rectangle of patterned paper; mat with patterned paper and adhere.
3. Cut strip of patterned paper; adhere.
4. Cut rectangle of patterned paper; attach brad and spell "Joy" with stickers. Adhere.
5. Cut out bird from patterned paper; adhere.
6. Cut wing shape from patterned paper; adhere with foam tape. Thread button with twine; tie bow and adhere.
7. Set eyelets; knot ribbon ends through eyelets to create hanger.

SUPPLIES: *Patterned paper:* (Grey Cube on Worn Background; Landings Way, Whitaker Street, River Walk, Lockwood Lane, Baywood Lane from Laurel collection) Scenic Route *Accents:* (pearlescent buttons) BoBunny Press; (assorted yellow, blue buttons) Darice; (orange, pink, blue brads) Jo-Ann Stores; (green, pink eyelets) We R Memory Keepers *Stickers:* (Tiny Alpha alphabet) Making Memories *Fibers:* (pink stitched, orange ribbon) We R Memory Keepers; (yellow twine) The Beadery *Adhesive:* (foam tape) 3M *Dies:* (snowflakes) Provo Craft *Tool:* (decorative-edge scissors) Jo-Ann Stores **Finished size: love 3" x 4½", noel 4¾" x 3¼", joy 3¼" x 4¾"**

Lacy Merry Christmas Card

Designer: Charlene Austin

1. Make card from cardstock.
2. Cut rectangle of patterned paper; mat with cardstock and adhere.
3. Adhere trim and button.
4. Tie twill bow and adhere. Adhere rhinestones.
5. Apply rub-on.

Bright Be Merry Card

Designer: Wendy Sue Anderson

1. Make card from patterned paper.
2. Cut rectangle of cardstock; adhere.
3. Cut rectangle of patterned paper; stitch border.
4. Tie ribbon around stitched piece; spell sentiment with stickers and adhere piece to card.
5. Apply glitter glue to tree; adhere with foam tape.
6. Tie ribbon bow and adhere.

SUPPLIES: *Cardstock:* (Vintage Cream, Ripe Avocado) Papertrey Ink *Patterned paper:* (Recipe Book from Noel collection) KI Memories *Accents:* (clear rhinestone) Darice; (clear mini rhinestones) Martha Stewart Crafts; (blue button) *Rub-on:* (Merry Christmas) Imaginisce *Fibers:* (white twill) Papertrey Ink; (white lace trim) Wal-Mart **Finished size: 4¼" x 5½"**

SUPPLIES: *Cardstock:* (white scalloped) Bazzill Basics Paper *Patterned paper:* (Number from Fa La La collection) Making Memories; (Sugar Cubes from Spring & Summer collection) American Crafts *Accents:* (silver glitter glue) Ranger Industries; (blue tree die cut) My Mind's Eye *Stickers:* (Shin Dig alphabet) Doodlebug Design *Fibers:* (teal ribbon) American Crafts **Finished size: 6" x 4"**

Snowman Noel Card

Designer: Rae Barthel

❶ Make card from cardstock; adhere strips of patterned paper.

❷ Punch border on cardstock strip; adhere strip of patterned paper.

❸ Tie ribbon on punched block. Adhere block to card.

❹ Thread button with string. Adhere with foam tape.

❺ Trim cardstock and adhere behind chipboard frame. Adhere frame with foam tape. Adhere pearls.

❻ Trim snowman from patterned paper. Adhere with foam tape.

❼ Apply rub-on to die cut; adhere with foam tape.

Winter Wonderland Card

Designer: Kristie Larsen

❶ Make card from cardstock.

❷ Cut square of cardstock; stamp snowflakes and emboss. Mat with cardstock and adhere.

❸ Adhere stickers with foam tape and tie on ribbon.

SUPPLIES: *Cardstock:* (black, cream) Hobby Lobby *Patterned paper:* (Sleigh Bells, Falling Snow from Good Cheer collection) October Afternoon *Accents:* (die cut tag) Jenni Bowlin Studio; (white pearls, mini pearls) Kaisercraft; (black chipboard frame) American Crafts; (red button) *Rub-on:* (noel) Creative Imaginations *Fibers:* (black ribbon) Offray; (white waxed string) *Tool:* (border punch) Fiskars **Finished size: 4¼" x 6"**

SUPPLIES: *Cardstock:* (Aqua Mist, Pure Poppy, Ripe Avocado) Papertrey Ink *Rubber stamp:* (Stunning Snowflakes Backgrounder) Hero Arts *Watermark ink:* Stampin' Up! *Embossing powder:* (silver) Papertrey Ink *Stickers:* (chipboard snowflakes, holly, flourish) Me & My Big Ideas *Fibers:* (red twill) Papertrey Ink **Finished size: 5¼" square**

DESIGNER TIP

When using colored pencils, color darkest at the edges along the stamped image to add subtle depth.

BONUS IDEA

Remove the holly and change the sentiment to use this card for any occasion!

5 STEPS · Gnome for the Holidays Card
Designer: Kim Hughes

1. Make card from cardstock; cover with patterned paper.
2. Cut strip of patterned paper, adhere, and trace seam with pen.
3. Stamp gnome, tree, cloud, and mushroom on cardstock; color with pencils. Outline with pen, trim, and adhere.
4. Spell "Gnome for the holidays" with label maker; affix.
5. Trim holly leaves from cardstock; adhere. Adhere rhinestone.

5 STEPS · Holiday Friends Card
Designer: Jennifer Buck

1. Make card from cardstock.
2. Trim rectangle from card front; adhere transparency sheet to inside cover.
3. Stamp sentiment on inside of card.
4. Using template, mark circle spots with pencil. Cover with glitter glue and paint. *Note: Paint and glitter dots appearing inside card and let dry before doing card front.*
5. Tie on ribbon.

SUPPLIES: *Cardstock:* (white) Cornish Heritage Farms; (Meadow) Core'dinations *Patterned paper:* (Travel Log from Fresh Print Traveler collection) Little Yellow Bicycle; (green flowers from Specialty Baby Girl pad) Me & My Big Ideas *Rubber stamps:* (gnome, tree, clouds, mushroom from Forest Friendzy set) Cornish Heritage Farms *Solvent ink:* (black) Tsukineko *Color media:* (assorted colored pencils) Prismacolor; (black pen) Sakura *Accent:* (orange rhinestone) Me & My Big Ideas *Sticker:* (black label tape) DYMO *Tool:* (label maker) DYMO **Finished size: 3¾" x 5"**

SUPPLIES: *Cardstock:* (white) *Transparency sheet; Clear stamp:* (sentiment from Believe set) Papertrey Ink *Dye ink:* (Tuxedo Black) Tsukineko *Paint:* (red dimensional) Ranger Industries *Accent:* (gold glitter glue) Ranger Industries *Fibers:* (red/brown striped ribbon) Stampin' Up! *Template:* (paper piercing circles) Bazzill Basics Paper **Finished size: 4¼" x 5½"**

BONUS IDEA

Make a fun family Christmas card by adhering your family photo onto the front. Allow room for a greeting on the inside.

Baby it's Cold Outside! Card
Designer: AJ Otto

❶ Die-cut and emboss two scalloped circles from cardstock. Fasten together with brad.

❷ Die-cut circle from cardstock, cover half with patterned paper, and tie on ribbon. Mat with die-cut cardstock circle.

❸ Mat with die-cut cardstock circle, adhere, and stamp sentiment. Pierce line.

❹ Thread button and adhere. Adhere rhinestones.

Let Us Adore Him Card
Designer: Susan R. Opel

❶ Make card from cardstock.

❷ Trim cardstock piece; adhere.

❸ Adhere border and church.

❹ Print sentiment on cardstock, trim, and round corners. Mat with cardstock; adhere.

❺ Adhere rhinestones.

❻ Tie on ribbon; attach brad.

SUPPLIES: *Cardstock:* (blue, vanilla) Stampin' Up! *Patterned paper:* (Frosty from Oh Joy collection) Cosmo Cricket *Rubber stamp:* (sentiment from Christmas in the City set) Lizzie Anne Designs *Dye ink:* (red) Stampin' Up! *Accents:* (red brad) Stampin' Up!; (red rhinestones) Me & My Big Ideas; (blue button) *Fibers:* (red gingham ribbon) Stampin' Up!; (white crochet thread) *Dies:* (scalloped circle, circles) Spellbinders **Finished size: 4¼" diameter**

SUPPLIES: *Cardstock:* (blue, brown, cream) Bazzill Basics Paper *Accents:* (chipboard church) K&Company; (brown rickrack border) Deja Views; (brown rhinestones) Glitz Design; (white pearl brad) Creative Imaginations *Fibers:* (cream ribbon) Offray *Fonts:* (Bernhard) www.fonts.com; (Chopin Script) www.dafont.com *Tool:* (corner rounder punch) Creative Memories **Finished size: 5" square**

Blue Hanukkah Card

Designer: Debbie Olson

1. Make card from cardstock.
2. Stamp circles grid and medallions on cardstock; adhere.
3. Score and punch edge of cardstock strip, adhere, and tie on ribbon.
4. Stamp menorah on cardstock, die-cut and emboss into circle, and adhere glitter. Adhere rhinestones; adhere using foam tape.
5. Adhere rhinestones.

Shalom to You Card

Designer: Jessica Witty

1. Make card from cardstock.
2. Cut candles from cardstock; adhere. Draw wicks with marker.
3. Cut flames from cardstock; ink edges and adhere with foam tape.
4. Stamp sentiment on cardstock; mat with cardstock and adhere.
5. Tie on ribbon.

SUPPLIES: *Cardstock:* (Spring Rain, white) Papertrey Ink *Clear stamps:* (circles grid, medallion from Guide Lines Two set; medallion from Guide Lines set; menorah from Mazel Tov set) Papertrey Ink *Pigment ink:* (Fresh Snow) Papertrey Ink *Chalk ink:* (French Blue) Clearsnap *Accents:* (clear, light blue rhinestones) A Muse Artstamps; (white glitter) Stampendous! *Fibers:* (blue ribbon) Papertrey Ink *Adhesive:* (foam tape) *Die:* (circle) Spellbinders *Tool:* (border punch) Martha Stewart Crafts **Finished size: 4¼" x 5½"**

SUPPLIES: *Cardstock:* (kraft, white) Papertrey Ink; (Night of Navy, Summer Sun) Stampin' Up! *Clear stamps:* (Simple Alphabet) Papertrey Ink *Dye ink:* (Chocolate Chip, Night of Navy, Pumpkin Pie) Stampin' Up! *Color medium:* (Chocolate Chip marker) Stampin Up! *Fibers:* (gray/brown ribbon) Martha Stewart Crafts *Adhesive:* (foam tape) **Finished size: 5½" x 4¼"**

Happy Kwanzaa Card
Designer: Teri Anderson

1. Make card from cardstock. Round bottom corners.
2. Create candles from cardstock and adhere. Freehand-cut flames from cardstock and adhere.
3. Stamp "Happy Kwanzaa" on card.
4. Cut cardstock strips and adhere.

The Candles of Kwanzaa Card
Designer: Layle Koncar

1. Make card from patterned paper.
2. Cut patterned paper square and adhere. Draw border.
3. Cut strips of patterned paper and cardstock; adhere. Cut flames from patterned paper; adhere and draw wicks with marker.
4. Spell "Kwanzaa" with stickers.

SUPPLIES: *Cardstock:* (red, green, yellow) Bazzill Basics Paper; (white, black) Provo Craft *Clear stamps:* (Williamsburg alphabet) Technique Tuesday *Dye ink:* (black) Marvy Uchida *Tool:* (corner rounder punch) Creative Memories **Finished size: 3½" x 5½"**

SUPPLIES: *Cardstock:* (light green shimmer) *Patterned paper:* (Forest Street from Roxbury collection; Young Street, Skyview Drive from Surprise collection; White Blue Grid Background) Scenic Route; (Boardwalk from Snorkel collection) Cosmo Cricket *Color medium:* (black marker) *Stickers:* (Quincy alphabet) Scenic Route **Finished size: 6" x 5¾"**

Totally Themed:
Trees, Sweets & Scrappy Projects

Trendy tree projects, cute cupcake
cards, and tips for using your scraps
round out this exciting themed chapter.

Lovely as a Tree

As the snow melts, tiny buds are beginning to form on the trees...and on
your paper projects! Discover how easy it is to add trendy tree product to
any spring occasion from birthday to thinking of you cards. And don't
forget Arbor Day and Earth Day are coming up—two great holidays to
incorporate some tree-lovin' into your card designs!

SUPPLIES: Cardstock: (Dark Chocolate, kraft, white) Papertrey Ink *Patterned paper:* (green grid from 2008 Bitty Box Basics collection) Papertrey Ink *Clear stamps:* (tree trunks, sentiment from Everyday Button Basics set, script background from Background Basics: Text Style set) Papertrey Ink *Chalk ink:* (Creamy Brown) Clearsnap *Specialty ink:* (Dark Chocolate hybrid) Papertrey Ink; (L'Amour hybrid) Stewart Superior Corp. *Accents:* (green buttons) Making Memories *Sticker:* (green polka dot badge) American Crafts *Fibers:* (red twine) Martha Stewart Crafts *Die:* (large rectangle) Spellbinders **Finished size:** 5½" x 4¼"

SUPPLIES: Cardstock: (white) WorldWin *Patterned paper:* (Tea Towel from Cherry Hill collection) October Afternoon *Accents:* (white frame die cut) My Mind's Eye; (tree, heart die cuts) October Afternoon *Stickers:* (Bristol alphabet) Scenic Route **Finished size:** 5" square

All Things Grow Card

Designer: Kimberly Crawford

1. Make card from cardstock. Stamp script background.
2. Stamp tree trunks and sentiment on cardstock, die-cut and emboss into rectangle, and mat with cardstock.
3. Adhere buttons and affix sticker; adhere.
4. Trim patterned paper strip, adhere, and tie on twine.

Gingham Tree Card

Designer: Teri Anderson

1. Make card from cardstock.
2. Adhere panel of patterned paper behind frame; adhere.
3. Adhere tree and heart die cuts. Affix stickers to spell sentiment.

DESIGNER TIPS

Mask off important words and stamp them in a different color from the rest of the sentiment to make the best words pop.

Use your stash of supplies to create different accents, such as buttons for tree tops.

DESIGNER TIP

Don't have a frame die cut? Use a picture of a frame and embellish it with patterned paper and other die cuts.

SUPPLIES: *Cardstock:* (Aqua Mist, Dark Chocolate, white) Papertrey Ink *Patterned paper:* (Relive from Earth Love collection) Cosmo Cricket *Clear stamps:* (tree trunks from Everyday Button Bits set, sentiment from Mailbox Greetings set) Papertrey Ink *Dye ink:* (Rich Cocoa) Tsukineko; (Chamomile) Papertrey Ink *Specialty ink:* (Ripe Avocado hybrid) Papertrey Ink *Color medium:* (lime green, clear blender markers) Copic *Accents:* (green buttons) Papertrey Ink; (bronze safety pin) Tim Holtz *Fibers:* (yellow ribbon, white twine) Papertrey Ink *Die:* (small tag) Spellbinders **Finished size: 5½" x 4¼"**

SUPPLIES: *Cardstock:* (Vintage Cream) Papertrey Ink; (dark brown) Hero Arts *Patterned paper:* (green polka dots from Tea Party pack) American Crafts *Clear stamps:* (planter, sentiment from Everyday Button Bits set, large polka dots from Polka Dot Basics set) Papertrey Ink *Watermark ink:* Tsukineko *Specialty ink:* (Dark Chocolate hybrid) Papertrey Ink *Embossing powder:* (clear) Ranger Industries *Color medium:* (light blue marker) Copic *Accent:* (green button) Papertrey Ink *Fibers:* (blue string) Prism *Dies:* (fancy frame, circle) Spellbinders **Finished size: 4¼" x 5½"**

⑤ Gifts of Spring Card

Designer: Debbie Olson

❶ Make card from cardstock.

❷ Trim patterned paper, sand edges, and adhere to cardstock. Mat with cardstock; stitch.

❸ Stamp tree trunks; thread buttons with twine and adhere.

❹ Tie on ribbon; adhere panel.

❺ Die-cut and emboss tag from cardstock. Stamp sentiment, ink edges, and thread with twine. Attach with safety pin.

⑤ Just a Little Something Card

Designer: Catherine Doucette

❶ Make card from cardstock.

❷ Stamp polka dots on cardstock panel; emboss. Tie string around panel and adhere.

❸ Die-cut and emboss frame from cardstock; stamp sentiment and planter. Die-cut circle from patterned paper; adhere, color, and adhere to card with foam tape.

❹ Thread string through button adhere.

DESIGNER TIPS

If you want a zigzag look but do not have a sewing machine, try using pinking shears to trim the hills.

SUPPLIES: *Cardstock:* (white) Papertrey Ink *Patterned paper:* (Saltwater Taffy from Lemonade collection) BasicGrey *Clear stamp:* (sentiment from Scattered Showers Additions set) Papertrey Ink *Chalk ink:* (Creamy Brown) Clearsnap *Specialty ink:* (Hibiscus Burst hybrid) Papertrey Ink *Accent:* (green button) Papertrey Ink *Sticker:* (chipboard tree) BasicGrey *Fibers:* (pink ribbon, white twine) Papertrey Ink *Die:* (label) Provo Craft *Other:* (glassine bag) Papertrey Ink; (seed packet) **Finished size: 3¾" x 5"**

SUPPLIES: *Cardstock:* (white, Hibiscus Burst) Papertrey Ink *Patterned paper:* (Sunday from Girl Friday collection) Cosmo Cricket *Rubber stamp:* (tree trio from Spring Trees set) Cornish Heritage Farms *Clear stamp:* (spring from Mailbox Greetings set) Papertrey Ink *Dye ink:* (Rich Cocoa) Tsukineko; (Chamomile) Papertrey Ink *Specialty ink:* (Hibiscus Burst hybrid) Papertrey Ink *Color medium:* (assorted markers) Copic *Accent:* (light green button) Papertrey Ink *Fibers:* (pink stitched ribbon, white twine) Papertrey Ink *Die:* (small tag) Spellbinders *Tools:* (decorative-edge scissors) Fiskars; (corner rounder punch) Marvy Uchida **Finished size: 4¼" x 5½"**

April Showers Packet

Designer: Betsy Veldman

1. Insert seed packet into bag. Trim strip of patterned paper and adhere around bag.
2. Tie on ribbon. Thread button with twine and tie to ribbon.
3. Fold top of bag over. Fasten flap by adhering tree die cut.
4. Die-cut label from cardstock. Stamp sentiment, ink edges, and adhere using foam tape.

Spring Trees Trio Card

Designer: Debbie Olson

1. Make card from cardstock; round right corners.
2. Round right corners and sand edges of patterned paper, mat with cardstock, and round right corners. Trim patterned paper strips with decorative-edge scissors, sand edges, adhere, and stitch.
3. Stamp trees on cardstock, color, and trim. Adhere using foam tape.
4. Tie ribbon around panel. Stamp sentiment on cardstock, die-cut into tag, and tie on tag and button with twine.
5. Adhere panel.

DESIGNER TIP

When coloring images, pick an arbitrary light source and be consistent with it. Make sure that your highlights and shadows are placed correctly according to that light source.

BONUS IDEA

Use this card for any season! Vary the color scheme to create a fall or summer card or white hills could be snow in the winter.

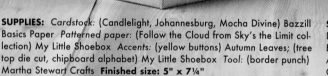

SUPPLIES: *Cardstock:* (Candlelight, Johannesburg, Mocha Divine) Bazzill Basics Paper *Patterned paper:* (Follow the Cloud from Sky's the Limit collection) My Little Shoebox *Accents:* (yellow buttons) Autumn Leaves; (tree top die cut, chipboard alphabet) My Little Shoebox *Tool:* (border punch) Martha Stewart Crafts **Finished size: 5" x 7¼"**

SUPPLIES: *Cardstock:* (white) Georgia-Pacific *Patterned paper:* (Wasabi Dot, Mint Dot from Double Dot collection) BoBunny Press; (Sunrise from Early Bird collection) Cosmo Cricket *Fibers:* (yellow polka dot ribbon) American Crafts; (white crochet thread) Coats & Clark *Font:* (Avant Garde) www.fonts.com *Die:* (leaf) QuicKutz *Tools:* (corner rounder punch) We R Memory Keepers; (decorative-edge scissors) Fiskars *Other:* (twig) **Finished size: 5" x 7"**

Buttons & Clouds Card

Designer: Robyn Weatherspoon, courtesy of My Little Shoebox

❶ Make card from cardstock. Punch edge of cardstock piece; adhere.

❷ Adhere patterned paper pieces; stitch edges.

❸ Adhere tree top die cut. Trim tree trunk from cardstock; adhere.

❹ Adhere letters and buttons.

Miss You Card

Designer: Heidi Van Laar

❶ Make card from cardstock. Cover with patterned paper. Round top corners.

❷ Round top corners of cardstock, adhere, and stitch with crochet thread.

❸ Trim patterned paper with decorative-edge scissors, distress edges, and adhere.

❹ Print sentiment on cardstock, trim into tag, and mat with patterned paper.

❺ Adhere ribbon to twig; adhere to card. Adhere sentiment tag with foam tape, knot ribbon, and adhere.

❻ Die-cut leaves from patterned paper; adhere.

DESIGNER TIP

When choosing a twig from your yard, pick a fresh one rather than one that has been on the ground. Fresh ones are less brittle and won't break as easily.

SUPPLIES: *Cardstock:* (Raspberry Fizz, white) Papertrey Ink; (Crystal Blue) Close To My Heart *Patterned paper:* (Alfresco from Abode a la Mode collection) TaDa Creative Studios *Clear stamps:* (tree from Treetops set) Close To My Heart *Dye ink:* (Sweet Leaf) Close To My Heart *Accents:* (clear buttons) Autumn Leaves; (clear glitter glue) Ranger Industries *Fibers:* (green striped ribbon) American Crafts *Dies:* (rectangle, scalloped rectangle) Spellbinders **Finished size: 4¼" x 5½"**

SUPPLIES: *Cardstock:* (white) Neenah Paper *Patterned paper:* (Kitchen Green) A Muse Artstamps *Rubber stamps:* (Swing Girl, Clouds, The Sky's the Limit) A Muse Artstamps *Dye ink:* (black) A Muse Artstamps *Chalk ink:* (Ice Blue) Clearsnap *Color medium:* (brown, light blue pencils) Lyra; (light brown, light peach pencils) Prismacolor *Other:* (blue, green note cards) A Muse Artstamps **Finished size: 5" x 3½"**

Picket Fence Tree Card

Designer: Katie Renz, courtesy of TaDa Creative Studios

1 Make card from cardstock.

2 Mat patterned paper with cardstock, tie on ribbon, and adhere.

3 Die-cut and emboss rectangle from cardstock, stamp tree, and mat with die-cut cardstock scalloped rectangle. Adhere buttons with glitter glue.

4 Adhere using foam tape.

The Sky's the Limit Card

Designer: Katie Stilwater

1 Stamp Swing Girl, Clouds, and sentiment on cardstock; color.

3 Trim strip of patterned paper, cut to make grass, and adhere. Mat with piece from note card; adhere to note card.

4 Stamp Swing Girl on patterned paper, trim tree top, and adhere using foam tape.

DESIGNER TIP

Give your coloring a smooth look by using a blending pencil.

Yummy sweets and treats are best sellers at the bakery and in the paper crafting world! From scrumptious cards to decadent albums, dessert-themed paper and accents are now tastier than ever! Plus at zero calories, you'll never feel guilty for making "just one more!"

SUPPLIES: Cardstock: (white) Accents: (red, pink, white polka dot flowers) Prima; (clear sequins) Nicole Crafts; (red, pink buttons) Autumn Leaves Digital elements: (yellow dot, multi-stripe, red squares, floral, green dot, pink plaid patterned paper from Boom I Got Your Boyfriend kit) www.sweetshoppedesigns.com Fibers: (green ribbon) My Mind's Eye; (aqua polka dot ribbon) Offray; (white felt rickrack) Creative Café Software: (photo editing) Tools: (decorative-edge scissors) Provo Craft; (dotted scallops border punch) Fiskars Other: (circle boxes) Nicole Crafts; (candle) Target **Finished sizes: big box 4½" diameter x 2" height; middle box 4" diameter x 1¾" height; small box 3" diameter x 1½" height**

SUPPLIES: Cardstock: (white, pink shimmer) Bazzill Basics Paper Patterned paper: (Glittered Dots from Ella Animal Crackers collection) Making Memories; (pink polka dots) Vellum: The Paper Company Rubber stamp: (Happy Birthday Background) Hero Arts Pigment ink: (Rosebud) Clearsnap Embossing powder: (Bubble Gum Yum!) Gel-a-tins Accents: (pink glitter) Stampendous!; (chipboard heart) Making Memories Fibers: (pink rickrack) American Crafts Font: (Satisfaction) www.fontbros.com Other: (pink, brown felt) Michaels **Finished size: 4¼" x 5½"**

DETAIL

Eat Cake Card
Designer: Mary MacAskill

1. Make card from cardstock.
2. Stamp Happy Birthday Background on card, emboss.
3. Trim strips of patterned paper and rickrack. Adhere and stitch.
4. Cut circle from vellum; adhere.
5. Cut cupcake top and bottom from felt. Stitch cupcake. *Note: Secure felt pieces with double-sided tape before stitching to prevent felt from moving.* Apply glitter; adhere.
6. Print sentiment, trim, and mat with cardstock; adhere. Adhere heart.

Birthday Cake Gift Box Tower
5 STEPS
Designer: Cindy Gilchrist

1. Open patterned paper in software; print on cardstock.
2. Cover boxes and lid tops with printed paper.
3. Trim paper strips to fit around lips of box lids. Punch or trim with decorative-edge scissors and adhere.
4. Embellish boxes with fibers, buttons, and sequins.
5. Punch hole in top box lid. Attach ribbon, flowers, and candle.

SUPPLIES: *Cardstock:* (light green, hot pink) *Patterned paper:* (Die Cut Scalloped Stripe, Pattern Stripe from Addie Noteworthy collection; Ledger Circle, Die Cut Stamp Glitter from Delaney Noteworthy collection; Glitter Dots from Garden Party collection) Making Memories *Clear stamps:* (sentiment from Frilly Sweet set) Darice *Chalk ink:* (pink) *Accents:* (pink rhinestones) Creative Crystal; (cherry rhinestone) Heidi Swapp *Adhesive:* (foam tape) *Template:* (chipboard ice cream cone) Magistical Memories **Finished size: 5¼" x 6¼"**

SUPPLIES: *Cardstock:* (white, Kevin, Apple Crush) Bazzill Basics Paper *Patterned paper:* (Nursery, Special Delivery from Little One collection) Li'l Davis Designs *Rubber stamp:* (happy birthday from On Your Birthday set) Stampin' Up! *Chalk ink:* (Peony) Clearsnap *Accents:* (sweet lovin' badge) American Crafts; (yellow glitter) Art Institute Glitter; (white binder clip) *Sticker:* (little one epoxy) Making Memories *Fibers:* (pink polka dot ribbon) May Arts *Other:* (cupcake chipboard book) EK Success; (photo) **Finished size: 6½" x 8½"**

💠 *Pure Sweetness Card*

Designer: Sherry Wright

❶ Make card from cardstock. Trim patterned paper slightly smaller than card front; mat with patterned paper and adhere.

❷ Trace chipboard ice cream cone on patterned paper; trim around. Stitch cone; ink edges. Sand ice cream edges and adhere pieces by layering with foam tape.

❸ Stamp sentiment on patterned paper. Trim into tag shape, adhere

❹ Adhere rhinestones.

💠 *Cupcake Album*

Designer: Kim Kesti

❶ Cover album pages with patterned paper and cardstock.

❷ Adhere photo.

❸ Stamp sentiment on cardstock, trim around, ink edges and adhere.

❹ Affix sticker and adhere badge. Apply glitter.

❺ Attach clip and tie on ribbon.

SUPPLIES: *Cardstock:* (white) *Patterned paper:* (Upbeat from Moda Bella collection) American Crafts *Color media:* (white gel pen) Ranger Industries; (black pen) American Crafts; (pink chalk) Craf-T Products *Accents:* (wiggle eyes) Darice *Fibers:* (pink ribbon) Offray **Finished size: 3¾" x 4"**

SUPPLIES: *Cardstock:* (white) *Patterned paper:* (Floral, Ledger Circle from Delaney Noteworthy collection) Making Memories; (orange polka dot) *Accents:* (green star button) Jesse James & Co.; (lime green brads) Making Memories; (chipboard numbers) Maya Road; (turquoise glitter) Jo-Ann Stores *Rub-ons:* (All Mixed Up alphabet) Doodlebug Design *Fibers:* (white floral printed ribbon) Offray; (white twine) *Tools:* (decorative-edge scissors, ⅛" circle punch) *Other:* (pink glitter foam) Michaels **Finished size: 8" x 5¾"**

5 STEPS *Happy Cupcake Card*

Designer: Teri Anderson

❶ Cut cupcake top, bottom, and base, from cardstock and patterned paper. Adhere together.

❷ Draw cheeks, highlights, and mouth.

❸ Adhere eyes.

❹ Tie ribbon bow and adhere.

Celebrate 16 Card

Designer: Shanna Vineyard

❶ Make card from cardstock.

❷ Cut patterned paper to fit card front. Distress and stitch edges; adhere.

❸ Cut cardstock panel; trim bottom edge with decorative-edge scissors. Stitch three sides, attach brads, and adhere. Tie on ribbon.

❹ Spell "Celebrate" with rub-ons. Cover chipboard numbers with glitter; adhere.

❺ Cut cake layers and frosting scallops, from patterned paper and foam. Stitch edges of cake layers and adhere. Punch holes in frosting scallops; adhere. Thread button with twine; adhere.

❻ Cut heart from foam, following pattern; adhere.

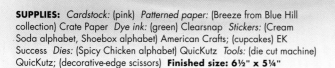

SUPPLIES: *Cardstock:* (pink) *Patterned paper:* (Breeze from Blue Hill collection) Crate Paper *Dye ink:* (green) Clearsnap *Stickers:* (Cream Soda alphabet, Shoebox alphabet) American Crafts; (cupcakes) EK Success *Dies:* (Spicy Chicken alphabet) QuicKutz *Tools:* (die cut machine) QuicKutz; (decorative-edge scissors) **Finished size: 6½" x 5¼"**

SUPPLIES: *Cardstock:* (green, pink, white) *Chalk ink:* (Lime Pastel) Clearsnap *Accents:* (orange flower) We R Memory Keepers; (pink, clear rhinestones) The Beadery *Rub-ons:* (Simply Sweet alphabet) Doodlebug Design *Stickers:* (sweet epoxy) Die Cuts With a View *Fibers:* (green floss) Karen Foster Design; (striped ribbon) American Crafts *Dies:* (popsicle, popsicle card, circle tag) Provo Craft *Tools:* (die cut/embossing machine) Provo Craft **Finished size: 3½" x 5"**

5 STEPS *Sweet Card*

Designer: Kalyn Kepner

❶ Make card from cardstock; trim edges with decorative-edge scissors.

❷ Trim patterned paper slightly smaller than card front. Ink edges and adhere.

❸ Affix cupcake stickers.

❹ Die-cut "ee" from cardstock. Spell "Sweet!" with stickers and die-cut letters.

DESIGNER TIP

If you run out of alphabet stickers to spell your sentiment, mix letters from other sticker sets or die-cuts to create a fun and fresh look.

5 STEPS *Sweet Summer Card*

Designer: Betsy Veldman

❶ Die-cut card from cardstock. Die-cut popsicle and sticks from cardstock; adhere.

❷ Adhere flower and tie on ribbon.

❸ Die-cut and emboss tag from cardstock. Ink edges, affix sticker, and adhere rhinestones. Tie tag to ribbon with floss.

❹ Spell "Have a summer" with rub-ons.

So Very Sweet Card
Designer: Ashley Harris

1. Make card from cardstock.

2. Trim patterned paper to fit card front; stitch edges with floss and adhere.

3. Tie ribbon around card. Stamp so very.

4. Cover cupcake pieces with cardstock, stamp sweet, and apply glitter. Adhere cupcake to card. *Note: Adhere top of cupcake with foam tape.*

5. Paint chipboard heart and apply glitter; let dry. Adhere to button; adhere button to card.

SUPPLIES: *Cardstock:* (white, Twig) Bazzill Basics *Paper Patterned paper:* (Plaid from Sharon Ann Delightful collection) Little Yellow Bicycle *Rubber stamps:* (so very, sweet from So Very set) Stampin' Up! *Dye ink:* (black) *Paint:* (Strawberries & Cream) Making Memories *Accents:* (red button) Creative Café; (chipboard cupcake, heart) Maya Road; (iridescent glitter) *Fibers:* (pink floss) DMC; (red polka dot ribbon) *Adhesive:* (foam tape) **Finished size: 4¼" x 5½"**

SUPPLIES: *Cardstock:* (white) *Patterned paper:* (Clown Nose, Surprise, Make a Wish from Cupcake collection) BasicGrey *Transparency sheet:* 3M *Accents:* (chipboard ice cream cone) BasicGrey; (red pearls, red felt stars) Queen & Co. *Rub-ons:* (celebrate) BasicGrey *Tool:* (decorative-edge scissors) **Finished size: 5" square**

Celebrate Card
Designer: Anabelle O'Malley

1. Make card from transparency sheet.

2. Trim patterned paper to fit card front; stitch edges and adhere to inside of card.

3. Cut circle from patterned paper; mat with cardstock and trim with decorative-edge scissors.

4. Trim strip of patterned paper; adhere felt stars.

5. Adhere chipboard cone and apply rub-on. Adhere pearls.

SUPPLIES: *Cardstock:* (red, kraft, white) *Rubber stamps:* (ice cream cone from Little Gal set; you're from Sweet Thang set; Open Plaid Backgrounder) Cornish Heritage Farms *Pigment ink:* (Onyx Black) Tsukineko *Color medium:* (markers) *Accents:* (pink, red buttons) BasicGrey *Rub-ons:* (Lil Girl alphabet) My Mind's Eye *Fibers:* (kraft lace trim) Making Memories; (brown floss) *Adhesive:* (foam tape) *Dies:* (oval embossing) Spellbinders *Tools:* (die cut/embossing machine) Spellbinders; (corner rounder punch) EK Success *Other:* (dimensional glaze) Ranger Industries **Finished size: 5½" x 4¼"**

SUPPLIES: *Cardstock:* (natural white) *Patterned paper:* (Be Mine, Milk Chocolate from Blush collection) BasicGrey *Rubber stamps:* (cupcake, cake from Sweet Celebration set) Taylored Expressions; (sentiment from Baking set) JustRite *Dye ink:* (black, brown) *Color medium:* (markers) Copic Marker *Accents:* (brown flat marbles) The Robin's Nest *Fibers:* (pink ribbon) Papertrey Ink *Adhesive:* (foam tape) *Dies:* (circle) Spellbinders *Tools:* (water brush) Copic Marker; (dotted scallops border punch) Fiskars; (die cut/embossing machine) Spellbinders; (corner-rounder punch) **Finished size: 4¼" x 5½"**

You're Sweet Card

Designer: Julie Campbell

❶ Make card from cardstock; sand edges.

❷ Stamp Open Plaid Backgrounder on cardstock; trim. Distress edges, adhere, and stitch edges.

❸ Trim strip of cardstock. Round bottom corners and adhere. Stamp you're and spell "Sweet" with rub-ons.

❹ Thread buttons with floss; adhere. Adhere lace.

❺ Stamp ice cream cone on cardstock; color. Die-cut/emboss stamped piece. Adhere using foam tape. Apply dimensional glaze.

So Much Chocolate Card

Designer: Debbie Olson

❶ Make card from cardstock; round right corners.

❷ Trim patterned paper slightly smaller than card front; round right corners and adhere.

❸ Trim strip of patterned paper. Punch edge, adhere, and zigzag-stitch edge.

❹ Tie ribbon around card.

❺ Die-cut/emboss circle from cardstock. Stamp sentiment and adhere with foam tape.

❻ Stamp cupcake and cake on cardstock. Color, trim around, and adhere with foam tape.

❼ Adhere marbles.

Hey Sweetie Card

Designer: Ana Wohlfahrt

1. Make card from cardstock. Trim patterned paper slightly smaller than card front; mat with cardstock and adhere.

2. Trim patterned paper, mat with cardstock, and adhere. Adhere pearls.

3. Stamp cupcakes, stand, and sentiment on cardstock; trim. Color with markers. Stamp frosting and sprinkles on cardstock. Trim around, adhere with foam tape.

4. Add glitter and dimensional glaze.

5. Pierce under sentiment. Double-mat piece with cardstock. Attach ribbon, flowers, and pearl. Adhere with foam tape.

SUPPLIES: *Cardstock:* (white, Lavender Moon, Plum Pudding, Sweet Blush) Papertrey Ink *Patterned paper:* (floral, stripe from Sprout collection) Memory Box *Clear stamps:* (cupcakes, frosting, sprinkles, stand, sentiment from What's Up Cupcake set) My Favorite Things *Dye ink:* (brown) *Pigment ink:* (Onyx Black) Tsukineko *Color medium:* (markers) Copic Marker *Accents:* (peach flowers) Prima; (iridescent glitter, pearls) Stampin' Up! *Fibers:* (green polka dot ribbon) Papertrey Ink *Adhesive:* (foam tape) *Other:* (dimensional glaze) Stampin' Up! **Finished size: 5½" x 4¼"**

Let Them Eat Cake Card

Designer: Andrea Gourley

1. Make card from cardstock. Create 4" x 5¼" project in software.

2. Drag patterned paper and sentiment to canvas; print on cardstock. Trim and doodle edges with pen.

3. Open template in software. Drag patterned paper onto template and resize to make paper strips. Print on cardstock, trim, doodle edges, and adhere.

4. Create new project in software. Drop in patterned paper, dotted circle border, and cupcake. Print on cardstock, punch into scalloped circle, and adhere with foam tape.

5. Tie ribbon around piece; adhere.

SUPPLIES: *Cardstock:* (bright pink, white) *Color medium:* (black pen) EK Success *Digital elements:* (plaid patterned paper from Birthday Wishes kit) www.shabbymissjenndesigns.com; (pink, white lined patterned paper; cupcake, dotted circle border, sentiment from Occasions kit) www.theshabbyshoppe.com; (rectangle template from Paper Strips #1 Card Templates kit) www.thedigichick.com *Fibers:* (pink ribbon) *Software:* (photo editing) *Adhesive:* (foam tape) *Tools:* (1¾" scalloped circle punch) Stampin' Up! **Finished size: 4½" x 5¾"**

Crafting the Scraps

We all have scraps lying around. Patterned paper, cardstock, ribbon, leftover stickers—the list goes on and on. Think twice before throwing them in the trash. Scraps and even product packaging are the perfect solutions for making your projects one-of-a-kind masterpieces while saving money, and doing your part to save the planet.

SUPPLIES: *Patterned paper:* (Garden Chair from Daydream collection) October Afternoon; (Go Jumpina Lake, Happy Campers from Mr. Campy collection) Cosmo Cricket *Chalk ink:* (Chestnut Roan) Clearsnap *Accents:* (blue buttons) Making Memories *Stickers:* (Noteworthy flocked alphabet) Making Memories *Fibers:* (tan floss) DMC **Finished size:** 4¼" x 4¾'

SUPPLIES: *Cardstock:* (green) *Accent:* (pink glitter glue) Ranger Industries *Rub-ons:* (Ginger alphabet) American Crafts *Stickers:* (bee) BasicGrey; (green, blue buttons) Crate Paper *Fibers:* (green floss) DMC; (jute) *Adhesive:* (foam tape) *Other:* (patterned paper image from packaging) BasicGrey; (kraft gift bag) **Finished size:** 4" x 5¼"

Lucky CARD

Designer: Kim Hughes

Ink all paper edges.

1 Make card from patterned paper. Trim patterned paper slightly smaller than card front.

2 Draw shamrock on back of patterned paper; trim and adhere.

3 Hand-stitch stem with floss and adhere piece to card.

4 Trim small strip of patterned paper. Loop and adhere. Thread buttons with floss and adhere.

5 Affix stickers. Stitch bottom of card.

USE YOUR SCRAPS

Trimming small accents and shapes from scraps of patterned paper is a great way to incorporate different designs and patterns in your card.

For You Gift Bag

Designer: Kalyn Kepner

1 Trim patterned paper image from packaging; mat with cardstock and adhere.

2 Apply rub-ons to spell "For you".

3 Adhere bee sticker using foam tape; apply glitter glue.

4 Thread button stickers with floss and adhere.

5 Tie jute around handles.

USE YOUR SCRAPS

Look for examples of paper patterns or embellishments on the packaging of paper, stickers, and other paper crafting supplies.

SUPPLIES: *Patterned paper:* (assorted patterns from Certainly Celery, Crushed Curry, Dusty Durango, Merry Moments, Old Olive, Pumpkin Pie, Razzleberry Lemonade, So Saffron Designer Series collections) Stampin' Up! *Tools:* (¾" circle punch) Stampin' Up! *Other:* (foam balls) **Finished size: 3" diameter**

Designer: Arika Bauer,
courtesy of Stampin' Up!

❶ Punch circles from patterned paper.

❷ Adhere to foam balls.

USE YOUR SCRAPS

Using small punches on paper scraps makes even the littlest scrap go a long way.

SUPPLIES: *Cardstock:* (yellow) *Patterned paper:* (Grove from Ambrosia collection) BasicGrey; (Rockin from About a Boy collection) Fancy Pants Designs *Accents:* (orange rhinestones) Kaisercraft *Rub-ons:* (sentiment) Melissa Frances *Sticker:* (chipboard butterfly) BasicGrey *Fibers:* (orange floss) *Adhesive:* (foam tape) *Other:* (sticker packaging) BasicGrey **Finished size: 4" x 6¼"**

SUPPLIES: *Cardstock:* (orange, blue, white) *Patterned paper:* (Hip to the Jive from Times Nouveau collection) Graphic 45; (Snowfall Polar Blue from Dasher collection) BasicGrey *Accents:* (white pearls) Mark Richards Enterprises *Rub-ons:* (zigzag stitches) Die Cuts With a View *Stickers:* (Basic epoxy alphabet) Creative Imaginations *Template:* (Floral Fantasy) Provo Craft *Tools:* (die-cut/embossing machine) Provo Craft; (butterfly punch) Martha Stewart Crafts; (corner-rounder punch) EK Success **Finished size: 4¾" x 6½"**

Dream BIG Card

Designer: Anabelle O'Malley

1. Make card from cardstock.

2. Trim packaging into strips; adhere.

3. Trim patterned paper; adhere.

4. Trim patterned paper. Stitch edges with floss and adhere.

5. Apply rub-on. Adhere sticker with foam tape.

6. Adhere rhinestones.

USE YOUR SCRAPS

Using images from product packaging is a great way to save money on supplies, while still getting a stylish effect.

Butterfly HELLO Friend Card

5 STEPS

Designer: Linda Beeson

1. Make card from cardstock.

2. Trim cardstock strip; adhere. Trim patterned paper. Round outside corners and adhere. Apply rub-on.

3. Emboss cardstock. Punch butterflies from embossed cardstock; adhere.

4. Spell "Hello friend" with stickers.

5. Adhere pearls.

USE YOUR SCRAPS

After you've embossed and cut out a piece of paper, you're bound to have scraps. Those scraps are the perfect size for punching small accents.

SUPPLIES: *Cardstock:* (kraft) *Patterned paper:* (Brianna, Nancy, Jenny, Carol Ann, Tori) Melissa Frances; (Flutterby from Feather Your Nest collection) Webster's Pages; (green polka dot) *Dye ink:* (Old Paper) Ranger Industries *Paint:* (cream) Ranger Industries *Accents:* (cream button, flower) *Rub-ons:* (sentiment) Melissa Frances *Sticker:* (baby tag) Melissa Frances *Fibers:* (twine, cream lace trim) *Tools:* (decorative-edge scissors, ⅞" square punch) *Other:* (white felt) **Finished size: 3¾" x 5½"**

SUPPLIES: *Patterned paper:* (green damask scalloped from Chelsea's Place collection) Michaels; (Teal Ledger from Passport collection) Making Memories; (Peace from Believe collection) BoBunny Press; (Red Love Song from Trendy collection) Jenni Bowlin Studio *Transparency sheet:* (Polka 2 scalloped from Sheer Delights collection) KI Memories *Rubber stamps:* (cake, heart, sentiment from I Thee Wed set) Cornish Heritage Farms *Pigment ink:* (Oasis Green, Red Magic, Aegean Blue) Tsukineko *Color medium:* (white gel pen) Sakura *Accents:* (light blue brad) Queen & Co.; (light blue, light green flowers) Prima *Fibers:* (twine, white tulle) **Finished size: 4½" x 4"**

OUR Little Girl CARD

Designer: Beatriz Jennings

❶ Make card from cardstock. Paint edges; let dry.

❷ Trim felt slightly smaller than card front using decorative-edge scissors; adhere.

❸ Punch patterned paper into squares. Adhere and stitch.

❹ Affix sticker. Adhere lace and flower. Apply rub-on.

❺ Thread twine through button, adhere.

USE YOUR SCRAPS

Even the tiniest of scraps can be used in bulk to make a statement on a precious card by punching the same shape repeatedly and adhering in a pattern.

BEST Wishes Card

Designer: Kim Hughes

❶ Make card from patterned paper; sand edges.

❷ Trim transparency sheet into strip; adhere.

❸ Trim patterned papers into strips; adhere.

❹ Stamp cake, sentiment, and heart. Color cake with pen.

❺ Tie twine around card. *Note: Tie bow over tulle.*

❻ Attach flowers with brad.

USE YOUR SCRAPS

Trimming patterned paper scraps into strips for cards is a great way to mix and match patterns.

SUPPLIES: *Patterned paper:* (pink doodles, blue doodles, notebook from Lucky You collection) Colorbok *Accents:* (pink chipboard flower, red chipboard sentiment) Colorbok; (chipboard letter negative) Cosmo Cricket; (silver staples) *Adhesive:* (foam tape) *Other:* (ruler-edged sticker packaging) Colorbok **Finished size: 6" x 7"**

SUPPLIES: *Cardstock:* (Baja Breeze) Stampin' Up!; (white, tan, dark red) *Rubber stamp:* (Sanded) Stampin' Up! *Dye ink:* (Baja Breeze) Stampin' Up! *Chalk ink:* (Chestnut Roan) Clearsnap *Accents:* (dark red, teal, plum, navy buttons) *Fibers:* (brown floss, twine) *Font:* (Ditzy) www.twopeasinanbucket.com *Dies:* (Owl, Moonlight alphabet) QuicKutz *Tools:* (die cut machine) QuicKutz *Other:* (corrugated cardboard) **Finished size: 5½" x 4¼"**

Designer: Charity Hassel

❶ Make card from patterned paper.

❷ Trim strips of patterned paper; adhere.

❸ Adhere sticker packaging.

❹ Staple chipboard letter negative; adhere.

❺ Adhere chipboard accents with foam tape.

USE YOUR SCRAPS

When using chipboard letters think of it as getting twice the letters! Both the positive and negative portions of the chipboards work great for card accents.

Designer: Samantha VanArnhem

❶ Make card from cardstock. Stamp background and ink edges.

❷ Print "Another year" twice on cardstock. Distress edges, tie twine around and adhere.

❸ Tear-off top layer of corrugated cardboard scrap. Die-cut owl from cardboard and cardstock. Piece together and adhere.

❹ Die-cut "Older" and "Wiser"; adhere.

❺ Tie twine through buttons; adhere.

USE YOUR SCRAPS

Lots of paper craft product packaging comes with cardboard. Samantha slightly distressed the cardboard for her card and used it with her die cut machine.

SUPPLIES: *Cardstock:* (black, white, yellow) *Patterned paper:* (Fresh, Au Naturel from Moda Bella collection) American Crafts *Stickers:* (Loopy Lou alphabet) Doodlebug Design **Finished size:** 3½" x 5½"

SUPPLIES: *Cardstock:* (red, kraft) *Patterned paper:* (Straw from Urban Prairie collection) BasicGrey; (White Blue Grid Background) Scenic Route *Accents:* (gray, red felt hearts) Jenni Bowlin Studio *Rub-on:* (love) Rusty Pickle *Stickers:* (assorted A, Z) SEI, BasicGrey, Scenic Route, Cosmo Cricket, Doodlebug Design *Fibers:* (black ribbon) Maya Road *Adhesive:* (foam tape) **Finished size:** 4" x 5¾"

Floral Hi Card

Designer: Teri Anderson

❶ Make card from cardstock.

❷ Trim patterned paper slightly smaller than card front; mat with cardstock and adhere.

❸ Adhere strip of patterned paper.

❹ Trim negative portions of stickers to spell "Hi". Adhere to cardstock. Trim and adhere.

USE YOUR SCRAPS

Instead of throwing away your sticker sheets when all the stickers have been used, create another alphabet by using the negative portion and adhering it to cardstock or patterned paper.

Love From A to Z Card

Designer: Charity Hassel

❶ Make card from patterned paper.

❷ Cut cardstock piece, mat with cardstock.

❸ Affix stickers to matted piece. Adhere ribbon; adhere to card.

❹ Adhere felt hearts.

❺ Apply rub-on to patterned paper; trim around and adhere with foam tape.

USE YOUR SCRAPS

Using up letter stickers can be as simple as using lots of the same letters to make your own sentiment. Or, try using someone's initials or mix-and-match letters in a sentiment for an eclectic look.

SUPPLIES: *Cardstock:* (red) *Patterned paper:* (Dapper Dan, Jumping Jack, Handsome Henry from Lil' Man collection) Cosmo Cricket *Dye ink:* (black) *Paint:* (tan) *Color medium:* (black pen) *Foam stamp:* (harlequin pattern) Making Memories *Accents:* (pearlescent buttons) *Rub-ons:* (All Mixed Up alphabet) Doodlebug Design *Other:* (photo) **Finished size: 12" x 12"**

One LOOK Layout

Designer: Lisa Guidry

❶ Trim patterned paper into different sized squares. Distress and ink edges; adhere.

❷ Adhere photo.

❸ Stitch along photo, paper pieces, and layout.

❹ Apply rub-ons for sentiment.

❺ Write journaling.

❻ Stamp harlequin pattern.

USE YOUR SCRAPS

Using small bits of paper from a collection, trimming into small shapes, and sewing together in a patchwork pattern is a great way to dress up a layout or card.

Just a Little Note Card Set

Designer: Jennifer Watson

PURSE BOX

1. Cut purse from 10" x 12" cardstock, following diagram.
2. Adhere strip of patterned paper to handle.
3. Cut rectangle of patterned paper to fit purse front; round corners and adhere.
4. Cut strip of patterned paper; mat with cardstock and adhere to purse front.
5. Spell "For you" with stickers on journaling card; adhere.
6. Tie bow and adhere.
7. Assemble purse, attaching handle with brads.

CARD

1. Make card from cardstock.
2. Cut rectangle of patterned paper; round corners and adhere.
3. Stamp image and sentiment on cardstock; round corners and adhere.
4. Adhere strip of cardstock; adhere strip of patterned paper punched with border punch.
5. Thread twine through button; adhere to flower. Adhere flower to card.
6. Adhere baubles; color stamped image as desired.

Finished sizes: purse box 6" x 5" x 2", cards 4¼" x 5½"

PURSE DIAGRAM

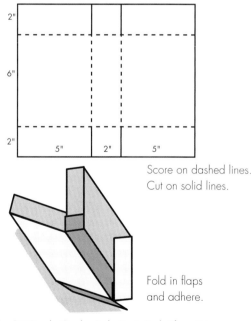

Score on dashed lines.
Cut on solid lines.

Fold in flaps and adhere.

SUPPLIES: *Cardstock:* (maroon, light blue, pink, green, beige) Bazzill Basics Paper *Patterned paper:* (Gazebo, Dirt Roads, Garden Path, Picnic Basket from Detours collection) October Afternoon *Clear stamps:* (just a little note) Technique Tuesday; (chick) Imaginisce *Solvent ink:* (Jet Black) Tsukineko *Color medium:* (watercolor pencils) *Accents:* (acrylic baubles) Stamping Bella; (pink felt flower, buttons) Making Memories; (maroon, blue, green, beige flowers) Prima; (maroon brads) BasicGrey; (journaling card) October Afternoon *Stickers:* (Sotheby's alphabet) American Crafts *Fibers:* (brown stitched ribbon, hemp twine) *Tools:* (border punch) Martha Stewart Crafts; (corner rounder punch)

Enjoy Card Set

Designer: Debbie Seyer

CARD BAG

1. Cut rectangles of cardstock to fit front and back of bag; round corners, punch rounded rectangle to create handle, and adhere.

2. Cut rectangle of patterned paper, round corners, mat with cardstock, and round corners.

3. Adhere ribbon around piece; adhere to bag.

4. Stamp sentiment on cardstock; mat with cardstock. Tie ribbon around and adhere.

5. Stamp image on cardstock circle; adhere with foam tape.

ONE OF A KIND CARD

1. Make card from cardstock.

2. Cut cardstock slightly smaller than card front; adhere.

3. Cut rectangle of patterned paper; mat with cardstock and adhere.

4. Stamp sentiment on cardstock; mat with cardstock. Punch holes, thread ribbon through, and adhere.

5. Stamp image on cardstock; cut out and adhere with foam tape.

KNOW LIFE CARD

1. Make card from cardstock.

2. Cut cardstock slightly smaller than card front; adhere.

3. Cut rectangle of patterned paper; mat with cardstock. Wrap ribbon around and adhere.

4. Stamp sentiment on cardstock; mat with cardstock.

5. Punch photo corner; adhere to sentiment piece and attach brad.

6. Stamp image on cardstock; cut out and adhere with foa

Finished sizes: card bag 5½" x 8", one of a kind card 4¼" x 5½", know life card 5½" x 4¼"

SUPPLIES: All supplies by Stampin' Up! unless otherwise noted. *Cardstock:* (Kiwi Kiss, Pink Pirouette, Whisper White) *Patterned paper:* (plaid, floral from Bella Rose collection) *Rubber stamps:* (sentiment, flower from Enjoy Every Moment set; sentiment, flower from One of a Kind set; sentiment, butterfly from Dreams du Jour set) *Dye ink:* (Riding Hood Red, Pink Pirouette) *Specialty ink:* (Noir hybrid) Stewart Superior Corp. *Accent:* (gold brad) no source *Fibers:* (olive, pink striped, red ribbon) *Adhesive:* (foam tape) 3M *Tools:* (rounded rectangle, circle, photo corner punches); (rectangle slit punch) Fiskars *Other:* (brown paper bag) no source

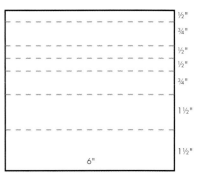

INSIDE

Enjoy Box & Card

Designer: Anabelle O'Malley

BOX

1. Cover inside and sides of box with patterned paper.
2. Adhere patterned paper to cover.
3. Adhere tag to patterned paper; cut out and adhere.
4. Tie on ribbon. Adhere rhinestone.
5. Place gift card inside box.

CARD

1. Make card from cardstock; adhere patterned paper pieces.
2. Adhere circle flower and affix stickers.
3. Adhere rhinestones; apply rub-on.

Finished size: box 5¾" x 4½", card 5" x 4½"

For You Card

Designer: Kimberly Crawford

OUTSIDE

1. Make card from cardstock; adhere patterned paper pieces.
2. Die-cut/emboss circle from cardstock. Stamp circle; adhere to card.
3. Spell "For you" with stickers.
4. Cut star from patterned paper and adhere.

INSIDE

1. Adhere patterned paper pieces. Cut stars from patterned paper and adhere.
2. Make pop-up mechanism, following diagram. Adhere to card.
3. Stamp sentiment on cardstock. Trim, ink edges, and adhere. Adhere star and insert gift card into pop-up.

Finished size: 5½" x 4¼"

POP-UP DIAGRAM

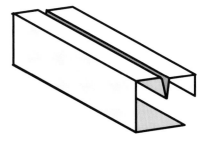

½"
¾"
½"
½"
¾"
1½"
1½"
6"

Cut from green cardstock; fold along lines

SUPPLIES: *Cardstock:* (orange) The Paper Company *Patterned paper:* (Ledger Circle, Die-Cut Circle Flower from Delaney collection) Making Memories; (Pop Culture Gossip) KI Memories *Accents:* (circle flower, enjoy tag die-cuts) Making Memories; (orange rhinestones) Kaisercraft *Rub-on:* (thank you) Crate Paper *Stickers:* (butterflies) Petaloo *Fibers:* (orange stitched ribbon) Making Memories *Other:* (clear stationery box) Emma's Paperie; (gift card)

SUPPLIES: *Cardstock:* (white) Papertrey Ink; (green) Duluth Paper *Patterned paper:* (Cover Band, Musical Chairs, Disco Ball from Celebration collection) American Crafts *Rubber stamp:* (Happy Birthday to You) Hero Arts *Clear stamp:* (circle from Christmas Memories Circles set) Creative Imaginations *Chalk ink:* (Warm Red, Blue Lagoon) Clearsnap *Stickers:* (Surprise Headline alphabet) KI Memories *Die:* (embossed circle) Spellbinders *Tools:* (die cut/embossing machine) Spellbinders *Other:* (gift card)

BONUS IDEA

Find a paper collection
you like, and use all
the various patterns to
create a colorful—but
coordinated—gift set.

Monogrammed Bridal Card Set

Designer: Maren Benedict

CARD BOX

1. Cut patterned paper to fit each panel of box and lid; adhere.
2. Adhere ribbon around box window.
3. Apply decoupage to box and lid; let dry.
4. Adhere sentiment die cut to lid.
5. Stamp monogram on circle of cardstock; mat with scalloped circle, using foam tape.
6. Adhere length of thread to inside box front; adhere monogram circle to thread to hang in window. *Note: Secure thread on piece by adhering it between monogram circle and second cardstock circle.*

CARD

1. Make card from cardstock.
2. Cut rectangle of patterned paper; adhere.
3. Wrap ribbon around card front; tie bow.
4. Stamp monogram on cardstock circle; mat with scalloped circle, using foam tape. Adhere monogram to card with foam tape.

Finished sizes: card box 4¼" x 6½" x 1¾", cards 4" x 5½"

SUPPLIES: *Cardstock:* (white) Papertrey Ink; (Bravo Burgundy) Stampin' Up! *Patterned paper:* (Florabella, Maize, Vineyard, Dew Drops, Strip Tease from Fleuriste collection) Cosmo Cricket *Rubber stamp:* (Alpha E Formal alphabet) Unity Stamp Co. *Dye ink:* (Tuxedo Black) Tsukineko *Accent:* (sentiment die cut) Cosmo Cricket *Fibers:* (metallic weave ribbon) Martha Stewart Crafts *Adhesive:* (foam tape, decoupage) Plaid *Tools:* (scalloped circle, 1⅜" circle punches) Stampin' Up! *Other:* (photo box) Cosmo Cricket

tiny notes

It doesn't take much to let someone know how much you appreciate them—a kind word, a smile, or a simple "thank you" mean so much! Or better yet, let a tiny note of thanks show it for you. A teensy card decorated with a mini felt flower or button, a rub-on or hand-written sentiment, and you're all set!

{ Tiny Notes of Thanks }

Many Thanks

Envelope Envy

After all the time and creativity you put into your cards, don't stuff them into ordinary envelopes. Take your photos a step further by incorporating them into unique envelopes like *Paper Crafts* Pro Wendy Johnson has done here. You won't regret taking the time to create this simple, yet effective finishing touch!

CREATE A WINDOW.
Use a simple punch to create a window in your envelope. Add a fun photo so the recipient will instantly know who sent the cheerful greeting.

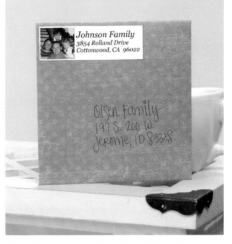

CUSTOMIZE YOUR RETURN ADDRESS.
Create custom return address labels with a photo and your computer. Creating your own labels is a great way to add a personal touch to envelopes, and it often costs less than buying them.

MAKE A SHAKER.
Transform a boring old envelope into an interactive shaker. Adhere a photo to the envelope, sprinkle glitter, and seal by stitching a transparency sheet over the top.

CUSTOMIZE YOUR ENVELOPE.
Print your favorite photo on cardstock and fold it into an envelope. This is a great way to use photos of landscapes and vacation scenes, and it will entice the recipient to see the coordinating card inside.

MAKE AN ENVELOPE SEAL.
Use those less-than-perfect photos of close up smiles, hands to the camera, and hidden faces to make envelope seals that are both functional and fun.

CREATE A CUSTOM STAMP.
Go to *www.stamps.com* to create your own photo stamps, approved by the United States Postal Service. Use any photo you want to add an official dose of personality to your envelope.

Beauties for Baby

Whether you're expecting a little one, or know someone who is this section is full of darling projects for baby girls and boys alike.

CARDS

blessings for baby box & cards

Designer: Jessica Witty

BOX

1. Remove hardware from box. Paint inside and lid; let dry.
2. Trim patterned paper to fit around box; adhere and replace hardware.
3. Apply rub-ons to spell "Baby's blessing box".
4. Dry-brush box, flowers, and charm.
5. Attach brads to flowers; adhere to box.
6. Tie ribbon around box, attaching charm.
7. Cut prongs from brads; adhere to box.

CARDS

1. Print sentiment (see "Simple Sentiments") and "Blessings for baby" on cardstock. Trim to fit in box; punch corners.
2. Dry-brush flower; attach to sentiment card with brad.
3. Loop ribbon on cards, attach with brad.

SIMPLE SENTIMENTS

Blessings for baby. Please write your blessing, prayer, or hope for baby and leave it in the blessing box for Mommy and Daddy to keep.

SUPPLIES: *Cardstock:* (Very Vanilla) Stampin' Up! *Patterned paper:* (Maroon Floral from Sisters collection) My Mind's Eye *Paint:* (Tapioca, Metallic Champagne, Basil Green) Plaid *Accents:* (flowers, charm) Making Memories; (pearl brads) K&Company *Rub-ons:* (Maternal alphabet) Scrappin' Creations *Fibers:* (green organdy ribbon) *Font:* (Stanzi FJ) www.myfonts.com *Adhesive:* (decoupage) Plaid; (foam tape) *Tools:* (corner rounder punch) EK Success *Other:* (paper mache box) Hobby Lobby **Finished sizes: box 6⅛" x 4⅛" x 4"; cards 5¼" x 3½"**

precious & pink topiary

Designer: Cheryl Kanenwisher, courtesy of One Heart One Mind

PAINT

1. Paint pot and dowel; let dry. Paint both with crackle medium; set according to manufacturer's directions.
2. Paint top-coat on pot with Pink Blush; let dry.
3. Paint top-coat on dowel with Spotlight.
4. Spray clear acrylic finish on pot and dowel; let dry.

CREATE

1. Cut 6 sheets of patterned paper into ½" x 3" strips.
2. Roll strips to curl.
3. Begin at top of topiary ball and attach curls using pins; cover entire ball. *Note: Place curls close together and alternate patterns.*
4. Apply small dots of dimensional glaze to scalloped edge; let dry. Adhere to pot.
5. Apply small dot of dimensional glaze to dot on flower rectangle. Let dry; adhere to pot.

FINISH

1. Adhere topiary base inside pot.
2. Adhere pink shred around base.
3. Tie ribbon on dowel.

SUPPLIES: *Patterned paper:* (Double-Sided Text from Cutie Patootie collection) One Heart One Mind *Paint:* (Meadow Green, Pastel Pink, Pink Blush) Plaid; (Spotlight) Making Memories *Finish:* (crackle medium) Delta; (clear acrylic matte coating spray) Crafts, Etc. *Accents:* (scalloped edge strip, flower rectangle) One Heart One Mind; (dressmaker pins) Prym-Dritz *Fibers:* (green wired ribbon) Michaels *Other:* (topiary form) Floracraft; (clay pot) Hobby Lobby; (pink paper shred) Cole & Ashcroft; (dimensional glaze) Ranger Industries **Finished size: 6½" diameter x 21" height**

things you should know book

Designer: Susan Neal

1. Trace album front cover onto cardstock. Leave extra 1" to wrap over binding on left-hand side. Cut out and adhere to cover.

2. Cut six petals from patterned paper; ink edges. Print sentiment on petals.

3. Adhere petals to cover using foam squares on every other one. Adhere strips of ribbon to petals.

4. Punch hole in each inside corner of petals. Insert brads and attach ribbon.

5. Attach brad and flower at edge of front cover. Punch hole in edge of last page, attach elastic, and wrap around flower to close album.

SUPPLIES: *Cardstock:* (white) Bazzill Basics Paper *Patterned paper:* (Hannah, Rosebud, Peapod from Oh, Baby! Girl collection) BasicGrey *Dye ink:* (Peeled Paint, Worn Lipstick) Ranger Industries *Accents:* (acrylic flower) Maya Road; (large, small crystal brads) Making Memories; (black elastic ties) 7gypsies *Fibers:* (green rickrack, white stitched ribbon) BasicGrey; (white grosgrain ribbon) Making Memories *Font:* (your choice) *Adhesive:* (foam squares) *Other:* (flower chipboard book) Maya Road **Finished size: 6½" diameter**

sweet baby frame

Designer: Wendy Johnson

❶ Trim patterned paper to fit frame; ink edges.
❷ Dilute paint with water and white-wash entire frame; let dry. ❸ Wrap ribbon around paper and tie knot; adhere to frame. ❹ Adhere chipboard; attach pin and flower to knot.

fluttering butterflies mobile

Designer: Nichole Heady

CREATE

❶ Cut five pieces of each pink ribbon.
❷ Punch ten butterflies from patterned paper; trim off antennae. ❸ Adhere ribbon between two butterflies; repeat with all punched butterflies. ❹ Score transparency butterfly in half, along body; punch near head.

ASSEMBLE

❶ Insert jump rings through holes in butterflies.
❷ Thread ribbon through jump rings and fold over to create loop; adhere. ❸ Adhere ribbons to hoop. ❹ Adhere ribbon border to outside and inside of hoop. ❺ Tie floss to hoop.

SUPPLIES: *Patterned paper:* (Parasol from LilyKate collection) BasicGrey *Dye ink:* (Chocolate Chip) Stampin' Up! *Paint:* (white) Delta *Accents:* (stick pin) Nunn Design; (flower) Doodlebug Design; (chipboard sentiment) Rusty Pickle *Fibers:* (green satin ribbon) Michaels *Other:* (wood frame) **Finished size: 8½" x 6⅜"**

SUPPLIES: *Patterned paper:* (Olive Garden Plaid) Chatterbox; (Parasol from LilyKate collection) BasicGrey *Accents:* (butterfly transparency die cuts) My Mind's Eye; (large jump rings) Making Memories *Fibers:* (pink dot organdy, satin ribbon) May Arts; (pink satin ribbon) Hobby Lobby; (celery grosgrain ribbon) Making Memories; (white floss) *Tools:* (butterfly punch) EK Success; (1/16" hole punch) Fiskars *Other:* (embroidery hoop) Hobby Lobby **Finished size: 8" diameter x 17" height**

sugar & spice
Designer: Heather D. White

❶ Make card from cardstock.
❷ Cover card front with patterned paper.
❸ Cut partial flower from patterned paper; mat with cardstock. Adhere button to flower.
❹ Print poem on vellum. Trim to fit width of flower; adhere poem and flower to card.
❺ Print "Congratulations on your new baby girl!" on cardstock; trim and adhere.

she's here sundress
Designer: Alice Golden

❶ Make card, from patterned paper. Chalk edges.
❷ Adhere trim to pocket and sundress. Stitch pocket to front.
❸ Die-cut "She's here" from cardstock; adhere to pocket.
❹ Adhere buttons to patterned paper circles; trim. Thread buttons with floss and adhere to sundress.

BONUS IDEAS
- Add birth details to a photo of the baby, then crop it to fit inside the pocket.
- Trim the sundress into overalls to announce the arrival of a baby boy.

SUPPLIES: *Cardstock:* (Lilac) Bazzill Basics Paper *Patterned paper:* (Sprinkles, Pretty Please from Sugar collection) 3 Bugs in a Rug *Vellum:* Provo Craft *Accent:* (pink button) Making Memories *Font:* (Girls Are Weird) www.dafont.com **Finished size:** 4¼" x 6"

SUPPLIES: *Cardstock:* (pink) Die Cuts With a View *Patterned paper:* (Sophie, Natalie from Oh, Baby! Girl collection) BasicGrey *Color medium:* (yellow chalk) Pebbles Inc. *Accents:* (clear buttons) 7gypsies *Fibers:* (lime floss) Karen Foster Design; (ivory eyelet trim) *Dies:* (Studio Classic alphabet) QuicKutz *Tools:* (die cut machine) QuicKutz **Finished size:** 7¾" x 7¾"

precious baby
Designer: Alisa Bangerter

1. Make card from cardstock.
2. Cut 2½" squares from cardstock; chalk edges.
3. Wrap each square with same color fiber; knot, tie bow, or adhere.
4. Attach safety pins to fibers. Adhere stickers to squares with foam tape. Adhere squares to card.

baby onesie
Designer: Alice Golden

1. Make card, from patterned paper; attach brads and mat with cardstock.
2. Spell "Boy!" with stickers and affix rickrack.
3. Adhere pajama sticker.

SUPPLIES: *Cardstock:* (Romance, Jet Stream, Pear, Lemonade) Bazzill Basics Paper; (white) *Color medium:* (blue, yellow, pink, green chalk) Craf-T Products *Accents:* (blue, yellow, pink, green safety pins) Making Memories *Stickers:* (metal baby word squares) Pressed Petals *Fibers:* (pink rickrack) Wrights; (blue organza, yellow gingham ribbon) Offray; (green trim) Hand-Dyed Hobbies *Adhesive:* (foam tape) **Finished size: 5½" square**

SUPPLIES: All supplies from Karen Foster Design unless otherwise noted. *Cardstock:* (Perfectly Baby Blue) Prism *Patterned paper:* (Blue Baby Collage) *Accents:* (car, boat, train brads) *Stickers:* (alphabet, pajamas, rickrack) **Finished size: 8½" x 8"**

5 steps *double stuff twin shower*

Designer: Wendy Johnson

INVITATION

❶ Cut 4¼" x 8½" piece of cardstock; fold 3" from bottom and adhere along sides to form pocket. ❷ Wrap ribbon around pocket. ❸ Punch two circles from brown cardstock; stamp "Oreo" on each. Crumple, flatten, and mat with white cardstock, using foam tape. Mat with brown and adhere to pocket. ❹ Print text on cardstock; trim into tag shape. Punch hole and tie with ribbon. Tuck in pocket.

PLACE CARD

❶ Make place card from cardstock. ❷ Print guest's name on cardstock; trim and adhere. ❸ Tie ribbon around front flap.

FAVOR BAG

❶ Place treats in bag. Fill with gift shred. ❷ Print text on cardstock; trim into tag shape. Mat with cardstock. ❸ Punch hole and tie tag to bag with ribbon.

SANDWICH COOKIE DESSERT RECIPE
Source: www.cooks.com

INGREDIENTS

½ c. butter
30 chocolate sandwich cookies
1 c. confectioner's sugar
1 small pkg. chocolate instant pudding
1 small pkg. vanilla instant pudding
1 (8 oz.) pkg. cream cheese
1 large container whipped topping
3 c. milk

Yields 8 servings

DIRECTIONS

Blend butter and cookies in food processor, one half at a time. Pour in 9" x 13" pan. Mix together confectioner's sugar, cream cheese, and half of the whipped topping. Layer over cookie mixture. Mix together puddings and milk. Layer over cream cheese mixture. Cover with remaining whipped topping. Garnish with sandwich cookies. Keep refrigerated.

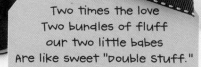

Two times the love
Two bundles of fluff
our two little babes
Are like sweet "Double stuff."

Two times the joy
Two times the Yum,
Two times the sweetness
Two times the fun.

Join us to celebrate
Abigail & Elizabeth Jones
Saturday, June 14th
2:00 p.m.
The Johnson Home

SUPPLIES: *Cardstock:* (brown, pink, white) Bazzill Basics Paper *Rubber stamps:* (Antique Uppercase alphabet) PSX *Dye ink:* (Basic Black) Stampin' Up! *Fibers:* (brown stitched ribbon) Michaels *Font:* (CK Handprint) Creating Keepsakes *Adhesive:* (foam tape) *Tools:* (1" circle punch) *Other:* (clear bag) ClearBags; (pink gift shred) **Finished sizes:** invitation 4¼" x 5½", place card 3½" x 3", favor bag approx. 4" x 5"

teddy
5 STEPS

Designer: Melissa Phillips

1. Make card from cardstock. Adhere patterned paper rectangle to card front.
2. Punch circle from card; adhere buttons around edge.
3. Apply rub-on inside card.
4. Tie knot with ribbon; adhere to card. Attach safety pin through knot.
5. Stitch edges of front flap.

twins
5 STEPS

Designer: Susan Neal

1. Make card from cardstock.
2. Trim patterned paper. Stamp "Boy twins" and "Boy, oh boy!" on cardstock; trim and attach to patterned paper with brads. Mat with cardstock and adhere to card.
3. Stamp strollers on cardstock; trim and stitch rickrack to top and bottom. Mat with cardstock and adhere.
4. Adhere chipboard letters to card.
5. Die-cut tag and x from white cardstock; mat with Apple Green cardstock. Adhere and tie to chipboard letter with string.

SUPPLIES: *Cardstock:* (white) DMD, Inc. *Patterned paper:* (paisley from Flutter collection) Autumn Leaves *Accents:* (green brads, pink safety pin) Making Memories; (pink buttons) *Rub-on:* (bear) American Crafts *Sticker:* (it's a girl label) Making Memories *Fibers:* (green gingham ribbon) American Crafts *Tools:* (1⅜" circle punch) **Finished size: 4" x 7½"**

SUPPLIES: *Cardstock:* (Apple Green, white) Bazzill Basics Paper *Patterned paper:* (Green Swirlies from Baby Boy collection) Provo Craft *Rubber stamps:* (stroller from Classic Baby collection) Provo Craft; (Antique alphabet) Inkadinkado *Pigment ink:* (Smoky Gray) Tsukineko *Accents:* (chipboard alphabet) Provo Craft; (square brads) Making Memories *Fibers:* (green rickrack) Provo Craft; (white string) *Dies:* (tag, x) Provo Craft *Tools:* (die cut machine) Provo Craft **Finished size: 3¾" x 8½"**

SUPPLIES: *Patterned paper:* (Chaps, Roper, Sheriff from Cowboy collection) Crate Paper *Dye ink:* (Old Paper) Ranger Industries *Paint:* (Light Ivory) Accent *Accents:* (tags, monogram, little boy label, border strips) Crate Paper; (white chipboard stars) Heidi Swapp; (yellow fabric-covered brads, pewter nail heads) Making Memories *Rub-ons:* (Heidi alphabet) Making Memories *Stickers:* (Cowboy alphabet) Crate Paper *Fibers:* (brown gingham ribbon) Close To My Heart *Font:* (Weathervane) www.twopeasinabucket.com *Other:* (album, wood skewers) **Finished sizes:** invitation 5½" x 4¼", advice book 7" x 5½", pinwheel 6¼" x 10¼"

adoption shower

Designer: Melissa Phillips

INVITATION

Apply paint and ink to edges of paper pieces.

OUTSIDE

❶ Make invitation from patterned paper. ❷ Trim and adhere polka dot border strip. ❸ Stitch edges of front flap. ❹ Cut piece of patterned paper; stitch edges. Adhere, solid side up. ❺ Attach little boy label with nail heads. Adhere "a" to square tag; adhere to invitation. ❻ Sand edges of stars; adhere. Spell "It's" on large star with rub-ons.

INSIDE

❶ Print shower details on solid side of patterned paper. Stitch edges and adhere. ❷ Sand edges of star; adhere. ❸ Adhere piece of patterned paper.

ADVICE BOOK

Apply paint and ink to edges of paper pieces.

Cover

❶ Remove covers from book and cut patterned paper to fit. ❷ Adhere striped and orange wave border strips. ❸ Stitch edges of piece and along center of orange wave strip. ❹ Spell "wisdom" on tag with rub-ons; stitch edges. Attach to piece with nail heads. ❺ Adhere "m" to round tag; zigzag-stitch edges. Adhere to piece. Spell "ommy" with stickers. ❻ Sand edges of star; attach brad and adhere to piece.

Assembly

❶ Adhere piece to cover. ❷ Adhere patterned paper to back cover. ❸ Place covers back on book. Tie ribbon on spiral binding.

PINWHEEL

Apply paint and ink to edges of paper pieces.

❶ Cut 4½" square of patterned paper. ❷ Cut in from corners 2½" (see Figure a). ❸ Fold corners and staple to center of piece (see Figure b). ❹ Tie ribbon in loose knot; adhere to center. ❺ Cut prongs off brad; adhere to center of knot. ❻ Adhere skewer to back.

PINWHEEL PATTERN

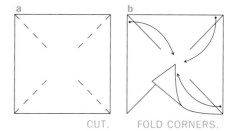

a   b

CUT.   FOLD CORNERS.

INVITATION INSIDE

tea party shower

Designers: Jennifer Nardone and
Beth Reames, courtesy of Ellison

INVITATION

❶ Die-cut card from cardstock.
❷ Cut strip of cardstock; trim with decorative-edges scissors. Adhere to bottom of front flap; stitch top edge.
❸ Die-cut circle from patterned paper; ink edges. Trim and adhere to invitation. ❹ Stamp sentiment.
❺ Die-cut tea set from cardstock; sand pieces and adhere to invitation.
❻ Apply rub-on and adhere gems.
❼ Tie ribbon around front flap.

FAVOR BOX/DECORATION

❶ Die-cut box and lid from patterned paper and/or cardstock; assemble. ❷ Die-cut leaf and flower layers from cardstock; curl petals with pencil. ❸ Layer leaf and flowers; attach to lid with brad.
❹ Adhere bead, button, or gem over brad, if desired.

TOPIARY

❶ Place floral foam in pot. ❷ Paint foam ball; let dry. Insert one end of stick in foam ball, and other end in pot. ❸ Die-cut flower layers from Build-A-Flower #1 set and leaf from cardstock. Punch hole in center of each flower layer; curl petals with pencil. ❹ Thread seed bead on pin; assemble flower layers and pin to foam ball. ❺ Create enough flowers to cover ball. ❻ Arrange moss in pot; tie with ribbon.

BONUS IDEA
Arrange the favor boxes in a dessert stand for an elegant decoration.

you're invited

SUPPLIES: *Cardstock:* (cream, blue shades, green shades, yellow shades) *Patterned paper:* (Imagine Polka Dots, assorted) My Mind's Eye *Rubber stamps:* (Providence alphabet) Making Memories *Dye ink:* (Peeled Paint) Ranger Industries *Paint:* (green) *Accents:* (small gems) Pure Allure; (clear seed beads; assorted beads, brads, buttons) *Rub-on:* (floral vine) American Crafts *Fibers:* (white organdy ribbon) Offray *Dies:* (Box #20; Build-A-Flower #1 set; Card Cover A2 #2; Circle; Flower Layers #1, #2, #3 sets; Flower, Daisies set; Girl set; Paper Sculpting, Hydrangea set) *Tools:* (die cut machine) Ellison; (⅛" circle punch, decorative-edge scissors) *Other:* (foam ball, stick, pot, floral foam, decorative moss, white ball point straight pins) **Finished sizes:** invitation 5½" x 4¼", favor boxes 2¼" cube, topiary approx. 7" diameter x 19" height

congrats trio

Design: courtesy of Ellison

GIRL CARD

1 Die-cut card from cardstock.
2 Cut strip of cardstock with decorative-edge scissors; adhere to card. Cut square of cardstock; adhere to card.
3 Die-cut teddy bear from cardstock. Draw stitching with pencil. Adhere cardstock behind eye holes and draw eyes with pen. Tie with floss and adhere to card.
4 Attach brads and ribbon.
5 Die-cut "Congrats" from cardstock; adhere.

BOY CARD

1 Die-cut card from cardstock.
2 Cut strip of patterned paper; adhere to card. Print "Sweet baby boy" on vellum; trim and adhere to card.
3 Adhere ribbon over seam. Stitch along center.
4 Die-cut rocket from chipboard and cardstock. Adhere cardstock pieces to chipboard; coat with dimensional glaze. Adhere to card with foam dots.

TWINS CARD

1 Make card from cardstock.
2 Cut patterned paper slightly smaller than card front; adhere.
3 Print sentiment on cardstock; trim with decorative-edge scissors and adhere.
4 Die-cut lambs from cardstock. Layer pieces; adhere. Draw eyes and with pen. Adhere lambs to card.
5 Knot ribbon around cover.

SUPPLIES: *Cardstock:* (orange, dark pink, light pink, light blue, dark blue) Bazzill Basics Paper; (yellow, green, cream) Die Cuts With a View; (white, silver) *Patterned paper:* (Stripes, Yellow Diamonds) *Vellum; Color media:* (white, colored pencils; black pen) *Accents:* (orange brads) Die Cuts With a View *Fibers:* (white organza, blue grosgrain ribbon) Offray; (pink satin, orange grosgrain ribbon; pink floss) *Adhesive:* (foam dots) Plaid *Fonts:* (Papyrus) www.myfonts.com; (Boulevard, Zapfino, Belwe) www.fonts.com *Dies:* (Card Cover A2 #2, Teddy Bear, Yarn alphabet, rocket from Boy set, lamb from Stuffed Animal set) Ellison *Tools:* (die cut machine) Ellison; (decorative-edge scissors) *Other:* (dimensional glaze) JudiKins; (chipboard) **Finished size: girl card 5⅜" x 4⅛"; boy card 5⅜" x 4⅛"; twins card 4¾" square**

star gift bag
5 STEPS

Designer: Emily Call, courtesy of Stampin' Up!

1. Stamp circles on cardstock square bottom.
2. Stamp Linen on cardstock; adhere.
3. Adhere patterned paper to chipboard star. Sand edges; adhere.
4. Stamp "Baby" on cardstock. Cut out letters and adhere using foam squares.
5. Attach cream ribbon with brad.
6. Adhere piece to gift bag.

sweet lollipop gift bag
Designer: Wendy Johnson

1. Adhere patterned paper to gift bag.
2. Punch two holes and thread ribbon through bag for handles.
3. Stamp lollipop on cardstock. Watercolor image, and cut into tag shape.
4. Mat tag with cardstock; trim.
5. Print sweet baby on cardstock. Trim; mat with cardstock.
6. Attach tag to gift bag with white twine; adhere sentiment to tag with foam squares.

SUPPLIES: All supplies from Stampin' Up! unless otherwise noted. *Cardstock:* (So Saffron, Whisper White) *Patterned paper:* (Blue Circles from Sarah collection) *Rubber stamps:* (Headline alphabet, Seeing Spots set, Linen) *Dye ink:* (Brocade Blue, Chocolate Chip, So Saffron) *Accents:* (chipboard star, vintage brad) *Fibers:* (cream grosgrain ribbon) *Adhesive:* (foam squares) *Other:* (white gift bag) **Finished size: 8" x 10¼"**

BONUS IDEA

Use pink-toned papers and ribbons to create this same bag for a baby girl.

SUPPLIES: *Cardstock:* (Old Olive) Stampin' Up!; (blue, white) *Patterned paper:* (Yellow Plaid from Fresh Paper collection) Sweetwater *Rubber stamp:* (lollipop) Paper Salon *Solvent ink:* (Jet Black) Tsukineko *Color medium:* (watercolor crayons) Stampin' Up! *Fibers:* (blue ribbon) Chatterbox; (white twine) Karen Foster Design *Font:* (Commercial Break) www.twopeasinabucket.com *Adhesive:* (foam squares) *Other:* (gift bag) **Finished size: 4" x 4¾"**

howdy pardner wall hanging

Designer: Kelly Keller

STAR

1. Cut star sections from patterned papers.
2. Ink edges.
3. Lay points flat; adhere to make flat star.
4. Once adhered together, re-fold to make star dimensional.

ACCENTS

1. Punch holes and attach eyelets to star.
2. Thread jute through eyelets to back of star, string beads, and thread back through eyelets; knot. Tie twig to star.
3. Apply rub-ons to tags. Ink edges; tie to twig with fibers and fabric scrap.

BONUS IDEA
Use girl-themed patterned paper to hang this star in a baby girl's nursery.

DESIGNER TIP

Score and fold on the lines before assembling the star, and then flatten it.

SUPPLIES: *Patterned paper:* (Cowboy, Stripe, Bandana, Diagonal Stripe, Cowboy Words from Kazoo Kids collection) K&Company *Dye ink:* (Pepperwood) Close To My Heart *Accents:* (wood tags) Blumenthal Lansing Co.; (wired twig) Sullivans Floral Supply; (eyelets, beads, fabric scrap) *Rub-ons:* (Wedding Monogram alphabet) K&Company *Fibers:* (red, blue, jute string; natural jute ribbon) May Arts **Finished size:** 10½" x 11"

SUPPLIES: *Cardstock:* (Flamingo, Watermelon, white) Bazzill Basics Paper *Fibers:* (pink dotted ribbon) May Arts *Fonts:* (CBX Chechee) Chatterbox; DW Oh Baby!) www.twopeasinabucket.com *Adhesive:* (foam squares) *Tools:* (corner rounder punch) EK Success **Finished size:** 2½" x 2¾"

SUPPLIES: *Cardstock:* (Banana, Parakeet) Bazzill Basics Paper *Patterned paper:* (Capture the Flag from Play collection) American Crafts *Dye ink:* (black) Stewart Superior Corp. *Accents:* (red brads, assorted buttons) Bazzill Basics Paper *Fibers:* (black waxed linen thread) Scrapworks *Font:* (Pussycat) www.getfreefonts.com *Tools:* (1" circle punch) EK Success *Other:* (white gift bag) **Finished size:** 7¾" x 9¾"

hello baby gift tag
Designer: Jennifer Miller

1 Make tag from cardstock; round corners.
2 Print text on cardstock. Cut text into circle and mat with cardstock; attach to tag with foam squares.
3 Punch hole in top of tag; attach ribbon.

big brother gift bag
Designer: Kim Kesti

1 Cover front of gift bag with patterned paper.
2 Print sentiment on cardstock; cut into pennant shape, and ink edges.
3 Adhere buttons.
4 Punch 1" circles from cardstock; ink edges.
5 Attach brads and circles to bag.
6 Punch two small holes on either side of pennant. Attach pennant to brads with thread.

flowers and frills mobile
Designer: Emily Smith

❶ Decorate chipboard pieces with card-stock, patterned paper, pen, accents, rub-ons, and sticker. ❷ Punch holes in finished accents and thread fishing line. ❸ Wrap fabric trim around embroidery hoop. ❹ Tie fishing lines to hoop. ❺ Thread beads on fishing lines. Tie fishing lines to silver hanging ring.

How to Create Paper Twirls
❶ Trim paper to ½" x 12"; fill shallow pan with warm water. ❷ Lay strips in pan; soak for five seconds. ❸ Remove from pan; squeeze off excess water. ❹ Wrap paper around various sized dowels and secure with rubber band; let dry.

sweet & sassy wall border
Designer: Alice Golden

❶ Adhere wallpaper border to wall. ❷ Trim strips from patterned paper. Adhere to top and bottom of border; affix stickers. ❸ Trim patterned paper; adhere. ❹ Cut squares from patterned paper; adhere.

SUPPLIES: *Cardstock:* (Fairy Tale Pink, Belgium Blue, Pure White Treasures) WorldWin *Patterned paper:* (Pixie Garden, Sky Lilac from Cottage collection; Rose Kelly Flower from Powder Room collection) Chatterbox *Color medium:* (black pen) Sakura *Accents:* (chipboard circles, chipboard flowers) Polar Bear Press; (pink, blue buttons; pink/white gingham fabric trim; chipboard hearts, chipboard alphabet, chipboard ornaments) Rusty Pickle; (pink, white flower buttons) Making Memories; (pink rhinestone flower) Prima; (blue rhinestones, blue/clear beads) Rub-ons: (border) Chatterbox; (flowers) Fontwerks *Sticker:* (round epoxy) Provo Craft *Other:* (embroidery hoop) Coats & Clark; (photo, fishing line, silver hanging ring) **Finished size: 6" diameter x 18" height**

SUPPLIES: *Patterned paper:* (Quilted Stripes, Alphabet Glitter, assorted patterns from mat pad from Small Wonders Girl collection) K&Company *Stickers:* (words, border) K&Company *Other:* (repositionable wallpaper border) Wall Pops **Finished size: 24" x 6½"**

refrigerator art clips

Designer: Wendy Johnson

1. Mat patterned paper rectangle with cardstock.
2. Die-cut 2½" and 3" stars from patterned paper. Adhere together, stitch edges, and adhere.
3. Punch circles from pattered paper, adhere together. Attach brad and adhere.
4. Print sentiment on paper; trim and adhere.
5. Spell "Art" with chipboard letters. Adhere block to clothespin.
6. Repeat for second clothespin.

SUPPLIES: Cardstock: (Blossom) Bazzill Basics Paper; (blue) Paper: (white) Patterned paper: (Sunny Paisley from Sun Room collection; Villa Plaid, Mini Gazebo Paisley) Chatterbox; (Simmons Street, Paradise Lane, Yasoda Street, Hillcrest Avenue, Carter Drive from Metropolis collection) Scenic Route Accents: (pink, orange brads) Making Memories; (chipboard alphabet) Chatterbox Font: (Papyrus) www.fonts.com Die: (star from George and Basic Shapes cartridge) Provo Craft Tools: (1" circle punch) EK Success; (die cut machine) Provo Craft; (⅛" circle punch) Other: (green jumbo magnetic clothespins) Stacks and Stacks **Finished size: 4" x 4¾" x 1¼"**

Groovin' Gifts & Clever Cards

Need a quick gift or a fun card? This chapter has everything you need to make a gasp-worthy project for anyone on your list.

Birthday Date List Gift Book

Designer: Carla Peicheff

COVER

1. Trim and layer patterned paper on tag. Stitch and zigzag-stitch.
2. Print "Date list" on cardstock; trim and adhere.
3. Attach brads.
4. Spell "B day" with stickers.
5. Attach tags together with metal ring. Tie button with twine; tie to twill.

INSIDE PAGE

1. Print lines on cardstock. Trim to fit tag. Adhere patterned paper and lined paper. Zigzag-stitch seams.
2. Punch tab from patterned paper. Fold in half and staple to tag.
3. Punch flower. Attach brad and adhere.
4. Print month abbreviation on cardstock. Trim and adhere.

5 STEPS — Moments in Time Notebook

Designer: Betsy Veldman

1. Trim two chipboard rectangles to same size as journaling cards. Adhere floss to one chipboard piece; attach brad to other. Adhere journaling cards to both sides of chipboard; trim. Sand edges.
2. Trim bird from patterned paper. Ink edges and adhere with foam tape.
3. Apply rub-ons. Thread button with floss; adhere flowers and button.
4. Trim several sheets of paper to fit inside album. Punch pages and cover; bind.
5. Tie ribbon, flower, and key to binding. Wrap floss around brad to close.

SUPPLIES: *Cardstock:* (white) Bazzill Basics Paper *Patterned paper:* (assorted from Detour collection) October Afternoon *Accents:* (assorted brads, staples) Making Memories; (green button) Hero Arts; (metal ring) *Stickers:* (felt alphabet) Making Memories *Fibers:* (blue twine) Michaels; (alphabet twill ribbon) Creative Imaginations *Font:* (Helvetica) Microsoft *Tools:* (tab punch, flower punch) Stampin' Up! *Other:* (manila tags) **Finished size: 5½" x 2½"**

SUPPLIES: *Cardstock:* (white) *Patterned paper:* (Natural Springs from Inspired collection) Webster's Pages *Chalk ink:* (Rouge, Chestnut Roan) Clearsnap *Accents:* (brown flowers, pink pearl brad) Imaginisce; (Passport alphabet, cream flower) Making Memories; (pink button) Autumn Leaves; (metal key) Tim Holtz *Rub-ons:* (brown, pink flourish) BasicGrey *Fibers:* (green iridescent ribbon) SEI; (natural floss) Karen Foster Design *Adhesive:* (foam tape) *Tools:* (binding machine) Zutter Zisters *Other:* (journaling cards) Webster's Pages; (binding wire) Zutter Zisters; (chipboard) **Finished size: 5" x 5½"**

Beautiful Life Journal & Pencil Holder

Designer: Tish Treadaway

JOURNAL

1 Adhere patterned paper to journal. Trim excess and sand edges.

2 Ink book binding tape; affix.

3 Trim patterned paper and tear bottom edge; adhere.

4 Trim patterned paper into square; adhere. Affix flourish sticker and adhere leaves.

5 Tie ribbon around journal.

PENCIL HOLDER

1 Paint pencil holder; let dry.

2 Trim patterned paper to fit around pencil holder; adhere.

3 Tie on ribbon and attach tag and leaf.

SUPPLIES: *Patterned paper:* (Dots, Life from Beautiful Life collection) BoBunny Press *Specialty ink:* (brown fabric) *Paint:* (Chocolate) Making Memories *Accents:* (fall leaves, happiness tag) BoBunny Press *Stickers:* (flourish) BoBunny Press; (book binding tape) Making Memories *Fibers:* (turquoise ribbon) *Other:* (wood pencil holder) Prima; (composition book) **Finished sizes: journal 7½" x 9¾"; pencil holder 3" x 5" x 3"**

DESIGNER TIP

Look for tiny vintage buttons on baby clothes in thrift stores and at yard sales.

5 STEPS On the Mend Flowers

Designer: Ann Powell

1. Cut tag from cardstock.

2. Print sentiment on cardstock; trim and adhere to tag. Adhere tag to spool; adhere button.

3. Tie on ribbon.

4. Cut lengths of wire 10"–12"and fold in half. String button, one or two flowers, and second button. Twist wire strands to ends.

5. Adhere in spool.

Little Princess Wall Hanging

Designer: Melissa Phillips

Ink all paper edges.

1. Cut patterned paper to fit inside and outside edges of box; adhere.

2. Cut patterned paper to fit inside box. Stamp flourish, stitch edges, and adhere.

3. Apply glitter to box edges.

4. Affix journaling oval inside box. Stitch edges of photo die cut; adhere. Affix little princess label; adhere crown.

5. Apply glitter to flower; adhere. Adhere button and rhinestones.

6. Thread chipboard heart on twine; tie around box. Adhere photo corners.

7. Adhere trim, affix border sticker, and adhere wired pearls. Tie on ribbon. Tie ribbon bow and adhere ends to box sides.

SUPPLIES: *Cardstock:* (yellow, white) *Accents:* (blue, white, yellow flowers) Prima; (assorted buttons) *Fibers:* (blue striped ribbon) Stampin' Up! *Font:* (Monotype Corsiva) www.fonts.com *Other:* (green wire, wood spool) **Finished size: 2¾" diameter x 5¼" height**

SUPPLIES: *Patterned paper:* (Anne, Brady, Julie) Melissa Frances *Clear stamps:* (flourish from Baroque set) Melissa Frances *Dye ink:* (Old Paper) Ranger Industries *Chalk ink:* (Dusty Plum) Clearsnap *Accents:* (pink glitter chipboard heart) American Crafts; (iridescent glitter; white resin crown, photo corners; vintage baby photo die cut) Melissa Frances; (pink rhinestones) Kaisercraft; (white button, wired pearls, yellow flower) *Stickers:* (journaling oval, little princess label, floral scalloped border) Melissa Frances *Fibers:* (white ribbon) Offray; (pink polka dot ribbon) May Arts; (cream crochet trim) Melissa Frances; (hemp twine) *Other:* (paper mache box) **Finished size: 3¾" x 6"**

DESIGNER TIP

Use a pencil to draw the heart shape and arrange the buttons before you start adhering.

The Sweetest Thing Photo Holder

Designer: Cathy List

POT

1. Paint flower pot; let dry. Apply rub-on. Apply two coats of decoupage to seal.

2. Cut floral foam; insert in pot. Adhere excelsior moss.

3. Tie on ribbon.

4. Cut three pieces of dowel to desired lengths. Adhere mini clothespins to one end of each dowel. Tie on ribbon.

5. Insert dowels in pot.

PHOTOS

1. Stamp happy on cardstock; punch into circle. Stamp always on patterned paper; punch into circle. Stamp delight on button; mat with punched patterned paper circle.

2. Mat pieces with punched cardstock circles. Mat with punched patterned paper and cardstock scalloped circles, using foam tape.

3. Adhere to mini clothespins. Sand edges of chipboard heart and star; adhere. Adhere button.

4. Mat photos with cardstock; insert in clothespins.

5 STEPS Button Heart Frame

Designer: Teri Anderson

1. Remove glass from frame. Cut cardstock to fit in frame.

2. Adhere buttons in heart shape. Place in frame.

SUPPLIES: All supplies from Stampin' Up! unless otherwise noted. *Cardstock:* (Real Red, Pumpkin Pie, Bashful Blue, Old Olive, Whisper White) *Patterned paper:* (floral, diamond from Real Red Designer Series collection; floral, diamond from Pumpkin Pie Designer Series collection; floral from Bashful Blue Designer Series collection) *Rubber stamps:* (happy, delight, always from Define Your Life set) *Dye ink:* (Old Olive) *Solvent ink:* (white, black) Tsukineko *Paint:* (red) Plaid *Accents:* (clear, red buttons; chipboard heart, star); (mini clothespins) no source *Rub-on:* (the sweetest thing) *Fibers:* (white, green ribbon) *Adhesive:* (foam tape); (decoupage) Plaid *Tools:* (1¼", 1⅜" circle punches, scalloped circle punch) *Other:* (flower pot, wood dowel, floral foam, natural excelsior moss, photos) no source **Finished size: 5" diameter x 9" height**

SUPPLIES: *Cardstock:* (white) Bazzill Basics Paper *Accents:* (assorted buttons) SEI, Oriental Trading Co., Bazzill Basics Paper *Other:* (white frame) Target **Finished size: 7¼" x 5¼"**

5 Smooth Sailin' Card

Designer: Jeanne Streiff

1 Make card from cardstock.
2 Trim slightly smaller piece of cardstock. Pierce edges and flourish, using template; adhere.
3 Trace flourish with marker
4 Stamp "Smooth sailin'".
5 Stamp sailboat on cardstock; color with markers. Trim and adhere to card with foam tape.

SUPPLIES: *Cardstock:* (Intense Mint, Iced Teal, white) Prism *Rubber stamps:* (sailboat from Bundle of Joy set) Whipper Snapper Designs; (Casual alphabet) Karen Foster Design *Dye ink:* (Tuxedo Black) Tsukineko *Color media:* (teal, red, yellow, orange markers) Copic Marker; (white gel pen) Ranger Industries *Adhesive:* (foam tape) *Template:* (flourish border piercing) Dandee Images **Finished size: 4½" x 3¼"**

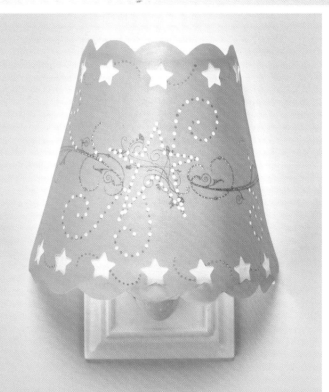

SUPPLIES: *Patterned paper:* (Blue Shimmer from Modern Milan collection) Me & My Big Ideas *Clear stamps:* (star from Twinkle-Twinkle set, flourish from WhirlyGigs set) Technique Tuesday *Dye ink:* (Twilight) Close to My Heart *Tools:* (corner rounder punch) EK Success; (star punch) McGill; (¹⁄₁₆" circle punch) Hyglo Crafts *Other:* (night light, lampshade pattern) Wisconsin Lighting **Finished sizes: 6" x 5" x 2¾"**

5 Starry Night Light

Designer: Alice Golden

1 Make lampshade from patterned paper, following pattern. *Note: Add extra ¼" to top and bottom edges.*
2 Trim top and bottom edges with corner rounder punch; punch stars.
3 Stamp star and flourishes; pierce along stamped lines.
4 Adhere to night light.

Thinking of You Card

Designer: Ashley Harris

1. Make card from cardstock; adhere patterned paper squares.
2. Stamp thinking of you on cardstock; trim and adhere to card.
3. Pierce scalloped border.
4. Tie ribbon around card; adhere butterfly and pearls.

Spring Rain Card

Designer: Kim Kesti

1. Make card from cardstock.
2. Print sentiment on cardstock; trim slightly smaller than card front.
3. Trim cardstock pieces to create umbrella; adhere.
4. Pierce raindrops; apply dimensional glaze.
5. Adhere piece to card; adhere button.

Create Motion

Add detail and interest to your projects by creating designs with paper piercing. Scatter a specific design, like raindrops, over the entire card, or add a gentle scallop that beautifully borders your project.

Into every spring
a little rain must fall

SUPPLIES: *Cardstock:* (white) Bazzill Basics Paper *Patterned paper:* (Enchanted, Butter Blossom from Ella collection) BoBunny Press *Clear stamp:* (thinking of you from Greetings set) Heidi Grace Designs *Solvent ink:* (Jet Black) Tsukineko *Accents:* (yellow felt butterfly) Heidi Swapp; (pearls) *Fibers:* (white sheer ribbon) Jo-Ann Stores **Finished size: 5" square**

SUPPLIES: *Cardstock:* (Lily White, Atlantic, Berrylicious, Limeade, Powder, Beetle Black) Bazzill Basics Paper *Accent:* (red button) *Font:* (MS Gothic) Microsoft *Other:* (dimensional glaze) Ranger Industries **Finished size: 7¼" x 5"**

INSIDE

Our Family Album

Designer: Roree Rumph

① Ink edges of chipboard circles. Cut patterned paper circles to cover both sides of chipboard circles. Adhere cardstock and patterned paper strips as desired. Ink edges. ② Stitch rickrack over some paper seams. ③ Stitch flower stems on cover circle. Sew on buttons and ribbon. Adhere rickrack stems. ④ Stamp "Our family". Adhere heart. Adhere to cover circle. ⑤ Adhere remaining circles to chipboard circles. Embellish with ribbon, accents, photos, and stamped captions as desired. ⑥ Tie circles together with hemp twine. Tie on ribbon and rickrack lengths.

Ladybug Backpack Tag

Designer: Sharron M. Hoff

① Make tag from cardstock; adhere patterned paper pieces and stitch edges. Zigzag-stitch seam. ② Punch ¾" and 1⅛" circles from cardstock. Adhere to tag to form ladybug body. Punch 1⅛" circle from cardstock; cut in half to make wings. Punch ⅛" circles from wings. Adhere. Draw antennae with marker. ③ Die-cut name from cardstock; adhere to tag. ④ Insert tag in name badge sleeve; tie on ribbon and attach bead chain.

SUPPLIES: *Cardstock:* (Parakeet) Bazzill Basics Paper *Patterned paper:* (Best Friends, Cutie Patootie, Girly Girl, Li'l Princess from Frou Frou collection) Fancy Pants Designs *Rubber stamps:* (Printer's Type Lowercase alphabet) Hero Arts *Dye ink:* (Peeled Paint) Ranger Industries *Accents:* (chipboard circles) Bazzill Basics Paper; (chipboard hearts) Heidi Swapp; (assorted buttons) Autumn Leaves; (assorted glitter brads) *Fibers:* (hemp twine; assorted rickrack, ribbon) *Tool:* (circle cutter) Fiskars *Other:* (photos) **Finished size: 5" diameter**

SUPPLIES: *Cardstock:* (white, black, red) Bazzill Basics Paper *Patterned paper:* (green polka dot, black gingham) *Color medium:* (black pen) *Accent:* (bead chain) *Fibers:* (sheer black polka dot, black gingham ribbon) Offray *Dies:* (Olivia alphabet) QuicKutz *Tools:* (die cut machine) QuicKutz; (⅛", ¾", 1⅛" circle punches) *Other:* (clear name badge sleeve) **Finished size: 4" x 2¾"**

Happy Birthday Bird Card

Designer: Danielle Flanders

CARD

❶ Make card from patterned paper; adhere patterned paper strips to edges.

❷ Adhere patterned paper strip to each side.

❸ Cut patterned paper with decorative-edge scissors; adhere reverse side up.

ACCENTS

❶ Cut bird, following pattern. Cross-stitch eye and whip-stitch edges. Staple ribbon loops for wing. Adhere.

❷ Create long stitches for legs. Draw feet.

❸ Draw quote bubble on patterned paper; trim and adhere. Affix sticker.

❹ Stamp stems. Affix circle sticker. Attach brad to flower sticker. Adhere remaining stickers with foam tape. Detail with pen.

BIRD PATTERN

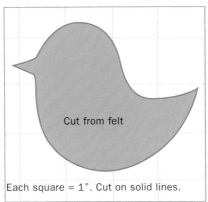

Cut from felt

Each square = 1". Cut on solid lines.

5 STEPS HiCard

Designer: Teri Anderson

❶ Make card from patterned paper.

❷ Affix wave sticker to reverse side of patterned paper; trim and adhere.

❸ Cut two half-circles from patterned paper; adhere. Adhere wiggle eyes.

❹ Cut two smaller half-circles for wings; adhere. Cut beaks from reverse side of patterned paper; adhere.

❺ Spell "Hi" with stickers.

SUPPLIES: *Patterned paper:* (Surprise Confetti, Surprise Giftwrap, Surprise Napkin) KI Memories; (White Line Scalloped from Antique Medley collection) Creative Imaginations *Clear stamps:* (stems from Build-a-Flower set) Autumn Leaves *Solvent ink:* (Jet Black) Tsukineko *Color medium:* (black marker) EK Success *Accents:* (light blue felt) CPE; (white brad) Jo-Ann Stores; (staple) *Stickers:* (circle, flower, happy birthday, oval) KI Memories *Fibers:* (patterned ribbon) KI Memories; (black, pink floss) DMC *Adhesive:* (foam tape) *Tool:* (decorative-edge scissors) Provo Craft **Finished size: 7" x 5¾"**

SUPPLIES: *Patterned paper:* (Buttercup Dot, Orange Citrus Dot, Pink Punch Dot from Double Dot collection) Bo-Bunny Press; (Franklin Stripe Pink from Hampton collection) Scenic Route *Accents:* (wiggle eyes) Darice *Stickers:* (Mumbo Jumbo alphabet) Sonburn; (wave) Bo-Bunny Press *Template:* (circle) Provo Craft **Finished size: 4½" x 5½"**

SUPPLIES: *Cardstock:* (white, brown) *Color medium:* (brown chalk) Craf-T Products *Accents:* (white brads) Making Memories *Fibers:* (brown polka dot ribbon) May Arts *Tools:* (decorative-edge scissors, ⅛" circle punch) Fiskars *Other:* (birthday card) Cherries Jubilee Creations; (pink tissue paper) **Finished size: 5" x 7"**

SUPPLIES: *Cardstock:* (purple, white) DMD, Inc. *Patterned paper:* (pink dots) Target; (yellow stripe from Super Slab collection) Provo Craft *Paint:* (white) *Accents:* (yellow brads) Making Memories; (jingle bells, white pompom) *Rub-ons:* (happy birthday) Making Memories *Fibers:* (purple polka dot ribbon) *Dies:* (party hat, scalloped frame) Provo Craft *Tool:* (die cut machine) Provo Craft **Finished size: 5" square**

Birthday Cupcake Card
Designer: Alisa Bangerter

① Make card from cardstock. Stitch edges; chalk.

② Cut cover off birthday card; chalk inside card piece and adhere. Attach brads.

③ Trim and gather tissue paper to create cupcake top; adhere.

④ Punch circles from cardstock; adhere.

⑤ Cut 2½" x 2¼" piece of cardstock to create cupcake base. Trim top with decorative-edge scissors; crumple.

⑥ Tie ribbon to cupcake base; adhere to card.

Birthday Jingles Card
Designer: Beatriz Jennings

① Make card from cardstock; adhere patterned paper.

② Die-cut scalloped frame; adhere to card. Stitch edges and attach brads.

③ Die-cut party hat from patterned paper and cardstock; adhere together. Die cut fringe and top of hat from cardstock; adhere. Adhere hat to card; stitch edges.

④ Apply rub-on.

⑤ Paint jingle bells; adhere.

⑥ Tie bow; adhere. Adhere pompom.

BONUS IDEA

Use different assortments of shapes and colors in this fun, alternating pattern to create endless variations for any occasion.

BONUS IDEA

Use this same technique to make all kinds of animal cupcake toppers. Use pink paper to make pigs, triangle shapes and yellow paper for chicks, or whatever cute animal the birthday boy or girl wants.

SUPPLIES: All supplies from Stampin' Up! unless otherwise noted. *Cardstock:* (Certainly Celery, So Saffron, Very Vanilla) *Patterned paper:* (daisy from Certainly Celery Designer collection, yellow stripes from So Saffron Designer collection) *Rubber stamps:* (Linen Background; happy birthday from It's Your Birthday set) *Dye ink:* (So Saffron, Basic Black) *Accents:* (black brads) no source *Adhesive:* (foam tape) no source *Tools:* (star punch); (¾" square punch) EK Success **Finished size: 4¼" x 5½"**

SUPPLIES: *Cardstock:* (brown, yellow, white) *Clear stamp:* (1 from Birthday Builder set) A Muse Artstamps *Dye ink:* (Chocolate) Close To My Heart *Color medium:* (black marker) *Tools:* (assorted circle punches, scalloped circle punch) Marvy Uchida *Other:* (toothpicks, brown lunch bag) **Finished size: 2" diameter**

Stars Card

Designer: Eleonor McGarry

1 Make card from cardstock.

2 Stamp Linen Background on cardstock piece; mat with cardstock, pierce, and adhere to card.

3 Punch squares from cardstock; adhere.

4 Punch stars from patterned paper; adhere with foam tape.

5 Stamp happy birthday.

6 Attach brads.

Funky Monkey Cupcake Toppers

Designer: Katie Stilwater

MONKEYS

1 Punch large circle from cardstock.

2 Punch medium circle from bag; cut in half. Adhere to punched circle.

3 Punch small circles from bag; adhere.

4 Draw eyes with marker.

5 Adhere to toothpick.

NUMBERS

1 Punch scalloped circle from cardstock.

2 Punch circle from cardstock; stamp. Mat with scalloped circle.

3 Adhere to toothpick.

INSIDE

Oh Happy Day Card

Designer: Maren Benedict

OUTSIDE

1. Make card from cardstock.
2. Cut star from patterned paper; adhere to card. Pierce edges.
3. Adhere tag with foam tape.
4. Tie on ribbon.

INSIDE

1. Apply rub-on.
2. Attach brads and photo turns; insert gift card.

5 STEPS Smart Cents Pocket

Designer: Sarah de Guzman

1. Adhere patterned paper pieces to felt pocket.
2. Adhere chipboard shapes and ribbon.
3. Spell "Smart" and "Cents" with stickers. Tie on ribbon.
4. Adhere coins; insert gift card.

SUPPLIES: *Cardstock:* (Summer Sunrise) Papertrey Ink *Patterned paper:* (Snappy from Get Happy collection) Cosmo Cricket *Accents:* (circle die cut tag) Cosmo Cricket; (brass brads, photo turns) We R Memory Keepers *Rub-on:* (circles) Cosmo Cricket *Fibers:* (green striped ribbon) Cosmo Cricket *Adhesive:* (foam tape) *Other:* (gift card) **Finished size: 7" x 7"**

SUPPLIES: *Patterned paper:* (Mania from Frenzy collection) We R Memory Keepers *Accents:* (chipboard circles, square) Target *Stickers:* (Sprinkles alphabet, Shoe Box alphabet) American Crafts *Fibers:* (blue ribbon, white ribbon) Offray *Other:* (felt pocket) Creative Imaginations; (gift card, penny, nickel) **Finished size: 5" square**

Wear them proudly.

INSIDE

Sometimes life gives you lemons.

Lemons Card & Earrings

Designer: Teri Anderson

CARD

1. Make card from cardstock.
2. Cover front and inside of card with patterned paper.
3. Print sentiments for front and inside of card on cardstock. Trim and adhere to card front.
4. Tie ribbon around card.
5. Trim patterned paper to fit inside metal-rimmed tag; adhere.
6. Adhere sentiment inside card.

EARRINGS

1. Thread yellow and green beads on headpins.
2. Loop tops of headpins above green beads, attaching to ear hooks. Wrap excess wire around loop; trim.
3. Attach earrings inside card.

5 STEPS Cheers Gift Bag

Designer: Susan R. Opel

1. Fussy-cut patterned paper and trim to fit bag; adhere.
2. Affix sentiment sticker.
3. Attach ribbon slide to ribbon; adhere ribbon to bag.

SUPPLIES: *Cardstock:* (white) *Patterned paper:* (Preppy from Moda Bella collection) American Crafts; (Grafton Tyson Street) Scenic Route *Accents:* (metal-rimmed rectangle tag) Making Memories; (headpins, French ear hooks) Darice; (green leaf beads) Halcraft; (yellow round beads) Fibers: (green polka dot ribbon) Offray *Font:* (Century Gothic) Microsoft **Finished sizes: card 3½" x 5½"; earrings 1" long**

SUPPLIES: *Patterned paper:* (Pomegranate from ala Carte collection) American Crafts *Accent:* (rhinestone ribbon slide) Making Memories *Sticker:* (rhinestone sentiment) Me & My Big Ideas *Fibers:* (black velvet ribbon) Target *Other:* (gift bag) **Finished size: 5¼" x 8½"**

SUPPLIES: *Patterned paper:* (Winsome, Tangy, Clementine, Citrus from Ambrosia collection) BasicGrey *Chalk ink:* (Chestnut Roan) Clearsnap *Accent:* (leaf brad) BasicGrey *Rub-on:* (you're the best) Scenic Route *Fibers:* (jute twine) *Other:* (kraft gift bag) **Finished size:** 3¼" x 6½"

SUPPLIES: *Patterned paper:* (Ode to Butterfly, Botanical News from Botanicabella collection) Graphic 45 *Chalk ink:* (Dark Brown) Clearsnap *Accents:* (tag, bookplate die cuts) Graphic 45; (pewter buttons) Daisy D's; (pewter brads) Imaginisce *Fibers:* (brown ribbon, copper ribbon) *Adhesive:* (foam tape) *Other:* (leather trimmed box) Jo-Ann Stores **Finished size:** 5¼" x 6" x 5¼"

You're the Best Gift Bag

Designer: Kim Hughes

Ink all edges.

1. Cut patterned paper to fit bag front. Adhere patterned paper strip and apply rub-on.
2. Tie on twine; attach brad.
3. Adhere panel to bag
4. Trim four patterned paper strips; adhere two back to back and repeat. Adhere to bag as handles.
5. Cut butterfly from patterned paper and adhere.

Botanic Box

Designer: Susan Neal

1. Unscrew lid. Cover box and lid with patterned paper; ink edges.
2. Ink edges of patterned paper strip; adhere ribbon and knot ends. Attach brads.
3. Adhere patterned paper strip to box.
4. Cut butterfly from patterned paper and adhere to bookplate die cut with foam tape; adhere buttons.
5. Adhere bookplate with foam tape.
6. Tie tag on with ribbon.

Butterfly Exhibit

Designer: Layle Koncar

1 Stamp, paint, and decorate chipboard butterflies as desired.

2 Adhere butterflies inside frame.

SUPPLIES: *Patterned paper:* (Laurel Rookery Road) Scenic Route *Rubber stamp:* (Alpha Collage K) Hampton Art *Clear stamp:* (swirl from Swirls v.2 set) Autumn Leaves *Solvent ink:* (black) Tsukineko *Color medium:* (black pen) *Paint:* (cream) Delta; (White Opal) Ranger Industries; (gold spray, black) *Accents:* (chipboard butterflies) Scenic Route; (iridescent gold glitter) Ranger Industries; (glass glitter) Art Institute Glitter; (butterfly mask) Heidi Swapp; (vintage buttons, clear rhinestones, gold microbeads) *Rub-ons:* (travel phrases) Scenic Route; (flowers) Three Bugs in a Rug *Stickers:* (assorted words) Making Memories *Other:* (crackle medium, dimensional glaze) Ranger Industries; (bingo card, frame) **Finished size: 13" square**

Live Your Dreams Card

Designer: Anabelle O'Malley

1 Make card from cardstock.

2 Cut patterned paper slightly smaller than card front Adhere patterned paper panel, zigzag-stitch edges, and adhere to card.

3 Adhere trim; pleat and adhere ribbon.

4 Ink edges of die cut and adhere. Affix sticker. Adhere swirls.

5 Cut butterfly from patterned paper; adhere to acrylic butterfly. Fold and adhere to card.

6 Adhere pearls.

SUPPLIES: *Cardstock:* (Fresh) Bazzill Basics Paper *Patterned paper:* (Drizzle, Cream, Yummy from Raspberry Truffle collection) Webster's Pages *Chalk ink:* (Creamy Brown) Clearsnap *Accents:* (acrylic butterfly) Heidi Swapp; (pearls) Kaisercraft; (black rhinestone swirls) Prima; (die cut tag) Scenic Route *Sticker:* (sentiment) Making Memories *Fibers:* (lace trim) Jo-Ann Stores; (pink ribbon) Making Memories **Finished size: 5" square**

Blue & Brown
Gift Ensemble

Designer: Nancy Davies

PAPER BEADS

1 Cut triangles of patterned paper ¾" x 12".

2 Beginning at widest end, wrap paper around a toothpick and secure with glue.

3 Coat with dimensional glaze; let dry.

EARRINGS

1 Make two paper beads, following instructions.

2 Place beads on earring posts. Attach beaded posts to earring hooks, twisting top of posts with needle nosed pliers.

BOX

1 Mat patterned paper with cardstock. Trim with decorative-edge scissors.

2 Stitch piece to cardstock and adhere to box.

3 Adhere flower and affix stickers to spell "Mom".

4 Ink chipboard circle and stamp Dot Circle.

5 Stamp especially for you on cardstock and trim with decorative-edge scissors. Adhere to chipboard.

6 Punch hole in tag. Tie tag and earrings to box with ribbon.

BRACELET

1 To make charm, cut oval image from patterned paper; mat with cardstock.

2 Loop wire and sandwich ends between matted piece and cardstock oval.

3 Coat charm with dimensional glaze; let dry.

4 Make eight paper beads, following instructions.

5 Thread beads and charm on elastic cording and knot.

SUPPLIES: *Cardstock:* (brown, white) *Patterned paper:* (Harvested from Mellow collection) BasicGrey *Rubber stamps:* (Dot Circle) Stampendous!; (Especially for You) K&Company *Dye ink:* (brown) Clearsnap; (turquoise) *Accents:* (chipboard circle) Deluxe Designs; (blue flower) Prima; (blue, brown glass beads) Westrim Crafts; (silver spacer, green glass beads) The Beadery *Stickers:* (Hat Box alphabet) American Crafts *Fibers:* (brown velvet ribbon) *Tool:* (decorative-edge scissors) *Other:* (dimensional glaze) Ranger Industries; (white metal container) Michaels; (elastic cording; blue wire; earring posts, hooks) **Finished sizes: earrings 2", bracelet 8½", box 5½" x 3¾" x 1"**

Floral Gift Bag

Designer: Sherry Wright

1. Trim pattered paper to fit bag front. Distress edges and adhere.
2. Adhere lace and rickrack to bottom of bag.
3. Fussy-cut flowers from patterned paper; adhere with foam tape.
4. Adhere rhinestones.
5. Stamp Thanks on patterned paper. Trim around and tie to handle.
6. Tie fibers on handle.

5 STEPS Elegant Wedding Box

Designer: Sherry Wright

Ink and distress edges of all patterned paper, accents, and sticker.

1. Trim pattered paper to fit box; adhere.
2. Punch oval from cardstock; adhere. Affix sticker.
3. Tie ribbon around box, trim with decorative-edge scissors.
4. Fussy-cut flowers from patterned paper; secure to ribbon with pin.

SUPPLIES: *Patterned paper:* (Flower Beds, Spring Flowers from Spring Fling collection) Pink Paislee *Clear stamp:* (thanks from Sentiment set) Inque Boutique *Chalk ink:* (red, Chestnut Roan) Clearsnap *Accents:* (green rhinestones) Creative Crystal *Fibers:* (green felt rickrack) Creative Café; (cream lace, green floss) *Adhesive:* (foam tape) *Other:* (gift bag) **Finished size: 4" x 8½"**

SUPPLIES: *Cardstock:* (brown) Bazzill Basics Paper *Patterned paper:* (Tranquility from Classical Garden collection; Twigs from Feather Your Nest collection) Webster's Pages *Accent:* (pearl head stick pin) *Sticker:* (Mr. & Mrs.) Melissa Frances *Fibers:* (brown ribbon) Offray *Tools:* (2" oval punch, decorative-edge scissors) *Other:* (paper mache box) Emma's Paperie **Finished size: 7" x 3½" x 2"**

SUPPLIES: All supplies from One Heart One Mind unless otherwise noted. *Cardstock:* (black, white scalloped) Bazzill Basics Paper *Patterned paper:* (I Believe from Merry Merry collection; Brighton, Preston, Bristol, Chatham from Designer Solids collection) *Color medium:* (green, yellow, blue pens) EK Success *Accents:* (assorted buttons, pink tag, green dotted squares, black brad); (medium black beads, black seed beads, cream button) no source *Rub-ons:* (mother, to:/from:) *Fibers:* (red floss) DMC *Font:* (your choice) no source *Adhesive:* (foam tape) no source *Other:* (silver ring back); (chipboard, wire, crimp beads, box) no source **Finished sizes: card 5¾" x 5½", bracelet 8½", ring 1½" diameter, box 3¾" x 3¾" x 1"**

Tweet Mother
Jewelry Ensemble

Designers: Stacey Triola and Dana Newsom,
courtesy of One Heart One Mind

CARD

1 Make card from cardstock. Adhere slightly smaller piece of cardstock.

2 Mat green dotted square with patterned paper; adhere.

3 Make bird and flourish, following pattern; adhere flourish to chipboard. Detail pieces with pens. Adhere flourish to card.

4 Insert brad and adhere bird to card with foam tape.

5 Adhere button.

6 Apply rub-on to patterned paper; trim. Adhere to tag and tie to flourish with floss; adhere.

BRACELET

1 Cut wire 12" in length.

2 Thread cream button 1½" from end, add crimp beads and crimp.

3 Thread eight black beads. Thread button on wire.

4 Repeat step 3 five additional times.

5 Thread eight black beads and crimp beads.

6 Thread 28 black seed beads. Thread excess wire back through crimp beads and pull tightly.

7 Crimp; trim excess wire.

RING

Adhere green button to ring back.

BOX

1 Cover box top with patterned paper.

2 Apply to:/from: rub-on to green dotted square; adhere.

3 Make flourish, following pattern; adhere to chipboard and detail with pen. Adhere.

4 Adhere button.

BIRD PATTERN

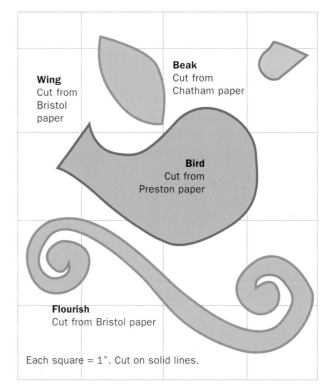

Wing
Cut from Bristol paper

Beak
Cut from Chatham paper

Bird
Cut from Preston paper

Flourish
Cut from Bristol paper

Each square = 1". Cut on solid lines.

Moms' P.E. Party

Designer: Tresa Black

INVITATION POCKET

① Cut two pieces of Blush cardstock to finished size.

② To make pocket front, trim 1" off top of one Blush piece; punch notch and ink top edge with Black. Stamp "Moms" with Black; adhere piece of Alpha Pistachio paper.

③ Apply adhesive to side and bottom of edges on pocket front; adhere to second piece of Blush. Stitch and ink outside edges with Black.

④ Adhere Bamboo cardstock behind P and E stencils; ink edges with Black. Adhere to pocket.

⑤ Punch two circles from Bamboo; adhere to stencils for periods.

⑥ Create "Need" and "Too." labels; affix to pocket.

INSERT

① Print Moms' P.E. details on Sweet Leaf cardstock. Trim and ink edges with Black.

② Adhere strip of Ochre paper.

③ Staple ribbon to top.

④ Tuck in pocket.

SUPPLIES: *Cardstock:* (Bamboo, Blush, Sweet Leaf) Close To My Heart *Patterned paper:* (Alpha Pistachio from Sublime collection, Ochre from Motifica collection) BasicGrey *Acrylic stamps:* (Precious Alphabet set) Close To My Heart *Dye ink:* (Black, Blush) Close To My Heart *Color medium:* (black pen) EK Success *Accents:* (metal-rimmed tag) Making Memories; (black label tape) Dymo; (alphabet stencils, large jump ring, staples) *Fibers:* (pink polka dot ribbon) Offray; (brown striped, polka dot ribbon) Michaels; (black hemp) Close To My Heart; (green thread) *Fonts:* (Arial) www.myfonts.com; (Bangle) www.bayfonts.com *Tools:* (label maker) Dymo; (¾" circle punch) *Other:* (small composition book) Wal-Mart; (water bottle, sandpaper) **Finished sizes: invitation 3¾" x 8½", journal 3½" x 4½", water bottle 2½" diameter x 10"**

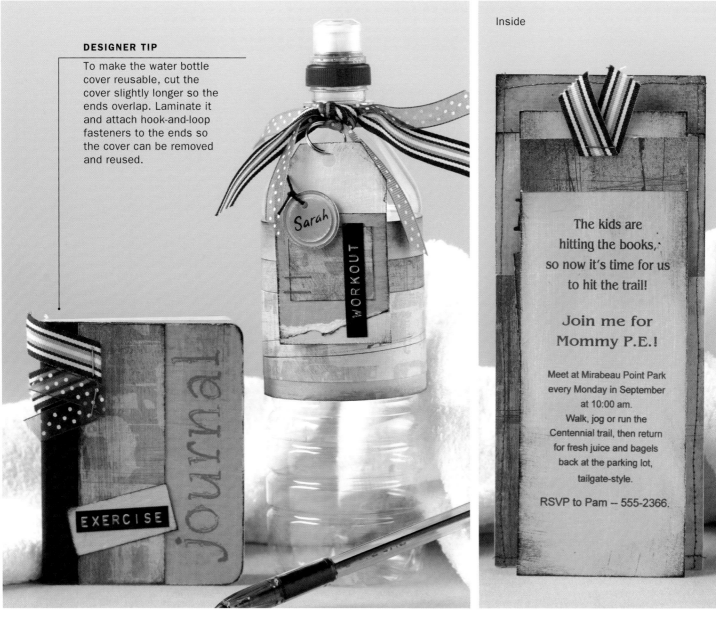

DESIGNER TIP

To make the water bottle cover reusable, cut the cover slightly longer so the ends overlap. Laminate it and attach hook-and-loop fasteners to the ends so the cover can be removed and reused.

The kids are hitting the books, so now it's time for us to hit the trail!

Join me for Mommy P.E.!

Meet at Mirabeau Point Park every Monday in September at 10:00 am. Walk, jog or run the Centennial trail, then return for fresh juice and bagels back at the parking lot, tailgate-style.

RSVP to Pam -- 555-2366.

JOURNAL

1 Adhere Blush cardstock to front and back covers of composition book. Sand and ink edges with Black.

2 Cut strip of Alpha Pistachio paper; ink edges with Black. Staple lengths of ribbon in place. Adhere to front cover.

3 Stamp "Journal" on front cover with Blush.

4 Create "Exercise" label; affix to piece of Bamboo cardstock. Ink edges and adhere.

WATER BOTTLE

1 Cut strip of Blush cardstock to fit around bottle; sand and ink edges with Black. Cut strip of Ochre paper; ink edges with Black. Cut wider strip of Alpha Pistachio paper. Adhere strips to Blush piece.

2 Cut tag from Sweet Leaf cardstock; sand and ink edges with Black. Cut piece of Blush; tear bottom edge. Cut smaller piece of Alpha Pistachio. Ink edges of both pieces and adhere to tag.

3 Create "Workout" label and affix to tag. Add two staples.

4 Write mom's name on Blush. Punch into circle, sand edges, and adhere to metal-rimmed tag. Tie hemp through hole. Adhere to paper tag.

5 Tie ribbon around neck of bottle; attach tag with jump ring.

SUPPLIES: *Cardstock:* (Dark Red, Light Red) Bazzill Basics Paper *Patterned paper:* (Argyle, Hex, Paisley/Striped from Swanky collection) All My Memories *Dye ink:* (Licorice) All My Memories *Accents:* (tan, red, pink brads; picture perfect metal label) All My Memories *Stickers:* (Swanky Monogram alphabet) All My Memories *Fibers:* (red striped ribbon, pink rickrack) All My Memories; (black thread) *Font:* (Squish) www.twopeasinabucket.com *Adhesive:* (decoupage, foam tape) *Tools:* (corner rounder punch) *Other:* (framed mirror, magnetic clipboard with notebook, pen, can) **Finished sizes: mirror 7½" square, clipboard 5"x 7½", pencil holder 4"diameter x 4½"**

Locker
Essentials Set

Designer: Tamara Jensen, courtesy of All My Memories

MIRROR

1 Cut strips of patterned paper to fit sides of mirror frame; ink edges.

2 Print "e true to yourself" on Light Red cardstock. Trim; ink edges

3 Coat frame with decoupage adhesive.

4 Ink edges of "b" monogram; adhere. Adhere metal label.

NOTEBOOK

1 Decoupage patterned paper to clipboard.

2 Print "hings to do" on Dark Red cardstock. Trim, ink edges, and attach brads. Adhere to notebook cover.

3 Ink edges of "t" monogram, tie with ribbon, and adhere to cover with foam tape.

4 Cut strips of patterned paper, ink edges, and adhere to cover.

5 Adhere loop of paper to back of notebook for pen holder.

PENCIL HOLDER

1 Cover can with patterned paper.

2 Print "ens & encils" on Light Red cardstock; mat with Dark Red cardstock and zigzag-stitch edges. Adhere to can.

3 Ink edges of "p" monogram and tie with ribbon and rickrack. Adhere with foam tape.

BONUS IDEA

Make a matching first aid kit and calculator with paper and stickers to complete the school ensemble.

Cheerful Blooms Magnets

Designer: Cindy Tobey

PLEATED CIRCLES

1. Cut three 1½" x 18" strips from fabric.

2. Punch two 2" circles and one 1⅛" circle from cardstock.

3. Stitch fabric to each circle, folding fabric over every ¼" to create pleats.

4. Affix magnet to back of each circle.

PHOTO MAGNET

1. Cut flower from patterned paper; ink edges and adhere to pleated circle.

2. Adhere photo to chipboard flower; trim and adhere.

3. Trim fabric pleats as desired.

SNAP MAGNET

1. Paint chipboard flower; let dry and sand edges. Punch circle from center; adhere flower to pleated circle.

2. Cut flowers from patterned paper; punch centers, ink edges, and adhere.

3. Adhere rhinestone snap.

4. Trim fabric pleats as desired.

RHINESTONE MAGNET

1. Paint chipboard circle; let dry.

2. Adhere rhinestones to circle.

3. Adhere circle to pleated circle.

4. Trim fabric pleats as desired.

SUPPLIES: *Cardstock:* (French Vanilla) Bazzill Basics Paper *Patterned paper:* (Brilliance, Sateen from Silver Lining collection) We R Memory Keepers *Chalk ink:* (Lipstick Red, Olive Pastel, Tangerine) Clearsnap *Paint:* (Cranberry) Making Memories *Accents:* (chipboard flowers, circle; orange rhinestone snap) We R Memory Keepers; (red rhinestones) Westrim Crafts *Tools:* (2", 1⅛", 1" circle punches) Marvy Uchida *Other:* (photo, yellow plaid fabric, adhesive magnets) **Finished sizes: photo magnet 3½" diameter; snap magnet 3¾" diameter; rhinestone magnet 2" diameter**

⁵Boo Crew Halloween Decor

Designer: Davinie Fiero

① Trim piece of barn wood.

② Mat photo with patterned paper and adhere to barn wood.

③ Tie ribbons around top and knot; adhere moon and affix badge.

④ Paint alphabet stickers and add glitter; let dry. Adhere to ribbon to spell sentiment.

⑤ Adhere stars to wire and attach behind photograph.

SUPPLIES: *Patterned paper:* (Nevermore from Haunted collection) Cosmo Cricket *Paint:* (black) Making Memories *Accents:* (chipboard moon) American Crafts; (black chipboard stars) Cosmo Cricket; (black glitter) Pink Paislee *Stickers:* (Hocus Pocus alphabet, date badge) American Crafts *Fibers:* (black striped ribbon) Creative Imaginations; (pink, orange ribbon) Making Memories *Other:* (photo, barn wood, craft wire) **Finished size: 11" x 7"**

I'M
BATTY
FOR YOU

stir up something

SPOOKY

Batty for You Treat Bag

Designer: Betsy Veldman

1 Cut cardstock, ink edges, and adhere to bag; adhere photo.

2 Die-cut large label from patterned paper, adhere to cardstock, and trim with decorative-edge scissors. Fold in half to make topper.

3 Die-cut and emboss oval label from cardstock, stamp sentiment, and attach with brads.

4 Die-cut large bat from cardstock, punch hole, and tie on with ribbon; adhere topper.

5 Create circular sentiment using word processor; print on cardstock and punch circle.

6 Adhere circle to cardstock and trim with decorative-edge scissors.

7 Die-cut small bat from cardstock and adhere. Adhere circle.

5 Stir Up Something Spooky Card

Designer: Susan R. Opel

1 Make card from cardstock. Print photo on photo paper; adhere.

2 Trim and adhere patterned paper and spell "Spooky" with stickers.

3 Print and mat sentiment on cardstock. Adhere rhinestone. Adhere to card using foam tape.

4 Tie on ribbon.

SUPPLIES: *Cardstock:* (Pumpkin, Slime) SEI *Patterned paper:* (Creepy Street from Eerie Alley collection) SEI *Clear stamps:* (Fresh Alphabet set; Simple Alphabet set; for you from Boxes, Bags & Tags set) Papertrey Ink *Specialty ink:* (True Black hybrid) Papertrey Ink *Accents:* (black brads) Making Memories *Fibers:* (green ribbon) Papertrey Ink *Font:* (Trajan Pro) www.fonts.com *Software:* (word processing) Microsoft *Dies:* (large label, bats, oval label) Provo Craft *Tools:* (die cut/embossing machine, decorative-edge scissors) Provo Craft; (circle punch) Marvy Uchida *Other:* (white coffee bag) Papertrey Ink; (photo) **Finished size: 4" x 6¾"**

SUPPLIES: *Cardstock:* (white) American Crafts; (green) Bazzill Basics Paper *Patterned paper:* (French Hens from Christmas collection) American Crafts *Specialty paper:* (photo paper) *Accent:* (purple rhinestone) Little Yellow Bicycle *Stickers:* (Roller Rink alphabet) American Crafts *Fibers:* (purple ribbon) Offray *Font:* (Antigoni) www.searchfreefonts.com *Adhesive:* (foam tape) *Other:* (photo) **Finished size: 5" x 7"**

Halloween Photo Collage

Designer: Wendy Sue Anderson

1. Use software to create photo collage. *Note: Leave spaces for patterned paper.* Print on cardstock.

2. Trim patterned papers to fill spaces; affix stickers.

3. Wrap floss around frame glass. Attach tag with brad and safety pin. Knot ribbon around safety pin.

4. Break prongs off witch brad and adhere to front of glass.

5. Place glass and collage in frame.

Happy Haunting Card

Designer: Layle Koncar

1. Make card from patterned paper. Trim cardstock and adhere.

2. Trim photo and patterned paper; adhere.

3. Affix sentiment sticker; adhere house sticker with foam tape.

SUPPLIES: *Cardstock:* (white) *Patterned paper:* (Argyle, Newsprint, Orange Brocade from Spellbound collection) Making Memories *Accents:* (witch brad, black brad, date tag) Making Memories; (silver safety pin) *Stickers:* (scalloped boo circle, Tiny Alpha alphabet) Making Memories *Fibers:* (orange floss) Bazzill Basics Paper; (black striped ribbon) May Arts *Software:* (photo editing) Adobe *Other:* (digital photos, frame)
Finished size: 7½" x 5½"

SUPPLIES: *Cardstock:* (rust) Bazzill Basics Paper *Patterned paper:* (Polka Dot Stripe from Spellbound collection) Making Memories; (Young Street from Surprise collection) Scenic Route *Stickers:* (sentiment) Scenic Route; (house) Creative Imaginations *Adhesive:* (foam tape) *Other:* (photo)
Finished size: 7¼" x 5"

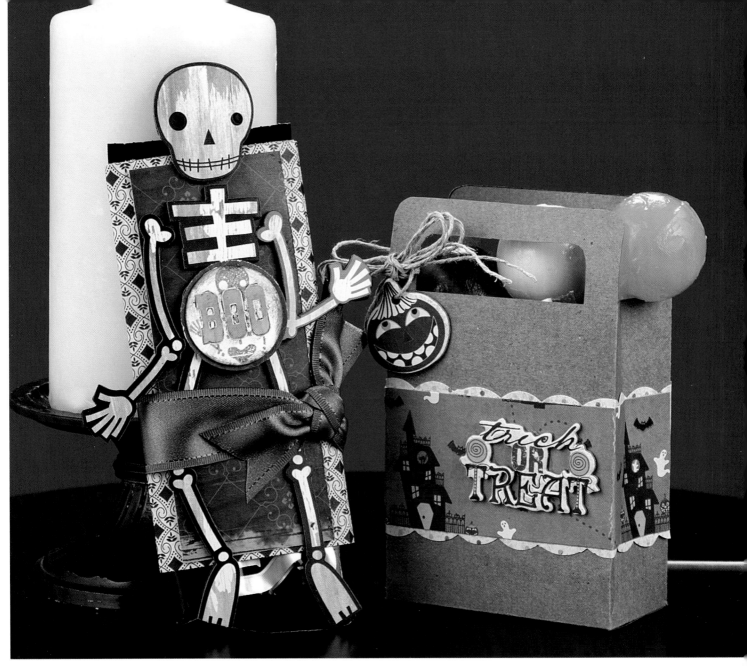

Skeleton Candy Bar Wrap

Designer: Maren Benedict

1 Wrap candy bar with patterned paper.

2 Adhere patterned paper rectangle.

3 Affix skeleton stickers to chipboard pieces. Adhere to wrap.

4 Punch patterned paper circle; apply rub-on. Stamp skeleton over rub-on. Mat with punched patterned paper circle; ink edges. Adhere.

5 Tie on ribbon.

Haunted House Treat Box

Designer: Daniela Dobson

1 Assemble box.

2 Cut strip of patterned paper; trim with decorative-edge scissors. Adhere to box.

3 Cut patterned paper strip and adhere.

4 Adhere chipboard sentiment. Punch hole in chipboard jack o' lantern; tie to box with hemp cord.

SUPPLIES: *Patterned paper:* (Nevermore, Ominous from Haunted collection) Cosmo Cricket *Clear stamps:* (small skeleton from Haunted set) Cosmo Cricket *Dye ink:* (Tuxedo Black) Tsukineko; (Pumpkin Pie) Stampin' Up! *Accents:* (chipboard skeleton) Cosmo Cricket *Rub-on:* (boo) Cosmo Cricket *Stickers:* (skeleton parts) Cosmo Cricket *Fibers:* (green ribbon) May Arts *Tools:* (1¼", 1½" circle punches) Stampin' Up! *Other:* (candy bar) **Finished size: 2½" x 7"**

SUPPLIES: *Cardstock:* (kraft) DMD, Inc. *Patterned paper:* (Velcome Inn, Pixie Sticks from Hallowhimsy collection) Imaginisce *Accents:* (chipboard sentiment, jack o' lantern) Imaginisce *Fibers:* (hemp cord) Darice *Tool:* (decorative-edge scissors) Other: (Kraft box) **Finished size: 3¼" x 5¼" x 1¾"**

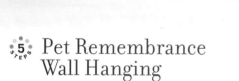

✦5✦ Pet Remembrance Wall Hanging

Designer: Kate Thaete

❶ Cut strip of cardstock; trim one edge with decorative-edge scissors. Adhere window tab and adhere to cardstock base. ❷ Adhere photo. Spell pet's name with stickers. ❸ Adhere hinge. Adhere flowers together. Adhere ribbon knot; adhere. ❹ Knot ribbon on frame. Thread ribbon through tags and charms; knot on frame. ❺ Write years of pet's life on tag.

SUPPLIES: *Cardstock:* (white, olive) Bazzill Basics Paper *Color medium:* (black marker) *Accents:* (adore, sweetheart tags; pewter hinge) Making Memories; (metal-rimmed circle tag) Avery; (remember window tab) Creative Imaginations; (heart, fire hydrant charms; red flowers) *Stickers:* (Runway alphabet) American Crafts *Fibers:* (red grosgrain, black gingham ribbon) Offray *Tool:* (decorative-edge scissors) *Other:* (frame) IKEA; (photo) **Finished size: 8¼" x 10½"**

✦5✦ Doggie Treats Box

Designer: Teri Anderson

❶ Crop photo, using software; print on photo paper. ❷ Trim photo, adhere to box, and sand edges. ❸ Spell "Treats" with stickers. ❹ Fill box with treats; tie with ribbon.

SUPPLIES: *Specialty paper:* (glossy photo) *Stickers:* (Kennedy Jr. alphabet) American Crafts *Fibers:* (black gingham ribbon) Pebbles Inc. *Software:* (photo editing) *Other:* (acrylic box) Provo Craft; (digital photo, treats) **Finished size: 2¼" x 4" x 2¼"**

✦5✦ Leash Hook

Designer: Teri Anderson

❶ Remove peg hook and screw from hanger. ❷ Adhere patterned paper to bottom half of hanger. Adhere photo. ❸ Cover hanger rim with patterned paper; sand edges. ❹ Spell "Leash" with chipboard alphabet. ❺ Attach metal hook.

SUPPLIES: *Patterned paper:* (Clover, Chocolate from Double Dot collection) Bo-Bunny Press *Accents:* (chipboard alphabet) Bisous *Other:* (wood hanger) Don Mechanic Enterprises; (metal hook, photo) **Finished size: 5¼" diameter**

DESIGNER TIP

The box in Wendy Sue's project used to hold a frame. Keep your eyes open when you are purchasing items. Their packaging can often be reused in unexpected (and gift-able) ways!

I Love Reading Ensemble
Designer: Wendy Sue Anderson

BOX

❶ Adhere patterned paper inside and outside box. ❷ Affix journaling frame sticker. Affix alphabet stickers and metal badge to spell sentiment.

BOOKMARKS

❶ Cut cardstock to finished size, round corners. ❷ Cut slightly smaller pieces of patterned paper, round corners, and adhere. ❸ Attach eyelet and tie on ribbon. ❹ Affix stickers to spell "Start here" and attach arrow with brad.

PAPER CLIP

❶ Punch two circles from cardstock. Adhere to either side of paper clip.
❷ Adhere flower and affix metal badge.

BOOK LABELS

❶ Print "This book belongs to:" on cardstock. Circle punch.
❷ Punch scalloped circle; adhere circle.

SUPPLIES: *Cardstock:* (black, white) *Patterned paper:* (Yo!, Good Morning, Hiya, Salut from Everyday collection) American Crafts *Accents:* (aqua flower) American Crafts; (orange eyelet) Making Memories; (silver paper clip) Wal-Mart; (pink brad, arrow) *Stickers:* (heart, flower metal badges; Daiquiri, JFK alphabets; clear journaling frame) American Crafts *Fibers:* (white printed ribbon) American Crafts *Font:* (Quicksand Book) www.abstractfonts.com *Tools:* (1¾" circle punch) EK Success; (2½" scalloped circle punch) Marvy Uchida; (corner rounder punch) *Other:* (white box with clear lid) **Finished sizes: box 4¾" x 1¼" x 7", bookmarks 2" x 6", paper clip 4" x 1½", book labels 2½" diameter**

Linked by Love Wall Hanging

Designer: Tricia Sproule

① Ink edges of cardstock base. Cut patterned paper slightly smaller; ink edges and adhere. ② Cut strip and piece of patterned paper; ink edges and adhere. ③ Stamp swirls. ④ Mat photo with cardstock; sand edges and adhere. ⑤ Remove F from puzzle piece. Paint piece; sand. Ink edges and tie with ribbon. Attach ribbon to hanger with brad; adhere. ⑥ Die-cut A, M, I, and two Y's from cardstock; ink and adhere. Trim F and turn upside down to become L. Ink and adhere. ⑦ Apply rub-on and insert into frame.

Our Family Bouquet

Designer: Heather D. White

① Cover flowers with patterned paper, some reverse side up. ② Paint edges of chipboard circles; let dry. Adhere photos to circles. Adhere to flowers. ③ Adhere flowers to stem caps; insert stems. ④ Cover vase with patterned paper. Adhere ribbon. ⑤ Print "Our family" on patterned paper, reverse side up. Trim and adhere to chipboard circle. Punch hole in circle, attach ball chain, and tie to vase with ribbon. ⑥ Fill half of vase with dry beans. Adhere foam center inside vase. ⑦ Arrange flowers as desired. Place gift shred around stems.

SUPPLIES: *Cardstock:* (brown, black, aqua, cream) Bazzill Basics Paper *Patterned paper:* (Stucco, Jade, Jade Pattern from Motifica collection) BasicGrey *Clear stamps:* (swirls from Swirls v.1 set) Autumn Leaves *Dye ink:* (Chocolate Chip, white) Stampin' Up! *Paint:* (Chocolate) Making Memories *Accents:* (pewter brad) Making Memories; (antique pewter hanger) BasicGrey; (F puzzle piece) Scrapworks *Rub-on:* (sentiment) BasicGrey *Fibers:* (brown polka dot ribbon) *Dies:* (George alphabet) Provo Craft *Tool:* (die cut machine) Provo Craft *Other:* (photo, frame) **Finished size: 11" x 8½"**

SUPPLIES: *Patterned paper:* (Botanic Blossom, Botanic Spray, Botanic Burst, Botanic Dot from Canvas collection) Scrapworks *Paint:* (white) Plaid *Accents:* (chipboard circles) Bazzill Basics Paper; (silver ball chain) Home Depot *Fibers:* (brown grosgrain ribbon) Offray *Font:* (Century Gothic) Microsoft *Other:* (chipboard bouquet kit) Doodlebug Design; (dry beans, photos) **Finished size: approx. 8" x 17"**

Family Name Wall Hanging

Designer: Susan Neal

1 Change photos to sepia, using software; print on photo paper. *Note: Print photos on plain paper first to check for placement.*

2 Mix white and Antique White paint (4:1); paint frame.

3 Cover chipboard letters with patterned paper. Mix Brown Iron Oxide and black paint (4:1); paint letter edges.

4 Adhere photos. Adhere letters.

SUPPLIES: *Patterned paper:* (Madison) Melissa Frances *Specialty paper:* (glossy photo) *Paint:* (Brown Iron Oxide, Antique White, black, white) Delta *Accents:* (chipboard letters) Making Memories *Software:* (photo editing) *Other:* (wood frame, digital photos) **Finished size:** 30¾" x 8¾"

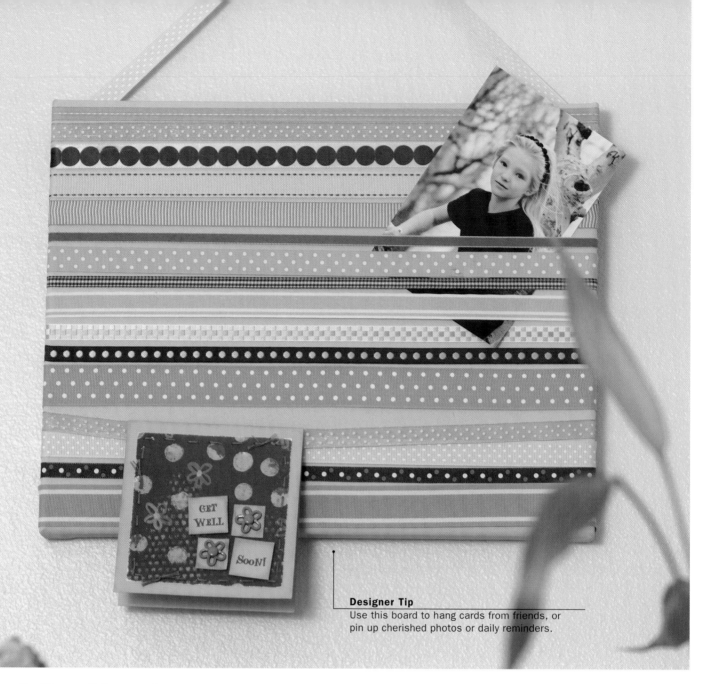

Designer Tip
Use this board to hang cards from friends, or pin up cherished photos or daily reminders.

⁵STEPS Be-ribboned Bulletin Board

Designer: Alisa Bangerter

❶ Paint canvas; let dry. ❷ Wrap ribbon tightly across canvas; staple ends to canvas edges. Repeat as desired. ❸ Staple folded ribbon to back of canvas for hanger.

SUPPLIES: *Paint:* (Baby Pink) DecoArt *Fibers:* (assorted ribbon) *Tool:* (heavy-duty staple gun) *Other:* (stretched canvas board) Canvas Concepts
Finished size: 14" x 10¾"

All-Star Hat Rack

Designer: Jennifer Miller

1 Paint hat rack; let dry. 2 Adhere strip of patterned paper around edge. 3 Cover metal strip with patterned paper. 4 Paint stars; let dry. Die-cut letters for name; adhere to stars. 5 Adhere magnet strips to mitt and stars. Attach to metal strip.

SUPPLIES: *Cardstock:* (black) Bazzill Basics Paper *Patterned paper:* (Wrapping Paper from Holiday collection) Rusty Pickle; (Baseball Texture) The Paper Studio *Paint:* (Sky Blue, white) Plaid *Accents:* (wood baseball mitt, stars) Provo Craft *Adhesive:* (decoupage) Plaid *Dies:* (Studio SkinniMini alphabet) QuicKutz *Tool:* (die cut machine) QuicKutz *Other:* (wood hat rack) Twelve Timbers; (magnet strips)
Finished size: 24" x 7"

Bonus Idea

Try matching the theme of your child's birthday party to create cute favors, or try a geography-themed book for a child to color on a long road trip.

Game Tins

Designer: Roree Rumph

① Cover tins with patterned paper. Sand and ink edges. ② Trim patterned paper to fit lids, round corners, and adhere. ③ Adhere patterned paper strips around tins. Tie on ribbon. ④ Cover chipboard alphabet negatives with patterned paper. Cut out letter portion with craft knife. Attach brads. Sand, ink, and adhere chipboard to cardstock. Trim and adhere to tins. ⑤ Create game labels; affix.

Color My World Book & Tin

Designer: Betsy Veldman

COLORING BOOK

① Cut several pages from cardstock to fit inside tin. Round corners. ② Stamp images on pages. ③ Ink staples with solvent ink. Score pages ½" from top edge; staple together. ④ Place in tin with crayons.

TIN

① Adhere transparency border around tin. *Note: Only adhere ends of transparency border so it will slide off the tin.* ② Adhere strip of patterned paper. ③ Print sentiment on cardstock; cut into circle. ④ Die-cut tag from cardstock, adhere sentiment circle, and stitch edges. ⑤ Stamp alien on cardstock, color with markers, and cut into tag. ⑥ Tie ribbon to stitched tag ends. Cut slit in alien tag; attach to star clip. Attach clip to ribbon. Adhere to transparency band.

SUPPLIES: *Cardstock:* (Red Devil) Bazzill Basics Paper *Patterned paper:* (North Shore Barrel Navy, North Shore Beach Break, North Shore Hang Ten) Scenic Route *Dye ink:* (Weathered Wood) Ranger Industries *Accents:* (chipboard alphabet) Making Memories; (red brads) *Sticker:* (label tape) Dymo *Fibers:* (red stitched ribbon) Morex *Tools:* (corner rounder punch) Marvy Uchida; (label maker) Dymo *Other:* (tins) Cost Plus World Market
Finished sizes: large 3" x 7¾", small 3" x 5¼"

SUPPLIES: *Cardstock:* (red) Bazzill Basics Paper; (white) Stampin' Up! *Patterned paper:* (Amusing Stripes from Amusement Park collection) Karen Foster Design *Transparency sheet:* (flourish border) Autumn Leaves *Clear stamps:* (Space Cadet set) Inque Boutique *Dye ink:* (black) Inque Boutique *Solvent ink:* (blue) Tsukineko *Color medium:* (markers) Inque Boutique *Accents:* (star clip) Creative Impressions; (staples) *Fibers:* (green ribbon) SEI *Die:* (tag) Provo Craft *Tools:* (die cut machine) Provo Craft; (corner rounder punch) The Paper Studio; (circle cutter) Creative Memories *Other:* (clear top hinged tin) Papertrey Ink; (crayons)
Finished size: 5½" x 3¾" x 1"

Little Boy's Fortune Teller

FOLD 1:

Fold paper in half lengthwise and then in half again widthwise to form square. Crease and unfold.

FOLD 2:

With patterned side of paper facing down, fold top corner diagonally to center of paper. Crease and leave corner folded. Repeat for three remaining corners.

FOLD 3:

Place piece so folds are facing down. Fold all four corners diagonally to center again.

FOLD 4:

Fold bottom edge to meet top edge. Crease and unfold.

FOLD 5:

Rotate square and repeat, keeping folded.

To Use:
Place thumbs into right and left front openings, and index fingers into back openings. Gently and slowly push all squares together so points meet in center.

SUPPLIES: *Patterned paper:* (Dainty from blue boutique collection) Sassafras Lass *Rub-ons:* (mommy-isms, spring words, numbers) Daisy D's *Finished size:* 6" square

Cut patterned paper to fit album cover; adhere. Cut strips of patterned paper; sand edges of blue rectangle. Adhere monogram to patterned paper; cut out. Cut heart from cardstock; sand edges. Apply rub-ons, and adhere monogram and heart to rectangle. Adhere rectangle and strip to album cover. Wrap ribbon around album cover and tie bow. Embellish inside pages of album, adding photos and journaling as desired.

SUPPLIES: *Cardstock:* (blue, light blue) *Patterned paper:* (paisley, stripe, blue words, polka dot, green large dot, criss-cross stripe) *Accents:* (paper daisies, spiral, regular paper clips, chipboard F, circled words square) *Rub-ons:* (our friendship…, just because, just about us, friend, small flowers) *Fibers:* (green polka dot grosgrain, light blue gingham, green gingham, blue flower ribbon) *Other:* (accordion mini-album) Lisa Bearnson **Finished size: 6½" square**

CARD INSDE

{ Happy, Laugh, & Smile Frame }

PAINT chipboard heart and flower. Let dry and sand edges. Adhere flower to heart and attach grommet. Cut patterned paper to fit frame. Adhere chipboard to patterned paper and place in frame.

SUPPLIES: *Patterned paper*: (Flowerful Words) Junkitz *Paint*: (red, light blue) *Accents*: (chipboard heart, flower) (white memories grommet) *Other*: (white shadow box frame) Target **Finished size: 10½″ square**

Bonus Idea
Create a similar frame for any occasion by doodling your own background. Try sweet, precious, and tiny in pinks and yellows for a baby girl or forever, love, and bliss in pastels for a wedding. When you doodle your own designs, the options are endless.

{ List Keeper Clipboard }

ADHERE patterned paper to clipboard; adhere strip of patterned paper. Sand edges. Adhere chipboard square and sticker. Adhere tab and heart. Knot ribbon around clip hook.

SUPPLIES: *Patterned paper:* (Orange Dot, Chicks and Hearts) Heidi Grace Designs *Accents:* (green chipboard heart, green square, blue tab) Heidi Grace Designs *Sticker:* (brown flower) Heidi Grace Designs *Fibers:* (assorted ribbon) *Other:* (mini clipboard) Staples **Finished size: 6" x 8¾"**

Bonus Idea
Use one of the ribbons to tie on a cute pen or pencil. Clip on an embellished to-do list to create a beautiful, ready-to-use gift.

Decorative Monograms

TRACE letter on back of patterned paper; cut out. Adhere to paper mache letter. *Note: Spray adhesive works best.* Decorate with ribbon and rub-ons. Sand edges.

SUPPLIES: *Patterned paper:* (stripe) *Rub-ons:* (alphabet) *Fibers:* (assorted) *Other:* (paper mache letters) **Finished size: approx. 4¾" x 8"**

SUPPLIES: *Patterned paper:* (Crown Jewels, Lyric, Windsor Castle from Formality collection) One Heart One Mind *Paint:* (black) Plaid *Accents:* (acrylic knobs) Home Depot *Other:* (wood plaques) Michaels **Finished size: 7" x 5"**

SUPPLIES: All supplies from Masterpiece Studios unless otherwise noted. *Patterned paper:* (Close Stripes, Scribble Daisies from Jennifer Closner Dream collection) *Paint:* (Parisian Pink) Plaid *Finish:* (matte sealer) USArtQuest *Rub-on:* (laugh love dream) *Stickers:* (dream, life, heart circle epoxy) *Other:* (paper mache jewelry box) USArtQuest **Finished size: 8" x 5¼" x 2"**

Black & White Hanger Trio

Designer: Kate Boetcher, courtesy of One Heart One Mind

① Sand plaques. Paint; let dry. ② Cut patterned paper slightly smaller than plaque fronts; adhere. ③ Drill through center of plaques. Attach knobs.

Dream Jewelry Box

Designer: Jennifer Lindemeier, courtesy of Masterpiece Studios

① Paint jewelry box inside and outside; let dry. *Note: Remove ribbon securing lid.* ② Cover lid and sides with patterned paper; apply finish. ③ Apply rub-on and affix sticker.

Designer Tip
Spray paint is easy to use, but it can be tough to make it stick and cover well on plastic. Look for spray paint that is made specifically for plastic surfaces.

Designer Tip
Spray paint is easy to use, but it can be tough to make it stick and cover well on plastic. Look for spray paint that is made specifically for plastic surfaces.

Designer Tip
Inking the inner edges of a frame die cut can be tricky. Try using a marker instead of the ink pad for better accuracy.

SUPPLIES: *Paper:* (white) *Paint:* (Tanzanite) Krylon *Fibers:* (solid, striped grosgrain ribbon) Strano Designs *Tools:* (½" circle punch) Punch Bunch; (1", 1¼" circle punches) EK Success *Other:* (white plastic trash can) Wal-Mart; (ribbon stiffener) Strano Designs **Finished size: 7½" diameter x 9" height**

SUPPLIES: *Patterned paper:* (Bristol, Chatham, Preston from Designer Solids collection) One Heart One Mind *Pigment ink:* (Graphite Black) Tsukineko *Accents:* (clear rhinestone stars) KI Memories *Rub-ons:* (Script ABC alphabet, Monogram letters) One Heart One Mind *Dies:* (Concentric Stars) Provo Craft *Tool:* (die cut machine) Provo Craft *Other:* (clock) Target **Finished size: 8" diameter**

⟨5⟩ Ribbon Dots Trash Can
Designer: Alice Golden

① Apply stiffener to ribbon; let dry. ② Mask upper third of can with masking tape and paper; paint. *Note: May need several coats.* ③ Adhere ribbon around can. ④ Punch circles from ribbon; adhere. *Note: Trim some circles to match can edge.*

⟨5⟩ Time Is on My Side Clock
Designer: Angie Hagist

① Remove clock hardware. ② Cover clock face with patterned paper. *Note: Punch hole for clock hardware.* ③ Spell "Time…is on my side" with rub-ons. ④ Die-cut stars from patterned paper; ink edges and adhere. ⑤ Adhere rhinestones. Replace hardware.

Flower Blocks

5 STEPS

Designer:
Diane D. Flowers,
courtesy of The Dow
Chemical Co.

① Cover blocks with patterned paper or cardstock. Decorate cardstock-covered sides with circles and/or strips of cardstock. ② Cover top of small blocks with moss. ③ Insert daisies in top of small blocks.

SUPPLIES: *Cardstock:* (black, white) *Patterned paper:* (Black & White Floral) Me & My Big Ideas; (Midnight Paisley from A Day to Remember collection) Bo-Bunny Press *Accents:* (pink gerbera daisies, reindeer moss) *Tools:* (assorted circle punches, circle cutters) *Other:* (foam cubes) The Dow Chemical Co. **Finished sizes: large block 8" cube, small block 3" cube**

Blessed Frame

5 STEPS

Designer: Julia Stainton

① Trim patterned paper. Adhere photo and place in frame. ② Apply rub-ons to front of glass.

SUPPLIES: *Patterned paper:* (pink floral) *Rub-ons:* (blessed, flourishes) BasicGrey *Other:* (floating frame) Michaels; (photo) **Finished size: 9" x 7"**

Cheerful Flower Jars

Designer: Marla Bird, courtesy of Crate Paper

1 Cut flowers, from patterned paper. 2 Mat some flower petals with patterned paper, as desired. 3 Arrange petals in circles to form flowers. *Note: Bend petals and use foam tape for dimension, as desired.* 4 Embellish flower centers with circles, flowers, and patterned paper fringe.

ASSEMBLE

1 Cut ¾" x 12" strips of patterned paper; adhere around wood skewers. 2 Adhere flowers to skewers. Tie with ribbon. 3 Insert flowers in jars.

SUPPLIES: Patterned paper: (Peony, Ivy, Poppy, Tulip, Lilac, Snapdragon from Samantha collection) Crate Paper Accents: (chipboard circles, chipboard flowers) Crate Paper Fibers: (green organza ribbon) Adhesive: (foam tape) Die: (circle frame) Ellison Tools: (die cut machine) Ellison; (½", ¾", 1", 1½" circle punches, flower punch) Family Treasures Other: (jars and rack, wood skewers) **Finished size: 15½" x 14" x 2½"**

Black & White Lampshade

Designer: Layle Koncar

1️⃣ Cut patterned paper to cover lampshade; adhere. 2️⃣ Adhere ribbon and trim.

Old-Fashioned Knob Key Holder

Designer: Lindsey Husmann

1️⃣ Remove knob and hooks from wall hanging. 2️⃣ Coat with paint; sand edges. 3️⃣ Cut patterned paper pieces to cover each section. Decoupage in place. 4️⃣ Reattach knob and hooks. 5️⃣ Tie ribbon around knob. 6️⃣ Affix sticker to knob.

SUPPLIES: *Patterned paper:* (Laurel Scrap Strip 3) Scenic Route *Fibers:* (black pompom fringe) Jo-Ann Stores; (black velvet ribbon) *Other:* (lampshade) Jo-Ann Stores **Finished size: 9" diameter x 7" height**

SUPPLIES: *Patterned paper:* (Piccadilly from Red, Black, & Cream collection) Autumn Leaves *Paint:* (Pure Black) Plaid *Sticker:* (floral epoxy) Creative Imaginations *Fibers:* (burgundy ribbon) Offray *Adhesive:* (decoupage) Plaid *Other:* (glass knob with hooks wall hanging) Creative Co-Op **Finished size: 6½" x 12"**

⁵ Enjoy the Journey Key Holder

Designer: Stefanie Hamilton

❶ Trim patterned paper; adhere. ❷ Cut border from patterned paper; adhere. ❸ Adhere flowers. ❹ Adhere chipboard tile behind bookplate; attach brads. Adhere. ❺ Affix photo corners.

SUPPLIES: *Patterned paper:* (Cape Town Table Bay Floral) Scenic Route; (Cream Floral) Creative Imaginations *Accents:* (red flowers) Jo-Ann Stores; (journey chipboard tile) Scenic Route; (black bookplate, brads) BasicGrey *Stickers:* (black photo corners) *Other:* (key holder) **Finished size: 9" x 10¼"**

Cute Cards Inspired by Lovely Layouts

Discover one-of-a-kind cards, bookmarks, and frames inspired by traditional scrapbook layouts.

AARGH
Jennifer Miller

A Pirate's Life For Me

When Aunt Shelley came out to visit us, she came bearing gifts. She brought me a pirate set, complete with hook, eye patch and telescope. It has quickly become my favorite toy. Nearly every day, I put on my eye patch and give my best pirate impersonation while attacking my mommy. She is always willing to run away from me in fear until I take off my eye patch and show her that it is just me... Joseph.

SUPPLIES: *Cardstock:* (white, black) Bazzill Basics Paper *Fonts:* (Papyrus, Century Gothic) www.fonts.com *Die:* (photo corner) QuicKutz *Tools:* (die cut machine) QuicKutz *Other:* (photo) **Finished size: 11" x 8½"**

AHOY GIFT BOX
Emily Call

AHOY, MATEY!
Wendy Johnson

The overall theme of the layout fired up Wendy's creativity. She borrowed the word "Arrrgh!" and the pirate theme for both the card design and sentiment for this unique get well card.

Emily found inspiration in the layout's photo. She imagined the boy in the photo was at a pirate-themed birthday party, and created a party favor for the receiver to treasure.

SUPPLIES: *Cardstock:* (Real Red, Basic Black, Whisper White) Stampin' Up! *Patterned paper:* (Midnight Diamonds from A Day to Remember collection) Bo-Bunny Press *Rubber stamps:* (treasure map, anchor from Ahoy, Matey set) Stampin' Up! *Pigment ink:* (white) Stampin' Up! *Solvent ink:* (Jet Black) Tsukineko *Rub-ons:* (French Quarter Mix alphabet) Heidi Swapp *Fibers:* (linen thread) Stampin' Up!; (black/white striped ribbon) *Adhesive:* (foam tape) 3M *Tools:* (¾" circle punch) Stampin' Up!; (⅝" circle punch) *Other:* (kraft paper takeout box) Westrim Crafts **Finished size: 3" x 2½" x 2¾"**

SUPPLIES: *Cardstock:* (white) Bazzill Basics Paper *Patterned paper:* (Pirate Collage, Treasure Map from Pirate's Life collection) Karen Foster Design *Dye ink:* (Frayed Burlap) Ranger Industries *Accents:* (hook charm) Karen Foster Design; (pewter brads) Making Memories *Font:* (Toxica) www.searchfreefonts.com *Adhesive:* (foam tape) **Finished size: 5½" square**

SUPPLIES: Cardstock: (brown) Patterned paper: (Harvest Chestnut Plaid) Scenic Route Paper Co.; (Winnie Blooms from Winnie's Walls collection) SEI; (Antique Cream from Narratives collection) Creative Imaginations Dye ink: (brown) Color medium: (brown pen) Accents: (chipboard flower) Fancy Pants Designs; (canvas flower, embroidered leaves) Autumn Leaves: (flower paper clip) EK Success Rub-ons: (xoxo, stars) Heidi Swapp; (friend, flower) KI Memories Stickers: (letter A) Creative Imaginations; (sentiments) 7gypsies Fibers: (brown rickrack) Creative Impressions Other: (photo) **Finished size: 11" x 8½"**

FRIENDS MAKE
MEMORIES
BOOKMARK
Anabelle O'Malley

SISTERS
Alisa Bangerter

Adding a photo to a bookmark is an easy way to personalize it, and it's also a friendly reminder of the people who are most important to you. Using photos in your card making is also an easy way to express your hard-to-say feelings for your loved ones. Show your sister that you forgive her for the hair pulling and drama of your childhood by sending her a photo card thanking her for being your best friend and greatest support in your adult life!

SUPPLIES: Cardstock: (brown) Patterned paper: (Birthday Paisley from Blossom collection) My Mind's Eye Transparency: 3M Dye ink: (brown) Paint: (cream) Delta; (pink, taupe) Accents: (flower coaster) Imagination Project; (chipboard scroll) Fancy Pants Designs Fibers: (brown trim) BasicGrey Font: (SuzanneQuillSH) www.fonts101.com Other: (photo) **Finished size: 2½" x 8½"**

SUPPLIES: Cardstock: (white) Patterned paper: (Rosey Villa Dots, Villa Swirls, Rosey Villa Vines) Chatterbox Color medium: (pink chalk) Accents: (chipboard flower) Pressed Petals; (orange buttons) Rub-on: (sisters) BasicGrey Fibers: (pink sheer ribbon) Offray Font: (Nueva Standard) Microsoft Other: (photo) **Finished size: 7" x 5"**

YOU

Dee Gallimore-Perry

My dear sweet husband... Thank you for everything you do for me and Brendan. I am so glad that I married YOU...because I know that there is NO ONE else in the world that is as patient, caring, considerate and giving as you. You have become an amazing man. You are a wonderful father and husband...a great provider...a source of strength and safety. I am so grateful every day that you are MY HUSBAND. It's been a wonderful journey over the past 22 years, watching you grow and become the wonderful man that you are. Your parents would be very proud of who you have become.
you are one of my nicest thoughts - georgia o'keefe
i love you just the way you are - billy joel
APR 16 2006
beautiful you
[you]

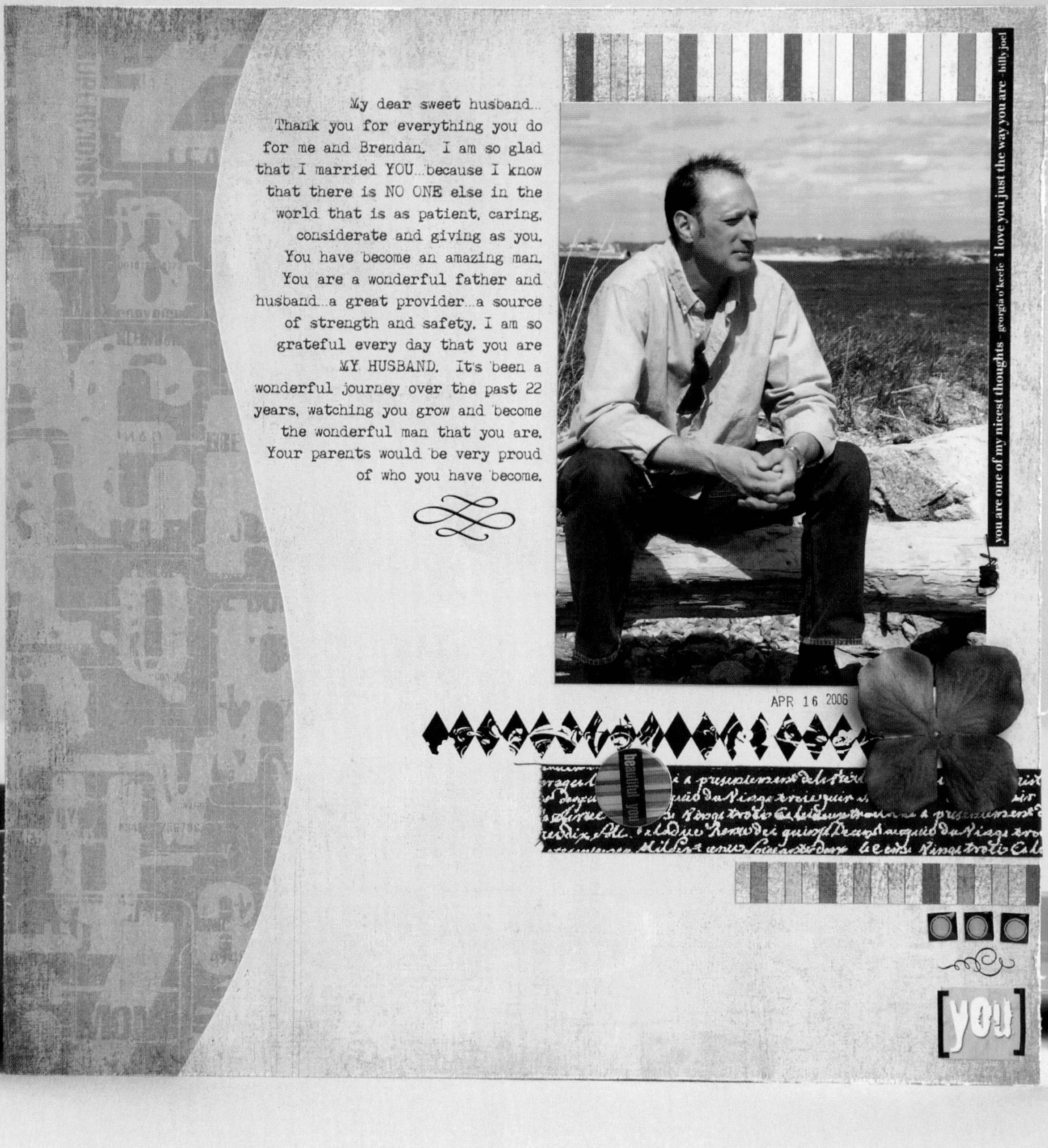

SUPPLIES: Patterned paper: (Drop In, Alias, Hemlock from Skate Shoppe collection) BasicGrey Rubber stamp: (date) OfficeMax Dye ink: (black) Accent: (blue flower) Stickers: (you) Daisy D's; (blue dots, beautiful you) Provo Craft; (black and white gaffer tape, sentiment strip) 7gypsies Rub-ons: (black flourishes) BasicGrey; (diamonds) Heidi Swapp; (parentheses) KI Memories Font: (Maszyna) www.fontica.com Other: (photo) **Finished size: 12" x 12"**

Use a heartfelt sentiment to add meaning and sincerity to your photo. Dee's well-worded quote tells her husband just how much she loves him and makes her card even more powerful. Use rich earth tones to paper-craft a masculine photo. A muted frame is a great way to showcase many different pictures of the special men in your life.

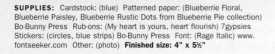

SUPPLIES: Cardstock: (blue) Patterned paper: (Blueberrie Floral, Blueberrie Paisley, Blueberrie Rustic Dots from Blueberrie Pie collection) Bo-Bunny Press Rub-ons: (My heart is yours, heart flourish) 7gypsies Stickers: (circles, blue strips) Bo-Bunny Press Font: (Rage Italic) www.fontseeker.com Other: (photo) **Finished size: 4" x 5½"**

SUPPLIES: Patterned paper: (Rawhide Floral from Horsin' Around collection, Harvest Houndstooth from Autumn Splendor collection) Flair Designs Chalk ink: (Chestnut Roan) Clearsnap Paint: (True Blue, Light Lavender, Parchment) Plaid Accents: (beads) Flair Designs Fibers: (leather trim) Other: (wood frame, photo) Adhesive: (decoupage) Plaid **Finished size: 8" square**

I AM
Kim Kesti

SUPPLIES: *Cardstock:* (kraft, white, yellow) *Patterned paper:* (Birdies/Stripe from Dulce Vintage collection) A2ZEssentials; (World Bazaar Circles from Gypsy Harvest collection) Daisy D's; (Citrus Burst from Canvas collection) Scrapworks *Accents:* (chipboard alphabet) Li'l Davis Designs; (buttons, letter tab) Autumn Leaves *Stickers:* (Boho Chic Tiny alphabet) Making Memories *Fibers:* (orange rickrack, striped grosgrain ribbon) *Other:* (photo) **Finished size: 9¼" x 9¼"**

WITH YOU
Alice Golden

BE YOURSELF
Stefanie Hamilton

Alice and her husband had just celebrated their 17th wedding anniversary, so when she saw the phrase "just where I want to be" on the layout, it made her think about Joe and how happy she is that they are together. With him is just where she wants to be, and that theme makes a wonderful card.

The layout's theme of being happy with yourself and where you are right now inspired Stefanie to make a card about being yourself. She hopes that the sentiment will inspire the recipient to be happy with herself as well.

with you...

is just where I want to be

BE yourself. [Who else is better qualified?]

INSIDE

SUPPLIES: *Cardstock:* (Tawny Light) Prism *Patterned paper:* (Memories Red, Large Textile Forest from Walter Knabe collection) Me & My Big Ideas *Specialty paper:* (Midnight Velvet) SEI *Dye ink:* (Black Soot) Ranger Industries *Color medium:* (black pen) American Crafts *Rub-ons:* (Sweetheart alphabet) Deja Views *Stickers:* (gel hearts) Me & My Big Ideas *Font:* (Monika) www.fryfonts.com *Adhesive:* (foam dots) **Finished size: 6¾" x 3¾"**

SUPPLIES: *Patterned paper:* (Preston, Buttercup, Blue Bonnet from Oh, Baby! Boy collection) BasicGrey *Accents:* (yellow/red silk flower) Michaels; (blue flower button) Autumn Leaves; (die cut sentiment) Around The Block **Finished size: 4½" x 5¼"**

SUPPLIES: *Cardstock:* (kraft) Bazzill Basics Paper *Patterned paper:* (Bold Stars from Bolded collection) CherryArte; (Cape Town Pentz Stripe) Scenic Route Paper Co. *Accents:* (Capitol Hill chipboard alphabet) Scenic Route Paper Co.; (clear plastic index tab) Avery; (rhinestone stars) *Rub-ons:* (Hand Drawn alphabet) EK Success; (Center of Attention alphabet) Heidi Swapp *Stickers:* (phrases) Making Memories; (fabric tape) 7gypsies *Font:* (Tom's New Roman) www.fontfinder.ws *Other:* (photo)
Finished size: 12" x 12"

LITTLE SUPER HERO GIFT BOX
Susan Neal

MY HERO
Linda Beeson

The superhero theme of the layout got Susan thinking: boys love super heroes and fantasize about being one. Susan thought it would thrill a little boy to not only be called a super hero, but to turn the gift box into a place for his treasures.

Linda played off the "hero" part of the superhero theme, transferring elements from the layout such as stars and descriptive word strips to this masculine card, suitable for a teen or man.

SUPPLIES: *Cardstock:* (Lava, Festive, Honeycomb, white) Bazzill Basics Paper *Accents:* (orange brads) Making Memories *Fonts:* (Arriere Garde) www.abstractfonts.com; (Seeing Stars) www.dafont.com *Dies:* (mini monograms, basic shapes, boxes, bags & tags) Provo Craft *Tools:* (die cut machine) Provo Craft *Other:* (black box) Provo Craft **Finished size: 7½" x 7½" x 3"**

SUPPLIES: *Cardstock:* (green, brown) Bazzill Basics Paper *Patterned paper:* (Polka Dot, Red from Full of Spunk collection) My Mind's Eye; (Merino from Urban Couture collection) BasicGrey *Dye ink:* (Coffee Bean) Paper Salon *Accents:* (die cut star, word strips) My Mind's Eye *Rub-ons:* (Hand Drawn alphabet, crown) EK Success *Adhesive:* (foam squares) *Tools:* (decorative-edge scissors) **Finished size: 8½" x 5½"**

SUPPLIES: *Cardstock:* (light olive) Bazzill Basics Paper *Patterned paper:* (Mixed Aqua Pansies, Frenzy Pinstripe Aqua) Provo Craft *Accents:* (clip, gem brad) Making Memories *Rub-ons:* (All Mixed Up alphabet, flower border, stitching) Doodlebug Design; (approved circles) Making Memories *Stickers:* (Mumbo Jumbo alphabet) American Crafts *Font:* (Century Gothic) www. fonts.com *Other:* (photo) **Finished size: 11" x 8½"**

Kim used the same paper, gem brad, and rub-ons on her card. In addition to get well and missing you cards from Wendy's layout, these cheerful supplies would work nicely for birthday, hello, or thinking of you cards

Wendy took maximizing her supplies to the limit on her card. Virtually every supply on this card was also on her original layout.

SUPPLIES: *Cardstock:* (light olive) Bazzill Basics Paper *Patterned paper:* (Mixed Aqua Pansies, Frenzy Pinstripe Aqua) Provo Craft *Accents:* (clip) Making Memories *Rub-ons:* (All Mixed Up alphabet, flower border, stitching) Doodlebug Design *Stickers:* (Mumbo Jumbo alphabet) American Crafts *Fibers:* (pink ribbon) Making Memories *Font:* (Century Gothic) www.fonts.com *Tools:* (decorative-edge scissors) Making Memories **Finished size: 4¾" x 5"**

SUPPLIES: *Cardstock:* (Cantaloupe) Bazzill Basics Paper *Patterned paper:* (Mixed Aqua Pansies, Frenzy Pinstripe Aqua) Provo Craft *Dye ink:* (Coffee Bean) Paper Salon *Accents:* (gem brad) Making Memories; (assorted flowers) Prima *Rub-ons:* (All Mixed Up alphabet) Doodlebug Design *Tools:* (1" circle punch) EK Success **Finished size: 7¼" x 3¾"**

a.k.a.
(maggie)

It started with Josh teasing. He'd say it, you would tattle & get mad & sometimes cry. Then I found out your friends called you Maggie. You told them about your nickname. Then I heard your prima & teachers call you Maggie. It seems you like it. So do I. Now maybe you should thank Joshua.

SUPPLIES: All supplies from Making Memories unless otherwise noted. *Patterned paper:* (Abby Dots, Abby Pink) *Color media:* (black pen) American Crafts; (white pen) Sanford *Accents:* (large pink flower, gem brad) *Rub-ons:* (Trademark alphabet) *Stickers:* (Simply Sweet alphabet) Doodlebug Design; (gems, dotted tape) *Other:* (photo) **Finished size: 9" x 9" circle**

Wendy's card uses the same paper, gem brad, stickers, and dotted tape from her layout. These bright colors and patterns translate effortlessly from a girl-themed layout to a happy birthday card.

Anabelle used the same paper, pink flower, gem brad, stickers, and dotted tape as Wendy's original layout. These cheerful supplies would work for almost any occasion or theme.

SUPPLIES: *Cardstock:* (white) Bazzill Basics Paper *Patterned paper:* (Abby Dots, Abby Pink, Abby Stripes) Making Memories *Accents:* (happy birthday tag, gem brad) Making Memories *Stickers:* (Simply Sweet alphabet) Doodlebug Design; (dotted tape) Making Memories *Other:* (tissue paper) **Finished size: 5" square**

SUPPLIES: *Cardstock:* (white) The Paper Company *Patterned paper:* (Abby Dots, Abby Pink) Making Memories *Color medium:* (white pen) Uniball *Accents:* (large pink flowers, gem brad) Making Memories *Stickers:* (Simply Sweet alphabet) Doodlebug Design; (dot patterned tape) Making Memories *Tools:* (circle cutter) Provo Craft; (decorative-edge scissors) Fiskars **Finished size: 5¾" square**

SUPPLIES: *Cardstock:* (kraft, Parakeet, Hot Pink, Apricot) Bazzill Basics Paper; (yellow, light green, fuchsia, orange) *Patterned paper:* (Rainbow Stripes) Provo Craft *Rubber stamps:* (Retro Daisy) Paper Candy; (small flower from Daisy Quartet set) Hero Arts *Solvent ink:* (Jet Black) Tsukineko *Paint:* (Spotlight, Capri) Making Memories; (purple, lime green) *Color media:* (white gel pen, black fine-tip marker) Sanford; (purple, blue, green markers) *Accents:* (blue, pink, orange, purple flowers) Prima; (chipboard flower) Maya Road; (green plastic, metal conchos) Scrapworks; (chipboard letters) Li'l Davis Designs; (assorted buttons) Doodlebug Design; (purple, pink brads) Junkitz; (metal bottle cap brad, metal tag) Making Memories; (metal hug tag) American Crafts; (acrylic you round) KI Memories; (cardstock bulls-eye die cut) Provo Craft; (metal number, chipboard tag, rhinestone) *Fibers:* (black floral print ribbon) *Rub-ons:* (so lucky) BasicGrey *Adhesive:* (foam squares) **Finished size: 12" x 12"**

M IS FOR MOM
Emily Call

I HEART U BOX
Valerie Pingree

Emily drew her ideas from the large chipboard letters on the layout, and created a simple and elegant card for Mom. The flower and beads give the card just a touch of girly pizzazz!

Valerie was inspired by the chunky chipboard letters and the painted dots. She used a hand-held punch to mimic the painted border on the layout. She then painted the acetate heart and matted it with a scalloped-edge heart to coordinate with the pink heart on the layout.

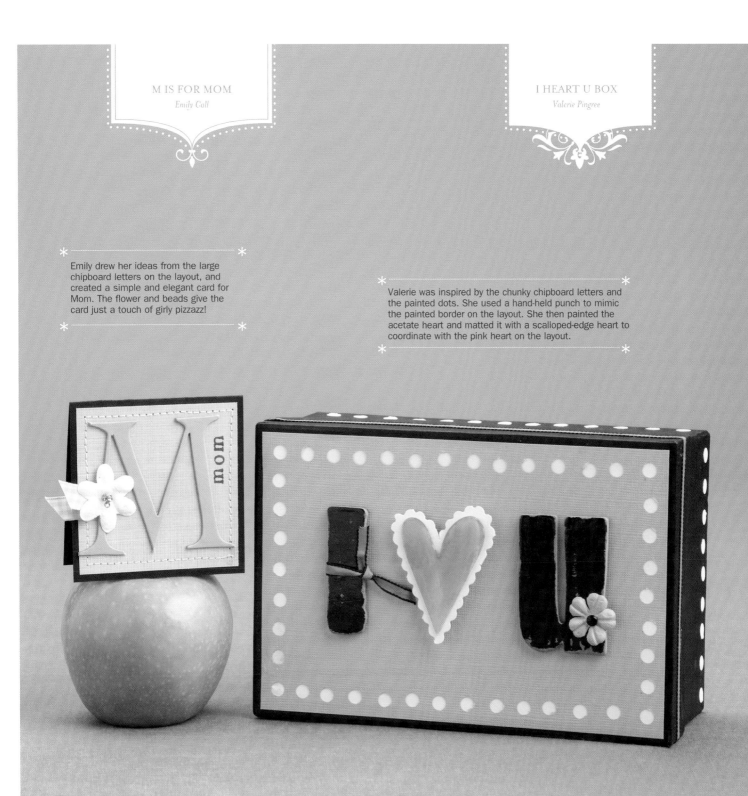

SUPPLIES: *Cardstock:* (black) *Patterned paper:* (Villa Bouquet) Chatterbox *Acrylic stamps:* (Williamsburg alphabet) Technique Tuesday *Solvent ink:* (Jet Black) Tsukineko *Accents:* (chipboard letter) Heidi Swapp; (white flower) Making Memories; (pink crystals) *Fibers:* (pink gingham ribbon) Li'l Davis Designs **Finished size: 3" square**

SUPPLIES: *Cardstock:* (cream, tan) Bazzill Basics Paper *Chalk ink:* (Charcoal) Clearsnap *Paint:* (Peony) Plaid *Accents:* (pink flower) Prima; (acetate heart) Heidi Swapp; (chipboard letters) Li'l Davis Designs; (black brad) All My Memories *Fibers:* (pink/black ribbon) Heidi Swapp *Adhesive:* (foam squares) *Tools:* (decorative-edge scissors) *Other:* (black cardboard box) **Finished size: 7½" x 5" x 3"**

SUPPLIES: *Cardstock:* (white, red, orange, pink) *Patterned paper:* (Posh Crowns) Autumn Leaves: (Harvest Daisies) Scenic Route Paper Co.; (Black & White Words) Provo Craft *Rubber stamps:* (Gothic alphabet) Post Modern; (dictionary text; map image) *Pigment ink:* (Graphite Black) Tsukineko *Chalk ink:* (Charcoal) Clearsnap *Paint:* (red, pink) *Accents:* (black brad, red leather flower) Making Memories; (good dog chipboard, wood letter) Li'l Davis Designs; (acetate stars) Heidi Swapp; (decorative border strips, chipboard circle letter) Provo Craft; (staples) *Rub-ons:* (5th Avenue alphabet) 7gypsies; (alphabet) Scenic Route Paper Co.; (Mixed Brite, Heidi alphabets) Making Memories; (letters, numbers) Li'l Davis Designs *Fonts:* (your choice) *Other:* (photo) **Finished size: 11" x 8½"**

The last line on the scrapbook layout—"Attitude is everything"—caught Michelle's eye and moved her to create a card that celebrates the everyday moments of our lives. With the bright colors and mix-and-match alphabets, the card carries an attitude all its own.

Michelle was inspired by the "dog" focus of the layout, so she created a quirky birthday card with a fun pun.

SUPPLIES: *Cardstock:* (Nautical Blue Dark) Prism; (Bazzill White) Bazzill Basics Paper *Patterned paper:* (Wild Berries, Mango Tango from Wild Berry collection) My Mind's Eye *Pigment ink:* (black) Clearsnap *Color medium:* (black pen) *Accents:* (chipboard alphabet) Imagination Project; (black brads) Making Memories; (die cut alphabet) My Mind's Eye *Rub-ons:* (enjoy each moment) Making Memories; (Hand Stamped alphabet) Polar Bear Press; (stitches) Die Cuts With a View *Stickers:* (Roadtrip alphabet) Sticker Studio; (Autumn Splendor alphabet) Flair Designs *Font:* (Blake) www.font-face.com *Fibers:* (green grosgrain ribbon) Die Cuts With a View **Finished size: 6" x 4"**

SUPPLIES: *Cardstock:* (Nautical Blue Medium) Prism *Patterned paper:* (Lemonade, Beach Ball, Capris from Summertime collection) We R Memory Keepers *Rubber stamp:* (Paw) Stampendous! *Pigment ink:* (Pinecone) Tsukineko *Accent:* (round metal-rimmed tag) Impress Rubber Stamps *Rub-ons:* (stitches) Die Cuts With a View *Sticker:* (dog) Me & My Big Ideas *Font:* (Good Dog) www.coolarchive.com **Finished size: 4" x 6"**

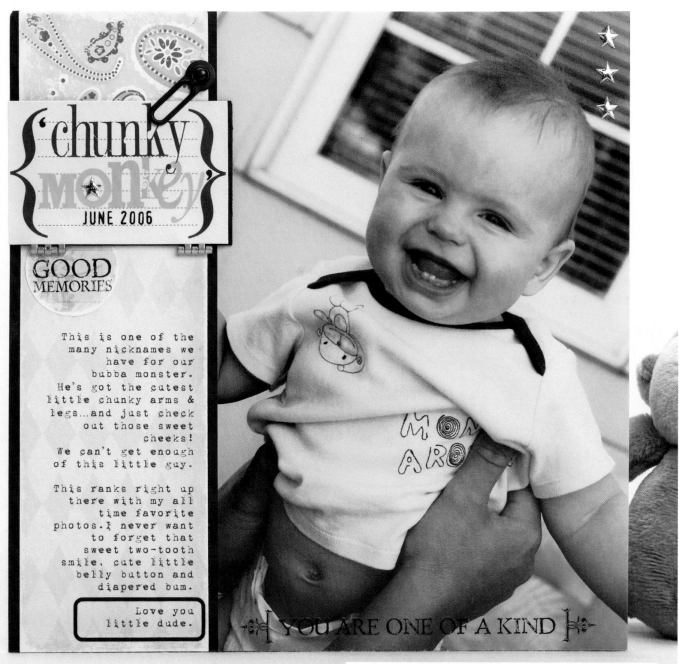

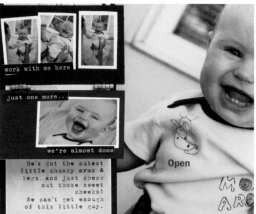

SUPPLIES: *Cardstock:* (Raven) Bazzill Basics Paper *Patterned paper:* (Summer Paisley) Autumn Leaves; (Harlequin) 7gypsies *Accents:* (red brad) Heidi Swapp; (photo turn, lined tag) 7gypsies; (pewter hinges) Making Memories *Rub-ons:* (One of a Kind sentiment and flourishes) Creative Imaginations; (Bordeaux alphabet) Heidi Swapp; (Mixed alphabet) Making Memories *Stickers:* (cardstock sentiments) Creative Imaginations; (stars) 7gypsies *Font:* (1492 Report) www.simplythebest.net *Other:* (photos) **Finished size: 9" x 9"**

SUPPLIES: *Cardstock:* (Summer Rain, Pomegranate, kraft) Bazzill Basics Paper *Patterned paper:* (Charlotte Canal Street Floral) Scenic Route Paper Co.; (Summer Paisley) Autumn Leaves *Accents:* (red brad) Heidi Swapp; (flashcard, photo turn) 7gypsies; (pewter hinges) Making Memories *Rub-ons:* (frame, accents, alphabet) American Crafts *Sticker:* (dad quote) Cloud 9 Design; (red tape) Heidi Swapp *Font:* (Supafly36) www.scrapnfonts.com *Other:* (photos) **Finished size: 4¼" x 5½"**

Take your interactive element to the max by creating a hinged accent using popular, new craft hinges or make your own with thick paper and decorative tape. You can also use new hardware hinges, pulls, knobs, and clasps to create unique hinged accents. Don't forget to keep the hinges closed using a photo turn or other fastener and make sure to have a special sentiment or photos on the inside to add pizzazz to your creation.

INSIDE

SUPPLIES: *Cardstock:* (Light Fairytale Pink) WorldWin *Patterned paper:* (Till There Was You, Hart Strings from He Sings at Weddings collection) Imagination Project *Accents:* (pink circles, flower, arrow, hearts coasters) Imagination Project; (photo turn) 7gypsies; (red brad) SEI; (black brads) Doodlebug Design; (love metal tag) Making Memories; (red, pink buttons) American Crafts; (black acrylic "o") KI Memories *Stickers:* (heart patch) Memories Complete (pink polka dot, brown diamonds, pink/brown flowers tape) Imagination Project *Rub-ons:* (Maggie, Natalie alphabets) Imagination Project *Fibers:* (cream and pink ribbon) SEI; (black floss) **Finished size: 6" square**

INSIDE

Cath EDVALSON

It's All Green to Me

Whether you're trying to save money or endeavoring to save the earth, the Green Movement has many oft-repeated words and catchy phrases. "Reduce, reuse, recycle" is a phrase I knew in my youth which has enthusiastically re-emerged as we come to terms with climate change and as we strive to make the best of tough economic times. At the same time, typography—creating art with letters, numbers, and words—has become a popular form of design. Here we're inspiring you by combining the two for purposeful projects that will put us all in the green.

SUPPLIES: *Cardstock:* (green, black) Bazzill Basics Paper; (kraft) *Patterned paper:* (Garland Parkman Road) Scenic Route *Color medium:* (black pen) *Accents:* (black chipboard letters) Scenic Route; (gel tree) October Afternoon *Stickers:* (Omaha alphabet) Scenic Route *Font:* (Impact) www.dafont.com **Finished size: 7¾" x 5"**

Reduce, Reuse, Recycle Card

Designer: Layle Koncar

1 Make card from cardstock.
2 Cut rectangle of patterned paper; adhere.
3 Print sentiment on cardstock; trim, mat with cardstock, and adhere.
4 Outline with pen.
5 Sand edges of black chipboard letters; adhere.
6 Affix stickers and adhere tree.

SIMPLE SENTIMENT

The inside sentiment reads, "It was a great age, why not reuse it?"

TRENDY TIP

As a Latin prefix, "re" means "again," "anew," or "back." I love the typographical treatment Layle has used on this card that emphasizes the "re" aspect of these three important activities. But what I love most of all is that she has connected this familiar phrase with one of the most common occasions in our lives—our birthdays.

SUPPLIES: *Cardstock:* (Green Tea, Sour Apple, Parakeet, Clover Leaf embossed) Bazzill Basics Paper *Digital element:* (recycle symbol) Microsoft *Fonts:* (Army) www.dafont.com; (Batang) www.ascenderfonts.com; (Arial) Microsoft *Software:* (word processing) Microsoft **Finished size: 6¼" x 4¼"**

SUPPLIES: *Cardstock:* (white) Provo Craft; (green, blue) Bazzill Basics Paper *Specialty paper:* (photo) *Accent:* (newspaper scrap) *Digital element:* (leaf brush) Adobe *Font:* (Stencil Distress) Autumn Leaves *Software:* (photo editing) Adobe *Fibers:* (jute) DCC **Finished size: 4¾" x 5½"**

Love Your Mother Card

Designer: Teri Anderson

1 Make card from cardstock.

2 Cut rectangles of cardstock; adhere.

3 Create 4" x 6" project in software.

4 Type "Love your mother"; angle sentiment. Change colors to match cardstock.

5 In new layer brush leaf; distress by applying filter.

6 Print on photo paper; trim. Tear bottom edge and adhere.

7 Crinkle and flatten newspaper scrap; adhere. Tie on jute.

TRENDY TIP

Are you old enough to remember the commercial in which there is a lightening bolt, and a crash of thunder, and a tunic-clad woman who appears and says, "It's not nice to fool Mother Nature"? This card has that same kind of power—as though it were stamped indelibly in our minds, we really should "love our mother."

5 STEPS The Ultimate Card

Designer: Kim Kesti

1 Make card from cardstock.

2 Cut rectangle of embossed cardstock; adhere.

3 Print symbol on cardstock, trim, and adhere.

4 Print sentiment on cardstock, trim, and adhere.

SIMPLE SENTIMENT

The inside of Kim's card solves the mystery of what "the absolute ultimate in recycling" is…"a recycled twenty" so place a $20 bill inside the card and your gift is wrapped and ready.

TRENDY TIP

Kim has used a familiar icon in this card while at the same time creating an ironic look at recycling—money!

EVERY THING GOES WITH GREEN

5 STEPS Everything Goes Tag

Designer: Susan Neal

❶ Die-cut tags from cardstock; adhere.

❷ Download digital element; print on cardstock, trim, and adhere with foam tape.

❸ Print sentiment on cardstock; trim and adhere with foam tape.

❹ Tie on ribbon.

5 STEPS Green Card

Designer: Beth Opel

❶ Make card from patterned paper.

❷ Create word collage in software; print on photo paper, trim, and adhere.

❸ Adhere accents.

❹ Draw stems with pen.

TRENDY TIP

This particular project captures the very essence of what this issue is all about: ecology and economy. As the design Susan has created shows, they each work together in harmony.

DESIGNER TIPS

Play with the word collage program until you achieve the design that you desire.

Customize! Because the words in this project are arranged randomly, no two designs will be alike. When creating your own project, select "green" words that are especially meaningful to you.

In order to make one word appear larger, type it multiple times.

The Wonderful World of Wood Grain

Rustic and natural, wood grain is working its way out of the forest and into the mainstream. And while its popularity is probably branching out from the green movement, you don't have to be a tree hugger to enjoy this look!

5 STEPS Adore Card

Designer: Melissa Phillips

1 Die-cut card from cardstock.

2 Die-cut circles from patterned paper and adhere.

3 Die-cut stroller outline from patterned paper, die-cut solid stroller from patterned paper, and adhere together.

4 Apply rub-ons and adhere stroller. Affix sticker; adhere flowers, buttons, and pearls.

5 Tie ribbon bow at top of card through fold.

TRENDY TIP

While you might not think of putting a wood grain element on a baby card, the fact that this hot wood grain pattern comes in pink and yellow makes for one trendy welcome!

SUPPLIES: *Cardstock:* (Iced Pink) Prism *Patterned paper:* (Noble, Lavish, Decadent, Dauphin from Eva collection) BasicGrey *Accents:* (green, purple, white buttons) BasicGrey; (pearls) Martha Stewart Crafts; (green polka dot, pink flowers) Making Memories *Rub-ons:* (flowers, adore) BasicGrey *Sticker:* (flourish) BasicGrey *Fibers:* (white ribbon) Offray *Dies:* (stroller, circle, scalloped circle card) Provo Craft *Tool:* (die cut machine) Provo Craft
Finished size: 5½" diameter

SUPPLIES: *Cardstock:* (Fire Hearts) Bazzill Basics Paper *Patterned paper:* (Branch Out from Pocket Full of Rosies collection) Sassafras Lass *Stickers:* (wood grain label, hedgehog) Sassafras Lass *Fibers:* (multi-colored striped ribbon) Making Memories *Font:* (Another Typewriter) www.dafont.com *Adhesive:* (foam tape) **Finished size: 4½" x 6"**

SUPPLIES: *Cardstock:* (Dragonfly, pink) Bazzill Basics Paper; (white) Papertrey Ink *Patterned paper:* (Stella from Retro Metro collection) Tinkering Ink *Rubber stamp:* (Wood Grain Backgrounder) Cornish Heritage Farms *Clear stamp:* (happy day from Simply Spring set) Tinkering Ink *Dye ink:* (Pink Passion) Stampin' Up! *Chalk ink:* (Lime Pastel) Clearsnap *Accents:* (chipboard vine) Cosmo Cricket; (felt flower with bird and button) American Crafts; (black mini brad) *Dies:* (Opposites Attract alphabet) Provo Craft *Tools:* (die cut machine, decorative-edge scissors) Provo Craft **Finished size: 4¼" x 5½"**

Hedging My Bets Card

Designer: Kim Kesti

1. Print sentiment on cardstock; make card.
2. Adhere patterned paper border to inside card edge.
3. Adhere label sticker to card with foam tape.
4. Tie ribbon around card and underneath sticker.
5. Adhere hedgehog sticker with foam tape.

Happy Bird Day Card

Designer: Betsy Veldman

1. Make card from cardstock.
2. Stamp Wood Grain Backgrounder on cardstock; trim and adhere.
3. Cut strip of cardstock, trim bottom edge with decorative-edge scissors, and stamp happy day. Adhere patterned paper strip.
4. Die-cut "Bird" from cardstock; adhere to strip. Attach brad and adhere strip to card.
5. Adhere chipboard vine and bird embellishment.

TRENDY TIP

Who knew that wood grain would make its way onto a sticker? I'm sure glad it did, because this is one easy and hip way to incorporate wood grain into your projects! Moxie fab!

TRENDY TIP

Not only is this wood grain stamp super cool, but the colors Betsy has chosen show us that there's so much more to wood grain than what meets the eye!

SUPPLIES: *Cardstock:* (Dark Terra Cotta) WorldWin; (orange, green) Bazzill Basics Paper; (white) Georgia-Pacific *Paint:* (Bark) Heidi Swapp *Accent:* (screw brad) Eyelet Outlet *Stickers:* (MoMA alphabet) American Crafts; (Center of Attention alphabet) Heidi Swapp *Fibers:* (jute) *Tools:* (wood graining tool) Hyde; (corner rounder punch) Marvy Uchida **Finished size: 5½" x 4¼"**

SUPPLIES: *Cardstock:* (black) Bazzill Basics Paper *Patterned paper:* (Skipping Stones from Mr. Campy collection) Cosmo Cricket *Clear stamps:* (Vintage Pop Alpha set) Pink Paislee *Dye ink:* (black) Ranger Industries *Color medium:* (black pen) *Rub-on:* (van) Cosmo Cricket **Finished size: 5½" x 5"**

To My Guy Card

Designer: Teri Anderson

1 Make card from cardstock.

2 Apply paint to white cardstock. Pull wood graining tool through paint; let dry.

3 Cut strip of cardstock. Spell sentiment with stickers.

4 Cut cardstock rectangle, knot jute, attach brad, and adhere.

5 Round bottom corners of card.

Daddy-O Card

Designer: Layle Koncar

1 Make card from patterned paper.

2 Cut square from patterned paper and stamp sentiment. Apply rub-on.

3 Mat with cardstock and adhere.

4 Draw lines around outside edges.

TRENDY TIP

DIY wood grain is super easy, super innovative, and super, super cool!

TRENDY TIP

This cartoonish wood grain goes perfectly with the van rub-on and the stylishly retro stamped letters! A moxie fab combination!

Gradient is Radiant

Like a moth to a flame, I am drawn to gradient color. It seems magical to me, as though my eyes move from one color to another like turning up the volume on a dial. Whether you call it monochromatic tie dye or you visualize a perpetual rainbow—its look is chic and sophisticated and it's never been trendier than now.

SUPPLIES: *Cardstock:* (black, orange, white) *Accents:* (tangerine glitter) Doodlebug Design; (garnet glitter) Martha Stewart Crafts; (orange felt flower) American Crafts; (orange flower) Prima; (orange button) *Digital element:* (Black Forest patterned paper from Jack kit) www.pclayers.com *Stickers:* (Block alphabet) BasicGrey *Fibers:* (orange, red, red dotted ribbon; orange floss) *Software:* (photo editing) *Adhesive:* (decoupage) Martha Stewart Crafts **Finished size: 5" square**

Shimmering Boo Card

Designer: Celeste Rockwood-Jones

❶ Cut cardstock to 5" x 10½".

❷ Print patterned paper on cardstock; adhere ½" from bottom of cardstock piece.

❸ Trim away negative space between trees.

❹ Cover stickers with glitter; stitch with floss and affix to spell "Boo". Adhere flowers; stitch button with floss and adhere. Apply glitter to flower center.

❺ Fold at 5" and 10" and adhere bottom flap to create pocket.

❻ Cut cardstock to fit in pocket; apply glitter; stitch ribbons to piece with floss to form pull-tab.

DESIGNER TIP

To achieve a gradient effect with the glitter, liberally apply the glitter at one end using less and less as you approach the bottom. Repeat the process with a darker color, starting at the opposite end.

TRENDY TIP

The gradient in this project moves from dark to light as your eye moves from the distant horizon to the sky for a moxie fab effect!

SUPPLIES: *Cardstock:* (Aloe Vera, Sprout, Green Tea, Parakeet, Whirlpool, Dragonfly, Blue Raspberry, Kachina, Blue Oasis) Bazzill Basics Paper *Rub-on:* (love yourself flourish) 7gypsies **Finished size: 4" x 7½"**

SUPPLIES: *Cardstock:* (white) Bazzill Basics Paper; (white) Georgia Pacific *Vellum:* WorldWin *Rubber stamp:* (hello friend from Friend Centers set) Cornish Heritage Farms *Clear stamp:* (damask from Damask set) Technique Tuesday *Pigment ink:* (Pink Grapefruit, Mango Madness, Thatched Straw) Tsukineko *Watermark ink:* Tsukineko *Embossing powder:* (clear) Ranger Industries *Accents:* (pink brad) Colorbok **Finished size: 4" x 6"**

Love Yourself Card

Designer: Kim Kesti

1. Make card from cardstock.
2. Cut strips of cardstock; tear bottom edges.
3. Adhere strips in layers.
4. Apply rub-on.

Hello Friend Card

Designer: Teri Anderson

1. Make card from cardstock.
2. Cut rectangle of cardstock; stamp repeatedly with damask; emboss.
3. Apply ink to panel; rub off excess with paper towel.
4. Stamp sentiment on cardstock; trim and adhere. Attach brad.
5. Adhere panel to vellum; tear edges. Adhere to card.

TRENDY TIP

I love how the colors in this card morph from blue at the bottom to green at the top, reminding me of the ruffles on a dress that would shimmer and shine with the motion of its wearer.

TRENDY TIP

The damask paired with these gradient colors reminds me of looking through a kaleidoscope when I was a child.

SUPPLIES: *Cardstock:* (Plum, Burgundy) Prism; (Vintage Cream) Papertrey Ink; (purple) Bazzill Basics Paper; (rose, brown, light brown) Die Cuts With a View *Patterned paper:* (Mousse from Chocolat colleciion) SEI *Chalk ink:* (Creamy Brown) Clearsnap *Accents:* (green chipboard swirl) Cosmo Cricket; (burgundy button) BasicGrey *Fibers:* (brown ribbon) Papertrey Ink; (purple twine) *Font:* (Trajan Pro) www.fonts.com *Software:* (word processing) Microsoft *Die:* (leaf) Provo Craft *Tools:* (die cut machine) Provo Craft; (1" circle punch) EK Success *Adhesive:* (foam tape) **Finished size: 7" x 4¼"**

SUPPLIES: *Cardstock:* (Going Gray) Stampin' Up! *Patterned paper:* (Love Dots, Love Song from Love Letters collection) Little Yellow Bicycle *Dye ink:* (Elegant Eggplant, Eggplant Envy, Baroque Burgundy, Pink Passion) Stampin' Up! *Accents:* (chipboard frame) Heidi Swapp; (black glitter) Martha Stewart Crafts *Stickers:* (Cheeky alphabet) Making Memories *Fibers:* (gray polka dot ribbon) American Crafts *Adhesive:* (foam tape) **Finished size: 5" x 4½"**

Season of Change Card

Designer: Betsy Veldman

❶ Make card from cardstock.

❷ Cut patterned paper; mat with cardstock and adhere.

❸ Adhere ribbon; trim.

❹ Print sentiment and frame on cardstock; trim and ink edges.

❺ Die-cut leaves from cardstock. Adhere chipboard flourish and leaves; punch left edge. Adhere with foam tape.

❻ Tie button with twine; adhere.

⑤ Love You Card

Designer: Jessica Witty

❶ Make card from cardstock.

❷ Cut patterned papers; adhere.

❸ Apply glitter to top and bottom edges of patterned paper.

❹ Ink chipboard from dark to light; adhere with foam tape.

❺ Spell sentiment with stickers; tie on ribbon.

TRENDY TIP

Betsy has applied the gradient effect brilliantly to the season of autumn. When you look at this card, it is as if the leaves are changing before your very eyes.

DESIGNER TIP

Applying ink is a great way to create the gradient effect and can be used with any set of colors. Just choose three colors that work well together and an extra color to blend in between the original three. Deepen the first color by applying more layers of ink if necessary.

Celebrate the Sassy Style of Anne Taintor

Anne Taintor is known for combining vintage images with hilarious sentiments that are reflective of what she thinks the people in the images might really be thinking. Found in every stationery shop in America, this style is all the rage. One of my favorites is a magnet I have on my fridge in which there's a picture of a woman from the '50s holding a martini glass with the sentiment, "Martinis: They're not just for breakfast anymore!" With the burst of vintage images on the paper crafting scene, I thought it would be fun to pair them up with our own sassy sentiments. Take a look at these Anne Taintor-style cards and use these ideas to create some attitude of your own.

Everything I Am Card

Designer: Stefanie Hamilton

1. Make card from cardstock.
2. Open new project in software.
3. Scan advertisement and import into software. Place on project.
4. Use marquee tool to cut out white boxes.
5. Type sentiment.
6. Print on photo paper, trim, and adhere to card.

SUPPLIES: *Cardstock:* (white) Creative Memories *Specialty paper:* (glossy photo) *Font:* (Typical Writer) www.fontspace.com *Software:* (photo editing) Creative Memories *Tool:* (scanner) *Other:* (vintage advertisement)
Finished size: 4½" x 3½"

TRENDY TIP

The trick in creating these Anne Taintor-inspired cards is to come up with a vintage image and a sassy sentiment. For inspiration, go directly to the source at *www.annetaintor.com*.

SUPPLIES: *Cardstock:* (Great Lakes, Tapioca) Bazzill Basics Paper *Patterned paper:* (Fashionista from Fashionista collection) Graphic 45 *Font:* (Courier New) Microsoft **Finished size: 4" x 6½"**

SUPPLIES: *Cardstock:* (black, white) WorldWin *Patterned paper:* (blue grid from Darcey collection) Anna Griffin *Specialty paper:* (glossy white) WorldWin *Rubber stamp:* (Fred Loves Lottie) Art Declassified *Solvent ink:* (Jet Black) Tsukineko *Accents:* (bracket tag) Anna Griffin; (black rhinestones) Kaisercraft *Fibers:* (black ribbon) May Arts *Font:* (MS Mincho) Microsoft **Finished size: 6¾" x 4¾"**

I Am Fashion Card

Designer: Kim Kesti

1 Make card from cardstock.

2 Trim strip of patterned paper; adhere. Trim patterned paper; adhere.

3 Print sentiment on cardstock; trim and adhere.

4 Trim figure from patterned paper, mat with cardstock, and adhere with foam tape.

Match Made in Heaven? Card

Designer: Teri Anderson

1 Make card from cardstock. Trim patterned paper and adhere.

2 Adhere tag.

3 Stamp image on specialty paper, trim, and adhere.

4 Print sentiment on cardstock; trim, mat with cardstock, and adhere.

5 Knot ribbon and adhere. Adhere rhinestones.

TRENDY TIP

I love how Kim used a variety of images from this piece of paper from Graphic 45. She's popped a focal point from the montage that makes it seem like the card is straight from a fashion show.

TRENDY TIP

This vintage photo image stamp is perfect for an Anne Taintor-style card. By paying special attention to the posture of the two people in the stamp, Teri was able to come up with a sassy sentiment that would make Anne proud.

SUPPLIES: *Cardstock:* (Buttercream) Bazzill Basics Paper; (white) Cornish Heritage Farms *Patterned paper:* (Pretty Rad Polka Dot, Teeny Weeny Stripe, Itsy Bitsy from Breaking Free collection) My Mind's Eye *Rubber stamps:* (Casual Conversation, Spanish Script Backgrounder) Cornish Heritage Farms *Dye ink:* (Watermelon, black) Ranger Industries *Color medium:* (assorted colored pencils) Prismacolor *Accents:* (pink, lavender, yellow flowers) *Font:* (Times New Roman) Microsoft **Finished size: 4¼" x 5½"**

SUPPLIES: *Cardstock:* (white) Bazzill Basics Paper *Patterned paper:* (Forget Me Not from Penny Lane collection; Geometric Pink from Bloom & Grow collection) My Mind's Eye *Chalk ink:* (Chestnut Roan) Clearsnap *Accents:* (vintage image) Crafty Secrets; (white button) *Sticker:* (laughter label) Making Memories *Fibers:* (blue printed ribbon) American Crafts; (white waxed floss) *Template:* (Swiss Dots embossing) Provo Craft *Tool:* (border punch) Stampin' Up! **Finished size: 4½" x 6"**

I Like You Card

Designer: Becky Olsen

1. Make card from cardstock.

2. Trim patterned paper to fit card front. Stamp Spanish Script Backgrounder and adhere.

3. Cut patterned papers, layer, and adhere.

4. Stamp Casual Conversation on cardstock, color, trim, and adhere.

5. Print sentiment on cardstock, trim, and adhere.

6. Adhere flowers.

Regular Guy Card

Designer: Melanie Douthit

Ink all edges unless otherwise noted.

1. Make card from cardstock. Cut patterned paper and adhere.

2. Cut patterned paper; adhere and stitch edges.

3. Cut strip of cardstock. Emboss and punch. Adhere without inking edges.

4. Tie on ribbon. Thread button with floss and adhere.

5. Trim vintage image and adhere with foam tape.

6. Affix label.

TRENDY TIP

In this card, Becky has juxtaposed two things women love: men and chocolate. To be true to the world of Anne Taintor, however, chocolate must be given the higher value.

TRENDY TIP

Melanie has capitalized on the sweetness of the era with the patterned papers, ribbon, and scalloped edges she has chosen to use on the card. All of these design elements help set the stage for the punny sentiment.

The Silhouette Movement

In the early 70s when I was in elementary school, I worked on an art project in which I cut out a profile of my face to give to my parents as a gift. In those days, silhouette images had become a standard feature on record albums, in Coke commercials, and as visuals on shows like Laugh-In, The Mod Squad, and Charlie's Angels. In the first decade of the 21st century, the modern adaptation of the silhouette was brought to life by iPod as we watched hip-swinging, hair-flipping dancers move in bright fluidity on our TV screens. Here we show you ways to create both effects: the modern, electric attitude of movement, and the traditional, vintage style of a bygone day. Both are equally moxie fab!

5 STEPS Silhouette Squirrel Tag

Designer: Kim Kesti

❶ Make tag from cardstock. Cut rectangles from cardstock; adhere.

❷ Cut Squirrel, Mushroom 1, and Mushroom 2, from cardstock. Cut out moon. Punch holes in mushrooms; adhere.

❸ Apply rub-on.

❹ Punch holes in tag top; tie with ribbon.

TRENDY TIP

Silhouettes are super easy to make yourself. Take any image you'd like to feature, draw or trace it onto cardstock, and voila!—instant, trendy silhouette!

SUPPLIES: *Cardstock:* (Vanilla, Espresso, Pretty Peach, Arizona, Light Chocolate) Bazzill Basics Paper *Rub-on:* (thinking of you) Scenic Route *Fibers:* (pink polka-dot ribbon) May Arts *Tools:* (⅛" circle punch) **Finished size: 4" x 7"**

TRENDY TIP

Silhouettes are a great way to show movement. In this card, Alisa has chosen a paper that shows skateboarders suspended in time. Whether the recipient of your card is a boarder, a basketball player, or a ballerina, silhouettes are great when your message is action.

TRENDY TIP

These funky motorcycle silhouettes add some edgy color and a tad of wicked detail for a moxie fab twist on traditional single-colored silhouettes!

1 Rad Dad Card

Designer: Alisa Bangerter

❶ Make card from cardstock.

❷ Cut rectangles of cardstock and patterned paper; adhere.

❸ Sew edges of patterned paper using zigzag and straight stitches.

❹ Ink chipboard letter; attach brads and adhere.

❺ Ink stickers; affix on cardstock to spell "Rad". Trim, mat, and adhere.

❻ Spell "Dad" with stickers. Attach brads.

U Da Bomb Frame

Designer: Betsy Veldman

❶ Cover front and sides of frame with patterned paper.

❷ Tear strip of patterned paper; adhere.

❸ Cut cycle silhouettes from patterned paper and adhere with foam tape.

❹ Apply rub-ons; affix stickers.

SUPPLIES: Cardstock: (brown, olive) Patterned paper: (Skaters from Skater collection) Karen Foster Design Dye ink: (Frayed Burlap) Ranger Industries; (Chocolate Chip) Stampin' Up! Accents: (chipboard letter) Cosmo Cricket; (bronze brads) Creative Impressions Stickers: (Smokey Joe's, Shoe Box alphabets) American Crafts **Finished size: 7" x 5"**

SUPPLIES: Patterned paper: (Word, Wack from Blur collection) Tinkering Ink Stickers: (black foam alphabet) Adorn It-Carolee's Creations Rub-ons: (circles, motorcycle, sentiment) Tinkering Ink Adhesive: (foam tape) Other: (wood frame) Provo Craft **Finished size: 8" square**

Happily Ever After Gift Bag

5 STEPS

Designer: Megan Hoeppner

❶ Cut rectangle from patterned paper. Trim piece along diamonds, flourishes, and the figure's shoes; adhere.

❷ Apply rub-on; adhere rhinestones.

❸ Punch holes at top of bag; thread and knot ribbon for handle.

TRENDY TIP

The posture of this girl speaks volumes. There is confidence in her stance. And youth in her build. There is an attractiveness to her, even though we can't see the details of her features. Yet details like the headband and the eyelashes let us know that she is as individual as they come.

Needs a Hand Card

5 STEPS

Designer: Teri Anderson

❶ Make card from cardstock.

❷ Cut rectangle of patterned paper; adhere.

❸ Adhere die cut.

❹ Print sentiment on cardstock; trim and adhere. Attach brads.

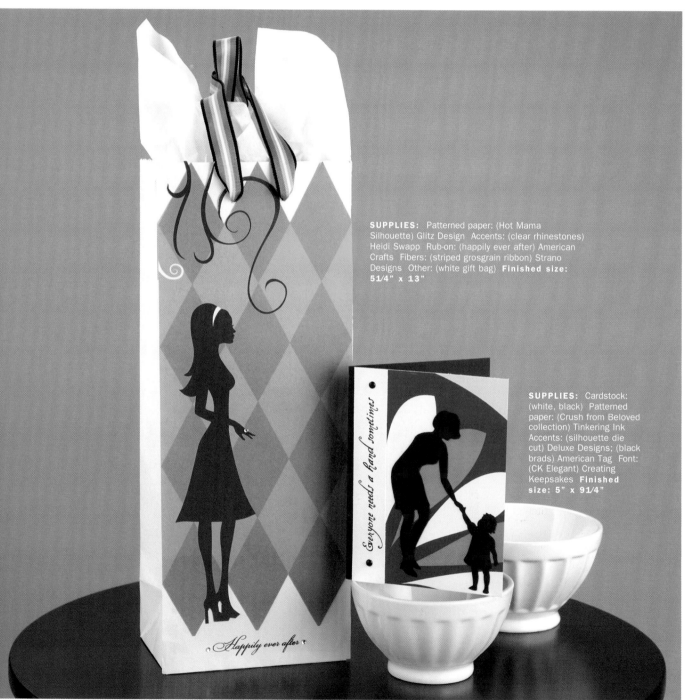

SUPPLIES: Patterned paper: (Hot Mama Silhouette) Glitz Design Accents: (clear rhinestones) Heidi Swapp Rub-on: (happily ever after) American Crafts Fibers: (striped grosgrain ribbon) Strano Designs Other: (white gift bag) **Finished size: 51/4" x 13"**

SUPPLIES: Cardstock: (white, black) Patterned paper: (Crush from Beloved collection) Tinkering Ink Accents: (silhouette die cut) Deluxe Designs; (black brads) American Tag Font: (CK Elegant) Creating Keepsakes **Finished size: 5" x 91/4"**

Happily ever after

Everyone needs a hand sometimes

What a Boy is Worth Wall Hanging

Designer: Melissa Phillips

1 Print silhouette on patterned paper; trim.

2 Print quote on vellum, trim, and stitch onto silhouette. Paint edges.

3 Paint scrolls. Let dry. Adhere behind silhouette. Tie top scroll with ribbon to create hanger.

4 Cut rectangle from patterned paper; paint edges. Adhere behind silhouette.

5 Stitch buttons with floss; adhere.

TRENDY TIP
While silhouettes can be very hip and modern, this card uses a vintage approach. Side facial profiles have been very popular in days of yore, and because silhouettes are so hot, we're seeing them in all their versatile formats.

SUPPLIES: Patterned paper: (Heartstrings from Vintage Brass collection, Café Curtains from In The Kitchen collection) We R Memory Keepers Vellum: WorldWin Paint: (Light Ivory) Delta Accents: (chipboard scrolls) Everlasting Keepsakes; (brown buttons) Creative Café Digital elements: (boy from Playtime Silhouettes collection) www.thevintageworkshop.com Fibers: (black/brown gingham ribbon) Morex; (tan floss) Fonts: (Audition, Old Type) www.twopeasinabucket.com **Finished size: 5" x 91/4"**

Surprisingly Simple Go-to Sketches

Feeling stumped? Revive your creativity by starting your design with an inspiring sketch from one of the *Paper Crafts* Go-to Gals.

Ready, Set, Sketch

Sketches are a great starting place for design. They're easy to use and all you have to do is change a few elements to create different projects for a variety of holidays, seasons, and recipients. Join Jessica Witty, this issue's Go-to Gal, and check out her fun sketches for some fabulous inspiration!

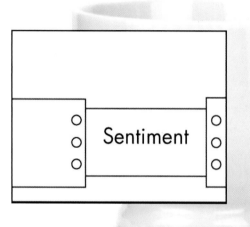

SUPPLIES: *Cardstock:* (white, kraft) Papertrey Ink *Patterned paper:* (Dishes from Nook & Pantry collection) BasicGrey *Clear stamps:* (sentiment from Damask Designs set; flourish from Vintage Labels set) Papertrey Ink *Dye ink:* (Pink Passion) Stampin' Up! *Pigment ink:* (white) Stampin' Up! *Specialty ink:* (Ocean Tides hybrid) Papertrey Ink *Accents:* (green, pink buttons) Papertrey Ink; (pink rhinestones) Kaisercraft *Fibers:* (cream twine) Papertrey Ink *Template:* (Swiss Dots embossing) Provo Craft **Finished size: 5" x 3½"**

5 STEPS Happy Birthday Card

Designer: Jessica Witty

1. Make card from cardstock. Cover with patterned paper.
2. Stamp flourish and sentiment on cardstock; adhere.
3. Emboss cardstock, ink, and adhere. Stitch edges.
4. Thread buttons with twine and adhere.
5. Adhere rhinestones.

Uniquely You Card

Designer: Kim Hughes

SUPPLIES: *Patterned paper:* (Waffles from Nook & Pantry collection) BasicGrey *Rubber stamp:* (wood grain from Artistic Windows set) Hero Arts *Pigment ink:* (Espresso) Ranger Industries *Accents:* (peach brads) Heidi Swapp *Rub-ons:* (mushrooms, bird, butterfly, sentiment) Cosmo Cricket *Sticker:* (bird label) Cosmo Cricket **Finished size: 5½" x 4¼"**

Happy Father's Day Hardware Card

Designer: Monika A. Davis

SUPPLIES: *Cardstock:* (kraft, white) Stampin' Up! *Rubber stamp:* (happy father's day from All Holidays set) Stampin' Up! *Dye ink:* (Not Quite Navy) Stampin' Up! *Other:* (self-adhesive drywall tape, metal lock washers, wire) **Finished size: 5½" x 4¼"**

Thinking of You Today Card

Designer: Sarah Martina Parker

SUPPLIES: *Cardstock:* (Blue Oasis) Bazzill Basics Paper; (Plum Pudding, white) Papertrey Ink *Patterned paper:* (Faye Needleworth from Craft Fair collection) American Crafts *Transparency sheet:* (Houndstooth) Teresa Collins Designs *Rubber stamp:* (Heart Winged Butterfly) Hero Arts *Clear stamps:* (sentiment from Everyday Classics set; tiles from Background Basics: Retro set) Papertrey Ink *Pigment ink:* (Fresh Snow) Papertrey Ink *Embossing powder:* (white) Ranger Industries *Accents:* (black buttons) Papertrey Ink; (purple rhinestones) Michaels *Fibers:* (twine ribbon) Michaels *Tool:* (corner rounder punch) EK Success **Finished size: 4¼" x 5½"**

DESIGNER TIP

It's a good idea to rub down your stamping area with an anti-static bag before applying embossing powder. This helps prevent the powder from clinging to the surface in places other than where you've stamped, giving you a cleaner image.

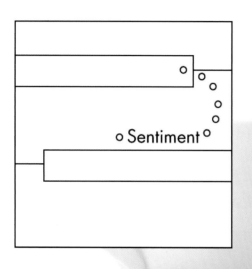

SUPPLIES: *Cardstock:* (Vintage Cream, Aqua Mist) Papertrey Ink *Patterned paper:* (yellow polka dots from 2008 Bitty Dots Basics collection) Papertrey Ink; (Mistletoe from St. Nick collection) BoBunny Press *Clear stamp:* (sentiment from Loving Words set) Technique Tuesday *Specialty ink:* (Aqua Mist hybrid) Papertrey Ink *Accents:* (silver brads) Making Memories; (white button) *Fibers:* (blue floss) DMC *Die:* (butterfly) Provo Craft *Tool:* (decorative-edge scissors) Creative Memories **Finished size: 5½" square**

Butterfly Blessing Card

Designer: Charlene Austin

1 Make card from cardstock. Adhere cardstock.

2 Attach brads to cardstock strip, adhere, and adhere patterned paper strip.

3 Trim cardstock strip with decorative-edge scissors, adhere to patterned paper strip, and adhere.

4 Stamp sentiment and stitch edges.

5 Die-cut butterfly from patterned paper and adhere.

6 Thread button with floss and adhere.

You Make Me Smile Card

Designer: Annaka Crockett

SUPPLIES: *Cardstock:* (white) Bazzill Basics Paper *Patterned paper:* (Ric Rac, Orchard from June Bug collection) BasicGrey *Accents:* (blue brads) Karen Foster Design *Rub-on:* (sentiment) Deja Views *Stickers:* (yellow border, large bird) BasicGrey *Other:* (chipboard) **Finished size: 5½" x 4½"**

Thank You Mom Card

Designer: Jessica Witty

SUPPLIES: *Cardstock:* (kraft) Papertrey Ink; (cream) Stampin' Up! *Patterned paper:* (Dishes from Nook & Pantry collection) BasicGrey *Specialty paper:* (Green/Blue Doilies die cut from Nook & Pantry collection) BasicGrey *Clear stamps:* (damask, sentiment from Damask Designs set) Papertrey Ink *Dye ink:* (Close to Cocoa) Stampin' Up! *Pigment ink:* (Vintage Cream) Papertrey Ink *Accents:* (white buttons) Papertrey Ink; (iridescent glitter) Stampin' Up! *Stickers:* (JFK alphabet) American Crafts *Fibers:* (natural twine) Papertrey Ink **Finished size: 5" square**

Birthday Treat Box

Designer: Vanessa Menhorn

SUPPLIES: *Cardstock:* (white) Papertrey Ink *Patterned paper:* (Blue Gingham, Pink Large Dot, Pink Branch from Spring Picnic collection) Jenni Bowlin Studio *Dye ink:* (Tattered Rose) Ranger Industries *Accents:* (blue button) Papertrey Ink; (pink rhinestones) BasicGrey *Rub-on:* (sentiment) Melissa Frances *Fibers:* (pink ribbon) Papertrey Ink; (pink floss) *Templates:* (Floral Screen embossing) Provo Craft; (box) Papertrey Ink *Dies:* (circle, scalloped circle, scalloped square) Spellbinders **Finished size: 3½" x 6½" x 1¾"**

DESIGNER TIP

An easy way to apply glitter to letter stickers is to pour a bit of glitter into the lid of the container, then dip the glue-coated letter into the glitter. If your container doesn't have a twist off lid, just pour a bit into a coffee filter and do the same.

Springtime Sketches

Sketches are a great starting place for design. They're easy to use and all you have to do is change a few design elements to create different cards for various holidays, seasons, and recipients. Join us as we explore the possibilities of these two sketches designed by Go-to Gal Teri Anderson.

SUPPLIES: *Cardstock:* (green, yellow, cream) Bazzill Basics Paper *Patterned paper:* (Butterfly, Stripe, Floral Stripe from Flower Patch collection) Making Memories *Dye ink:* (pink, blue, yellow) Clearsnap *Color medium:* (green gel pen) Sakura *Accents:* (pink, yellow buttons) Papertrey Ink; (blue flower) Prima; (yellow acrylic dots) The Robin's Nest; (yellow glitter glue) Ranger Industries *Fibers:* (white floss) DMC *Template:* (circle) Provo Craft *Dies:* (Reuse alphabet) QuicKutz *Tools:* (border punch) Fiskars; (decorative-edge scissors) **Finished size: 5½" square**

Happy Spring Card

Designer: Kalyn Kepner

Ink all edges.

① Make card from cardstock. Adhere patterned paper; stitch edges.

② Trim cardstock strip using decorative edge scissors; adhere to bottom.

③ Trim patterned paper strips, punch border on one, and adhere. Apply glitter glue.

④ Trim patterned paper into half-circle using template and mat with cardstock. Trim mat with decorative-edge scissors, zigzag-stitch seam, and adhere. Apply glitter glue.

⑤ Write "Happy" with gel pen. Die-cut "Spring" from cardstock and adhere.

⑥ Adhere flower and acrylic dot. Thread buttons with floss and adhere.

Baby Boy Card

Designer: Betsy Veldman

SUPPLIES: *Cardstock:* (Vintage Cream) Papertrey Ink *Patterned paper:* (Mushroom Fancy from Twitterpated collection) Imaginisce; (Peek-a-Boo from Ducks in a Row collection) October Afternoon; (Kettle from Urban Prairie collection) BasicGrey *Clear stamps:* (baby from Mega Mixed Messages set, star from Star Prints set) Papertrey Ink *Chalk ink:* (Creamy Brown) Clearsnap *Specialty ink:* (Aqua Mist, Smokey Shadow hybrid) Papertrey Ink *Accents:* (epoxy chick brad) BasicGrey; (melon buttons) Papertrey Ink; (cream cardstock border) Bazzill Basics Paper *Fibers:* (white twine) Papertrey Ink *Die:* (boy, b) Provo Craft *Tool:* (star punch) Fiskars
Finished size: 5" square

Thanks Sweetie Card

Designer: Teri Anderson

SUPPLIES: *Cardstock:* (white) WorldWin; (green) Bazzill Basics Paper *Patterned paper:* (Tea Towel from Cherry Hill collection) October Afternoon *Vellum:* WorldWin *Rubber stamps:* (thanks from Mainly Men set) A Muse Artstamps; (sweetie from The Birds and the Bees set) Cornish Heritage Farms *Dye ink:* (Tuxedo Black) Tsukineko *Accents:* (pink brads) Making Memories; (cherry, ruler die-cut) October Afternoon *Die:* (large circle) QuicKutz *Tool:* (border punch) EK Success
Finished size: 4½" square

DESIGNER TIP

Worried about brads showing inside your card? Create your card front on a separate piece of cardstock and adhere it to the card after attaching the brads. It also helps to poke holes with a paper piercer for the brads before inserting them into the card.

UR My Sunshine Card

Designer: Aly Dosdall

SUPPLIES: *Cardstock:* (Bluebell) Core'dinations *Patterned paper:* (Pink Wildflowers, Spiro Art, Ribbon Stripes from Duck Pond collection) Black River Designs *Accents:* (orange, red felt flowers; white journaling tag) Jillibean Soup; (blue, red, green buttons) The Paper Studio *Rub-ons:* (Alphas #1 alphabet) Black River Designs; (Midnight Kisses alphabet) Heidi Grace Designs *Fibers:* (red rickrack) Jillibean Soup *Tools:* (border punch) Fiskars; (circle cutter) EK Success **Finished size: 6" square**

DESIGNER TIP

Rather than cut out the sun rays by hand, save time by trimming the petals off your extra felt flowers.

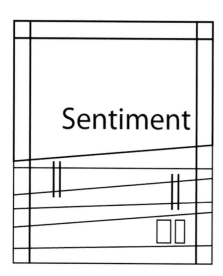

Sentiment

SUPPLIES: *Cardstock:* (white) WorldWin; (gray) *Patterned paper:* (Sunday Brunch, Breeze, Pavilion, Garden Tour, Tennis Court from Bridgeport collection) SEI *Accents:* (silver staples) *Stickers:* (Prudence alphabet) Crate Paper **Finished size: 4½" x 5½"**

5 STEPS Congrats Card

Designer: Teri Anderson

❶ Make card from cardstock. Cover with patterned paper.

❷ Trim patterned paper strips; adhere.

❸ Affix stickers to spell "Congrats".

❹ Trim two small rectangles from patterned paper, mat with cardstock, and adhere.

❺ Attach staples.

DESIGNER TIPS

To draw the viewer's eye toward the image, add a row of brads.

To add complexity and detail, paper piece images and stack using foam tape.

Sweetest Thing Card

Designer: Ryann Salamon

SUPPLIES: Cardstock: (Sahara Sand) Stampin'
Up! Patterned paper: (Something Old from
Everafter collection) Cosmo Cricket Accents:
(white, black buttons) BasicGrey Rub-on:
(sentiment) Stampin' Up! Fibers: (yellow floss)
Bazzill Basics Paper
Finished size: 4¼" x 5½"

Sending Love Card

Designer: AJ Otto

SUPPLIES: Cardstock: (white) Neenah
Paper Patterned paper: (Super Stack from
Monstrosity collection) Sassafras Lass Rubber
stamp: (sentiment from Sending My Love set)
Unity Stamp Co. Specialty ink: (Summer
Sunrise hybrid) Papertrey Ink Color medium:
(Certainly Celery marker) Stampin' Up!
Accents: (square orange rhinestones) Glitz
Design; (silver staples)
Finished size: 4¼" x 5½"

Friends Card

Designer: Stephanie Muzzulin

SUPPLIES: Cardstock: (white) Papertrey
Ink Patterned paper: (Multistripe, Vine Dot,
Brocade from Just Chillin: Girl collection)
Making Memories Accents: (silver pearls)
Michaels; (friends, stars die cuts) Making
Memories; (silver staples)
Finished size: 4½" x 5½"

DESIGNER TIP

The sentiment rub-on comes from the
Eastern Elegance set by Stampin' Up!,
which is a retired item. A comparable
substitute for this rub-on can be found in the
Wedding Words set, also by Stampin' Up!

Inspirational Sketches

Sketches are a great "go-to" resource when you're designing a project. They're easy to use and all you have to do is change a few elements to create different cards for various holidays, seasons, and recipients. Join us as we explore the possibilities of these two sketches designed by Go-to Gal Maren Benedict.

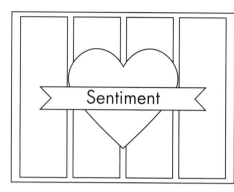

SUPPLIES: *Cardstock:* (white, beige) Bazzill Basics Paper *Patterned paper:* (Kate, Julie, Lindsay, Chelsey) Melissa Frances *Dye ink:* (Vintage Photo) Ranger Industries *Paint:* (Antique White) Delta *Accents:* (chipboard heart negative) Heidi Swapp; (sentiment banner die cut) K&Company; (white glitter) Martha Stewart Crafts; (red flower) Making Memories; (blue brad) **Finished size:** 5" x 4½"

Hugs & Kisses Card

Designer: Beatriz Jennings

❶ Make card from cardstock. Ink edges.

❷ Trim cardstock; paint edges and adhere.

❸ Trim patterned paper strips, ink edges, and adhere. Zigzag-stitch.

❹ Ink chipboard heart negative edges, cover with glitter, and adhere.

❺ Adhere banner die cut.

❻ Fasten brad to flower and adhere.

Beautiful Card

Designer: Betsy Veldman

SUPPLIES: *Cardstock:* (black, white) Papertrey Ink *Patterned paper:* (Farrow, Streisand from Tiffany's collection) We R Memory Keepers *Chalk ink:* (Creamy Brown) Clearsnap *Paint:* (white) Delta *Accents:* (pink buttons) Papertrey Ink; (clear rhinestones) Zva Creative; (chipboard butterfly) Scenic Route; (white glitter) Doodlebug Design *Rub-on:* (beautiful) American Crafts *Fibers:* (light blue, light green, pink, yellow ribbon; cream twine) Papertrey Ink **Finished size: 5½" square**

I Love You Card

Designer: Deb Rymer

SUPPLIES: *Cardstock:* (Pure Poppy, white) Papertrey Ink *Patterned paper:* (swirls, polka dots, dashed lines, retro wood grain from Black & White Basics collection) Papertrey Ink *Clear stamp:* (flourish from Fantastic Flourishes set) Hero Arts *Watermark ink:* (clear) Tsukineko *Embossing powder:* (clear) Hampton Art *Accents:* (red epoxy dots) The Robin's Nest *Fibers:* (black love ribbon) Making Memories **Finished size: 5½" x 4¼"**

Bold Thanks Card

Designer: Maren Benedict

SUPPLIES: *Cardstock:* (black) Papertrey Ink *Patterned paper:* (Ticket to Freedom, Dream Big from Anthem collection) Sassafras Lass *Clear stamp:* (thank you from Jack's World set) Cosmo Cricket *Dye ink:* (Black Soot) Ranger Industries *Accent:* (chipboard heart) Cosmo Cricket *Fibers:* (black stitched ribbon) Papertrey Ink **Finished size: 5½" x 4¼"**

BONUS IDEA

Looking for more ways to stretch this sketch? Use a pink palette and rhinestones for a fun teen card, or use vellum and pearls for an elegant wedding card.

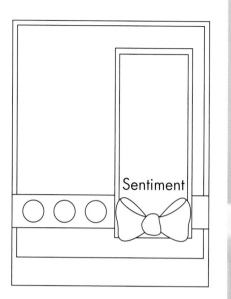

SUPPLIES: *Cardstock:* (white) Papertrey Ink *Patterned paper:* (Cosmos, Mimosa, Guava, Mango from Mimosa collection) SEI *Rubber stamps:* (happy birthday from Everyday Sayings set) Lizzie Anne Designs; (ice cream cone from Perfect in Every Way set) Unity Stamp Co. *Dye ink:* (Rich Cocoa) Tsukineko *Color medium:* (light, medium brown markers) Copic *Accents:* (white brads) American Crafts *Fibers:* (pink ribbon) Papertrey Ink **Finished size: 4¼" x 5½"**

Sweet Birthday Card

Designer: Maren Benedict

❶ Make card from cardstock. Adhere patterned paper.

❷ Attach brads to strip of patterned paper; adhere.

❸ Stamp sentiment on cardstock panel. Tie on ribbon.

❹ Stamp ice cream cone on cardstock and patterned papers.

❺ Trim pieces. Adhere scoops and cherry together. Color cone and adhere scoops with foam tape.

❻ Adhere cone to panel with foam tape. Adhere to card with foam tape.

DESIGNER TIPS

To draw the viewer's eye toward the image, add a row of brads.

To add complexity and detail, paper piece images and stack using foam tape.

Tea Time Card

Designer: Angela Robledo

SUPPLIES: *Cardstock:* (Vintage Cream) Papertrey Ink *Patterned paper:* (pink floral, simple tan from McKenna pad) K&Company; (Gilbert) Melissa Frances *Clear stamps:* (teapot, tea time, friend from Tea for Two set) Papertrey Ink *Solvent ink:* (brown) Tsukineko *Walnut ink:* (spray) Tsukineko *Paint:* (white) Making Memories *Accents:* (cream buttons) *Fibers:* (olive ribbon) May Arts; (twine) *Tool:* (decorative edge punch) Fiskars
Finished size: 4¼" x 5½"

All You Need is Love Card

Designer: Rae Barthel

SUPPLIES: *Cardstock:* (dark brown) Hobby Lobby *Patterned paper:* (Belgian, Blushing Pink, Brittle, Essence from Bittersweet collection) BasicGrey *Rubber stamp:* (All You Need is Love) Hampton Art *Accents:* (white pearls) Zva Creative *Fibers:* (pink polka dot ribbon) American Crafts
Finished size: 4" x 6"

Enjoy Life Card

Designer: Betsy Veldman

SUPPLIES: *Cardstock:* (Dark Chocolate) Papertrey Ink *Patterned paper:* (Wonderful from Enchanting collection) Pink Paislee; (Delaney Die-Cut Circle Flower from Noteworthy collection) Making Memories; (Flutterby from Feather Your Nest collection) Webster's Pages; (Winding Vine from Admire collection) My Mind's Eye *Clear stamp:* (sentiment from Star Prints set) Papertrey Ink *Chalk ink:* (Creamy Brown) Clearsnap *Specialty ink:* (Dark Chocolate hybrid) Papertrey Ink *Accents:* (white pearls) Zva Creative *Fibers:* (green ribbon) Papertrey Ink *Tool:* (decorative-edge scissors) Provo Craft
Finished size: 4¼" x 5½"

Paper Crafts 101: Tips & Tricks

Peruse this gallery of techniques before beginning your next crafting project. You'll be glad you did!

Fun with Floss

Embroidery floss is one of the most versatile supplies in your crafting stash. Available in nearly every color imaginable, floss can go far beyond threading buttons and tying around cards. Take a look at *Go-to Gal* Kim Hughes' nine amazing ways to embellish your projects with this wonderful fiber.

Stitch a design, anything from shapes to words.

Adhere floss directly to cardstock to **create a flat accent.**

Create a flower by looping floss.

Accentuate floss strands with beads.

Overlap strands to **create a plaid background.**

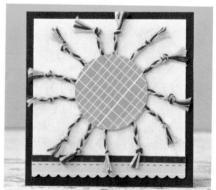

Braid floss for textured sun rays or even bird legs.

Ink floss and press on cardstock for one-of-a-kind stamps.

Create lacing with floss and a paper piercer.

Add stiffener **to form a unique hard floss accent.**

SUPPLIES: *Cardstock:* (French Roast) Core'dinations *Patterned paper:* (Wild Berry Red Dot from Double Dot collection) BoBunny Press; (Dancing Daisies from Plie collection) My Mind's Eye; (Sunday, Monday from Girl Friday collection) Cosmo Cricket *Accent:* (green button) Autumn Leaves *Fibers:* (brown, pink floss) DMC *Tool:* (decorative-edge scissors) Fiskars **Finished size: 5¼" x 3¾"**

SUPPLIES: *Cardstock:* (French Roast) Core'dinations *Patterned paper:* (Wild Berry Red Dot from Double Dot collection) BoBunny Press; (Rain from Blue Hill collection) Crate Paper; (Sunday, Monday from Girl Friday collection) Cosmo Cricket *Accent:* (cream button) Autumn Leaves *Rub-on:* (just because) American Crafts *Fibers:* (brown, green, red, cream floss) DMC *Tools:* (decorative-edge scissors) Fiskars; (⅛" circle punch) **Finished size: 5" square**

Stitched Love Card

Designer: Kim Hughes

❶ Make card from cardstock.

❷ Cut patterned paper rectangle, mat with patterned paper, and adhere.

❸ Write "Love" lightly in pencil on patterned paper and pierce along lines; erase pencil marks. Stitch with floss and adhere piece to card.

❹ Trim patterned paper strip with decorative-edge scissors; adhere. Trim heart from patterned paper and adhere.

❺ Thread button with floss; knot. Cut eight strips of floss, loop, and adhere behind button. Adhere to card.

Just Because Card

Designer: Kim Hughes

❶ Make card from cardstock.

❷ Adhere patterned paper.

❸ Cut patterned paper square. Adhere lengths of floss to create plaid pattern.

❹ Trim strip of patterned paper with decorative-edge scissors; adhere to square. Adhere square to card.

❺ Cut tag from patterned paper. Draw flower shape on back of tag; stitch with floss.

❻ Apply rub-on. Punch top of tag, tie on floss, and adhere to card.

DESIGNER TIP

Print the word you wish to stitch on the reverse side of your paper if you're not comfortable with your handwriting.

DESIGNER TIP

Trace a small chipboard flower to make a perfect flower pattern.

SUPPLIES: *Patterned paper:* (Monday from Girl Friday collection) Cosmo Cricket *Transparency sheet;* *Paint:* (Blank Canvas, Traditional Tan) Ranger Industries *Accents:* (brown brads) Bazzill Basics Paper *Fibers:* (green, red, pink floss) DMC *Tool:* (1/8" circle punch) *Other:* (white box) Innovative Stamp Creations **Finished size: 2¾" x 4" x¾"**

XOXO Heart Box

Designer: Kim Hughes

❶ Blend paint colors together and paint box.

❷ Cut heart window from box front. Adhere floss around edge. Adhere transparency sheet behind window.

❸ Stitch around box front with floss. Adhere patterned paper strip.

❹ Stitch "X" with floss three times on box lid. Attach brads.

❺ Braid floss. Punch side of lid and tie on braid.

DESIGNER TIP

Hand-stitching is easier when holes have already been pierced. For evenly spaced holes, run your paper through a sewing machine without thread.

Stunning Machine & Faux Stitching

Whether you are attaching ribbon, creating a pocket, or giving the illusion of a dimensional border, Wendy Sue Anderson shows you how versatile machine and faux stitching can be.

FAUX-STITCH WITH RUB-ONS. Stitch rub-ons are easy to use, come in several designs and colors, and won't add bulk to your prized project.

FAUX-STITCH WITH A WHITE PEN. Create a stitched look by paper piercing holes and then connecting them with lines drawn with a white pen.

FAUX-STITCH WITH A STAMP. Stamp stitched borders, squares, and circles with perfect spacing in the blink of an eye.

MACHINE-STITCH TO ATTACH RIBBON. Attach your ribbon and trims with strong and secure machine stitching.

MACHINE-STITCH TO ATTACH A TRANSPARENCY. Machine-stitch transparencies for a secure, atractive way to fasten them.

MACHINE-STITCH TO CREATE JOURNALING LINES. Put emphasis on your heartfelt sentiments by creating journaling lines with machine stitching.

MACHINE-STITCH TO CREATE FREESTYLE SHAPES. Machine-stitch random and freestyle designs for a doodled look.

MACHINE-STITCH AND COLOR THREAD WITH CHALK. Achieve a spectrum look without constantly changing your thread. Stitch lines with a neutral thread and color sections with different shades of chalk.

MACHINE-STITCH TO CREATE A POCKET. Create an interactive project by machine-stitching a pocket, perfect for a sentiment, photo, or gift card.

Button Up

Buttons are a great way to add dimension, color, and fun. Melissa Phillips reveals a variety of creative uses for buttons on any project.

FILL A SHAPE. Use buttons of different sizes, colors, and textures to fill any shape.

CREATE A FLOWER. Adhere buttons to create the petals and center of a flower.

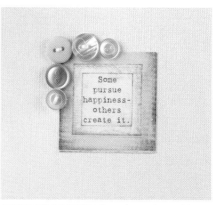

DECORATE A CORNER. Accent an element by adding a button photo corner. For a more homespun look, thread the buttons before adhering them.

FASHION A FLOWER CENTER. Add a button to create the center of a flower.

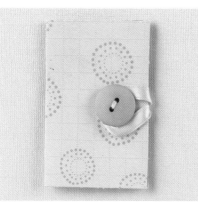

MAKE A CLOSURE. Combine a button with ribbon for a fun and functional closure.

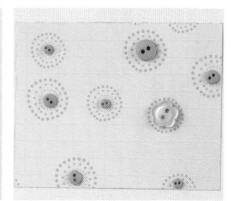

ACCENT PATTERNED PAPER. Spice up patterned paper by adding buttons of different sizes, shapes, and colors.

TIE WITH DIFFERENT FIBERS. Tie buttons with various fibers for a unique touch.

STACK. Stack buttons to create dimension.

STRING TOGETHER. Thread buttons together to create a unique border or a fun focal point.

Trendy Trims

Discover the versatility of trims as Melissa Phillips reveals inventive ways to incorporate these fun fibers into your projects.

COVER CHIPBOARD. Wrap wide lace or other trim around chipboard shapes to create delicate accents.

CREATE LETTERS. Combine various types of trims to spell sentiments and titles. For best results, make large letters so the trims take center stage.

FASHION A DECORATIVE EDGE. Adhere rickrack, pom-poms, or other trims for decorative edges that are both fun to look at and to feel.

COVER A BUTTON. Add additional color and texture to buttons by covering them with bold-colored trims. Select trims with loose weaves so some of the button still shows through.

BUILD A FRAME. Frame sentiments, photos, and accents with a mixture of assorted trims for an eclectic look.

MAKE TABS. Create quick and easy tabs by looping trims and adhering them to the edges of mini albums or cards. Fasten them with staples or brads for a finishing touch.

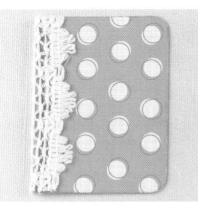

CREATE A BINDING. Bind mini books, cards, or tags with lace trim. Make sure you match the color of your trim to your patterned paper to make your design more uniform.

FORM A FLOURISH. Adhere delicate trims to cardstock or chipboard to create one-of-a-kind flourishes. To ensure the longevity of the flourish, use a heavy-duty adhesive.

MAKE A FLOWER. Loop and layer multiple trims to make a 3-D flower that is perfect for cards, gift bags, or tags.

A Rainbow of Ribbon

Nichol Magouirk shows us that ribbon is no longer just for tying pretty bows. From creating decorative fringes to weaving, explore the creative possibilities of this paper crafting staple.

GATHER AND SHAPE. Make one-of-a-kind shapes by gathering grosgrain ribbon and adhering it to your paper-crafted projects.

MAKE FLOWER LOOPS. Create a whimsical flower by looping lengths of ribbon and adhering them to and around a button or chipboard accent.

WEAVE. Weave two contrasting ribbons for a background that's ideal for cards or home décor items.

CREATE A TAB. Fold a coordinating ribbon over a tag and secure it with a brad or eyelet for a fashionable and functional tab.

FASHION FRINGE. Combine an assortment of ribbon to create a funky fringe. Adhere only the top of each ribbon length to give the completed fringe movement.

STAMP. Stamp sentiments and simple shapes on grosgrain ribbon for a textured look.

WRAP A FRAME. Wrap ribbon around a chipboard or metal frame, adhering as you go.

LAYER TO MAKE A TAG. Adhere layered ribbon to cardstock and place in a metal frame.

FORM FLOWER STEMS. Discover an entire garden of unique flowers by combining epoxy or acetate flowers with ribbon stems. Also, try fastening ribbon loops with brads to create leaves.

Totally Typography

Typography, the art and technique of printing with movable type, has been around for centuries. But today, this time-honored tradition is taking on a whole new life as it's used to create shapes, accents, and patterned paper. Learn how die cut letters, computer fonts, and much more can be transformed into truly terrific typographic creations.

Designer: Susan Neal

MONOGRAM

Make a monogram a major design element.

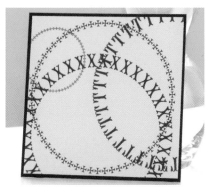

CIRCLE

Use a letter and your software's Word Art tool to make circles.

COLLAGE

Combine die cut letters, numbers, and punctuation to form a collage.

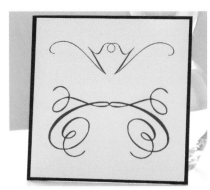

MIRROR

Flip script letters (in this case a V and a C) for a perfectly mirrored image.

SHAPE

Die-cut and combine letters to create familiar shapes.

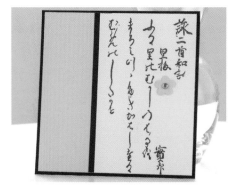

FOREIGN SYMBOLS

Stamp a vertical pattern with foreign symbols.

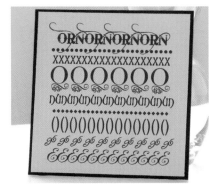

REPEAT

Duplicate punctuation, letters, and numbers to create one-of-a-kind designs.

PARTIAL MONOGRAM

Designate a focal point by isolating part of an oversized monogram (in this case an S).

TEXT BLOCKS

Digitally create and combine text blocks for a fashionable background.

Delightful Doodling

Nichol Magouirk shows off her carefree, creative streak as she doodles by hand, with stamps, via sewing machine, and on or around existing product. With no boundaries, the doodling possibilities are endless.

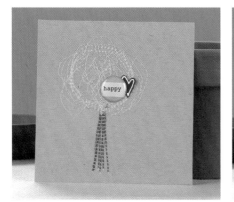

MACHINE-STITCH DOODLE. Use your sewing machine to create freestyle designs like a doodled tree.

HAND-STITCH DOODLE. Hand-stitch basic doodle shapes and then branch out with shapes like a winged heart.

STAMP & LAYER DOODLES. Stamp a doodle on multiple pieces of patterned paper and then layer the pieces to create a colorful mix of doodled fun.

DIGITALLY DOODLE. Manipulate doodley fonts and graphics for playful sentiment squares or titles.

ADD DOODLES TO DOODLED PRODUCTS. Add your own unique touch to commercially available doodled product by doodling on or around existing designs.

DOODLE ON FRAMES & BUTTONS. Doctor up trendy frames and buttons with your own doodling flair by using your favorite pens and markers.

DOODLE ON CHIPBOARD. Make your chipboard come alive with painted or hand-drawn doodling.

DOODLE AROUND STAMPED IMAGES. Let your imagination take over as you add your own doodling to stamped images.

DOODLE ON PHOTOS. Accent your favorite photos with doodling that can be drawn, stamped, or rubbed on.

Dreamy Digital Effects

Paper crafting is going high-tech! Celeste Rockwood-Jones shows how to add digital stamps, patterned paper, and other embellishments to the powerful text and photo editing options of your favorite software. With digital elements, ultra-cool effects are only a mouse click away.

CURVE TEXT. Text doesn't have to follow a straight line. Adjust text to follow a curved line and turn a sentiment into a design element.

BRUSH A PHOTO. With digital stamps called brushes, you can play with the color, position, size, and more—and wait to print until the effect is perfect.

LAYER TEXT. Do something special with a sentiment or quote by layering words. Change the color, font, size, and opacity of background text to create gorgeous embellishments.

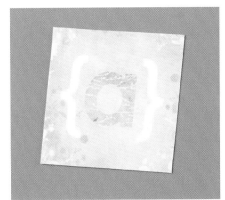

CUSTOMIZE LETTERS. Try applying digital rub-ons, brush effects, or patterns to create a truly unique monogram for your project.

CREATE A FRAME. Apply digital brushes to surround sentiments with a custom frame. Adjust the overall color of brushed images, or fill parts of the images with color for a perfectly coordinated embellishment.

MAKE A TEXT BORDER. Use a photo or frame as your focal point and bend the sentiment text around the edges as an attention-grabbing border.

ADD TEXT TO A PHOTO. Make the caption or sentiment a part of the photo by positioning text right in the picture. For a perfect color match, pick up a color in the photo and use it to color the text.

BRUSH PATTERNED PAPER. Use digital patterned paper and apply brushes to add an ideal accent. Adjust colors and opacity to mimic ink-and-paper stamping, without the mess.

ADD TEXTURE WITH BRUSHES. Digital brushes applied along the edges of a photo can add detail and interest, as well as create an aged or distressed look.

Stylish Sticker Designs

Alice Golden shows you the latest techniques for making the most of your stickers, including creating shadows, adding dimension, and more.

LAYER TO CREATE DIMENSION. Layer stickers with foam tape to add dimension to your designs.

CREATE A SHADOW. Affix two layers of different colored stickers (one layer slightly to the right) to create a shadow.

DOODLE DESIGNS. Add more depth and character to stickers by doodling around them.

ADD COLOR. Apply different colors of ink to stickers for a vibrant watercolor-like design.

USE AS A STENCIL. Mask paper with stickers, ink, and remove for a fun stenciled look.

MAKE PATTERNED PAPER. Design your own patterned paper by affixing stickers of multiple sizes and colors to cardstock.

DESIGN IMAGES. Use similar or different stickers to create images such as flowers, birds, etc.

ACCENT WITH STITCHING. Accentuate stickers by straight-stitching or zigzag-stitching on them.

STAMP ON DESIGNS. Give your stickers an artistic look by using rubber or clear stamps and different-colored ink to stamp designs on them.

Rockin' Rub-ons

Rub-ons have quickly become a necessity in the paper crafting world, as they adhere to just about anything and come in a multitude of designs. Try Dee Gallimore-Perry's easy tips for making them count.

ADORN WITH RHINESTONES. Add rhinestones or bling to rub-ons to make images really sparkle and shine.

APPLY TO BRADS. Make a bold statement by applying letters or image rub-ons to either large or small brads.

EMBELLISH CHIPBOARD. Dress up otherwise plain chipboard with a rub-on. To make the application easier, apply the rub-on to the chipboard before adhering it to your project.

CREATE PATTERNED PAPER. Apply rub-ons to coordinating cardstock to create custom patterned paper.

DRESS UP PATTERNED PAPER. Don't be afraid to apply rub-ons to patterned paper. Seeing the pattern peek through only adds to the charm of the rub-on.

ENHANCE PHOTOS. Add rub-ons to photos to tell a story in just a word or two. However, don't rub too hard or you may damage the photo.

ADD COLOR TO RUB-ONS. Use colored pencils and/or chalk to add color to rub-ons.

CREATE YOUR OWN DESIGN. Turn a sentiment sideways, and use the words themselves as part of your design. Add additional rub-ons to complete the image.

ACCENT WITH FLOWERS. Layer flowers over rub-ons or off to the side for more artistic flare.

Get Punchy with Punches

Discover the versatility of your paper punches. Whether you're punching materials like felt and vellum, or using simple circle punches to create background paper, the paper punching possibilities are virtually endless.

Designer: Wendy Johnson

CREATE 3-D IMAGES.

Punch paper, then curl the edges of the punched image for a three-dimensional effect.

PUNCH A BACKGROUND.

Use simple punches such as circles to make your own background designs.

COMBINE PUNCHES TO CREATE A MOTIF.

Combine different sized punches to create butterflies, flowers, or other basic designs.

LAYER PUNCHES TO CREATE A BORDER.

Layer different sized punches either horizontally or vertically for a designer-looking border.

ADD DEPTH TO PUNCHED DESIGNS WITH PATTERNED PAPER.

Adhere different paper behind punched images to give them a splash of color and more depth.

FILL A PUNCHED POCKET WITH PUNCHES.

Use an envelope punch to make a pocket to hold and display smaller punched elements.

STAMP AND PUNCH IMAGES.

Use a stamp set that comes with perfectly coordinating punches to stamp and punch shapes such as flowers, hearts, and more.

PUNCH DIFFERENT MEDIUMS.

Punch and layer paper, vellum, felt, and other paper crafting product for a multi-textured look.

FILL A SHAKER WITH PUNCHES.

Fill a shaker with basic circle punches or other shaped punches for a fun and interactive element.

Floral Just Because Card

1 Make card from cardstock; adhere patterned paper, reverse side up.

2 Mat strip of patterned paper with cardstock, trim with decorative-edge scissors, and adhere.

3 Apply rub-ons.

4 Stamp flowers on cardstock; punch. Affix stickers, adhere glitter, and adhere with foam tape.

SUPPLIES: *Cardstock:* (white) *Patterned paper:* (Garden Dots) Chatterbox; (Décor Stripe from Moonlight Meadow collection) Heidi Grace Designs *Rubber stamps:* (flowers from Looks Like Spring set) Stampin' Up! *Dye ink:* (Old Olive) Stampin' Up! *Accent:* (clear glitter) Ranger Industries *Rub-ons:* (just because, flourishes) American Crafts *Stickers:* (blue, teal circles) Heidi Grace Designs *Adhesive:* (foam tape) *Tools:* (flower punches) Stampin' Up!; (decorative-edge scissors) **Finished size: 4" square**

SUPPLIES: *Cardstock:* (white, light pink, medium pink, blue) *Patterned paper:* (Moonlight Flowers, Moon Song, Paisley from Moonlight Meadow collection) Heidi Grace Designs *Accents:* (pink brads) Happy Hammer *Rub-ons:* (pink flourish) Heidi Grace Designs; (Simply Sweet alphabet) Doodlebug Design *Sticker:* (floral bookplate) Heidi Grace Designs *Fonts:* (OttumHmk) www.fonts101.com; (Teen) www.dafont.com *Adhesive:* (foam tape) *Tools:* (envelope punch) McGill; (decorative-edge scissors; circle, heart punches) **Finished size: 5¼" x 4¼"**

Happy Mother's Day Card

1 Make card from cardstock; adhere patterned paper reverse side up.

2 Print "Happy" on reverse side of patterned paper. Trim printed piece and cardstock with decorative-edge scissors; adhere.

3 Apply flourish rub-on.

4 Punch envelope from reverse side of patterned paper, adhere cardstock to top flap, and adhere bottom flaps closed.

5 Adhere envelope. Punch hearts from cardstock; adhere.

6 Print "Mother's" on cardstock. Trim and adhere behind bookplate sticker. Attach brads and adhere with foam tape.

7 Punch circles from patterned paper, apply rub-ons to spell "Day", and adhere.

Love of Learning Tag

❶ Print sentiment on cardstock, trim into tag shape, and chalk edges.

❷ Punch sunflower from tag; adhere cardstock and patterned paper behind punched image.

❸ Adhere patterned paper strip, reverse side up, to create stem.

❹ Punch leaves from reverse side of patterned paper; chalk and curl edges, and adhere.

❺ Trim reverse side of patterned paper to create grass. Chalk edges and adhere.

❻ Punch hole through tag top and tie ribbon.

SUPPLIES: *Cardstock:* (teal, yellow) *Patterned paper:* (Garden Dots) Chatterbox; (Moonlight Flowers from Moonlight Meadow collection) Heidi Grace Designs *Color medium:* (green, blue chalk) Pebbles Inc. *Fibers:* (salmon grosgrain ribbon) American Crafts *Font:* (CluffHmk) www.fonts101.com *Tools:* (sunflower punch) McGill; (leaf punch) EK Success **Finished size: 3" x 5"**

Perfect Paper Piecing

Looking for a way to make your projects unique? Try paper piecing! This easy technique lets you add detail to stamped images, punch up focal points, and create just the right combination of patterns and colors on any project. Check out the nine inventive ways our Go-to Gal Betsy Veldman came up with to put paper piecing to work.

Use punches to create a flower.

Fussy-cut motifs from patterned paper to create a design.

Stamp images on multiple papers, then piece together.

Create a scene with punched and hand-cut pieces.

Piece a background with blocks of patterned paper.

Print downloadable coloring pages on several patterned papers, then piece the scene.

Cut apart punched shapes then piece together for a folk art look.

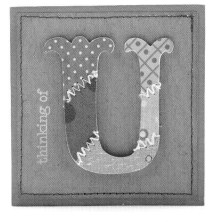

Create unique monograms by piecing on chipboard.

Die-cut the same image on different papers, then cut and piece together.

Finding the Fun in Fussy-Cutting

Fussy cutting is the act of making elaborate hand cuts to create a design. Whether you cut out a motif, a portion of a design, or create an image from your own technical cuts, fussy-cutting is all about creating something new from the original. Take a look at Kim Kesti's approach to fussy-cutting and let the inspiration begin!

CUT MOTIF AND POP. Cut out your favorite image from a piece of patterned paper and pop it with foam tape.

CUT AN EDGE TO CREATE A BORDER. Cut along the edge of a design and place a contrasting color behind it to create a border.

CUT FROM ONE PATTERNED PAPER AND LAYER ONTO ANOTHER. Layer cuts from a different patterned paper to create a new, unique design.

CREATE AN APPLIQUÉ BY REPEATING A MOTIF. Create a quilted look by cutting out a motif multiple times and arranging it in a geometric pattern.

ADD DIMENSION BY LAYERING IDENTICAL CUTS. Make an image appear 3-D by cutting out an image and layering it on top of itself with foam tape.

CREATE A SHADOW. After cutting out an image, place a contrasting color behind while moving the original image to the left or right, creating a shadow effect.

CUT OUT WHITE SPACE AND LAYER OVER A PATTERN. Cutting away the white space enables you to put a funky pattern or contrasting color behind, creating something altogether new and different.

CREATE A SILHOUETTE. Convey attitude and movement by creating your own silhouettes.

CUT A FRAME. Create a frame by cutting a shape that appeals to you.

Divine Die-Cut Designs

These days, just about anything can be die-cut, and there are oodles of attractive designs to choose from. With designer Nichol Magouirk's ideas for die-cutting a variety of different mediums and creating unique shapes, you'll fall in love with this longstanding technique all over again.

FELT. Create one-of-a-kind felt shapes in a number of different colors with your favorite dies.

VINYL. Make anything from cards to home décor with this appealing medium.

FABRIC. Add texture by die-cutting your favorite images from scraps of fabric.

RIBBON. Apply ribbon stiffener to ribbon and die-cut for colorful results that won't fray.

MAGNET. Create attractive embellishments with die-cut magnets. They will accentuate your paper crafts and give recipients extra keepsakes to remove from cards or gifts.

CHIPBOARD. Make your own chipboard accents. Check to see if your die cut machine will cut through chipboard before you begin, as all tools are different.

FOIL. Make your projects shine by die-cutting images from metal or foil.

TRANSPARENCY. Layer die-cut transparency sheets over a solid color for a slick finish.

LAYER. Select two shapes in different sizes, die-cut, and layer for decorative dimension.

Cheers to Chipboard

You can paint it, stamp it, stitch it, and more! Stefanie Hamilton shares her love of chipboard, and the many ways to use this popular paper crafting product.

CREATE A FAUX FINISH. Coat chipboard accents with a faux stone finish by applying multiple layers of texturing medium.

APPLY RUB-ONS. Apply rub-ons in a contrasting color to transform any chipboard accent into an instant journaling block or title.

ADD GLITTER. Make chipboard sparkle with glitter.

STAMP AND EMBOSS. Add sophistication and texture to chipboard by stamping and embossing a decorative image.

COVER WITH PATTERNED PAPER. Adhere your favorite patterned paper to chipboard to make accents that perfectly match your paper projects.

ATTACH EYELETS. Add eyelets to your chipboard shapes to add detail.

STITCH. Machine-stitch thinner chipboard shapes for a homespun, doodled look.

COVER WITH RIBBON. Adhere strips of ribbon to your chipboard pieces for custom, cozy accents.

EMBOSS. Emboss and ink plain chipboard to create unique impressions and textures.

Eyelets & Grommets

Adding just a few little eyelets or a not-so-little grommet to your project will leave it looking refined and delightful. And, as Wendy Sue Anderson demonstrates, these little guys have a practical and functional purpose, too.

REINFORCE A TAG. An eyelet not only gives this accent a finished look, but also helps keep the tag from tearing when ribbon is threaded through the hole.

CREATE BULLET POINTS. Use eyelets in place of bullet points in a list to draw attention to your words.

MAKE SHAPES. Use eyelets to create a simple shape. First draw a shape lightly with a pencil, then mark where each eyelet will go. This will ensure even spacing as you attach the eyelets.

ATTACH TRANSPARENCIES. Eyelets are great for attaching overlays and transparencies without adhesive showing through, as well as attaching vellum or any other sheer material.

CREATE A CLOSURE. Use eyelets and a bit of string to make a cute and simple closure. Simply line up the eyelets directly across from each other and tie them together.

ADORN A FLOWER CENTER. Add a hint of color to paper flowers by replacing the flower centers with eyelets.

EMBELLISH SCALLOPS. Scallops are always lovely, but adding eyelets to scallops really jazzes them up!

USE IN PLACE OF LETTERS OR NUMBERS. Use a grommet in place of letters in a word. The letter "O" and the number "zero" may be obvious choices, but also try replacing the bottom of a lower case "b", the dot over an "i", or others.

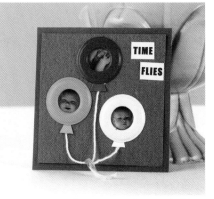

FRAME PHOTOS. Grommets make wonderful picture frames. They can also be used to create balloons, bicycle wheels, balls, and other shapes.

Creating Texture Naturally

What could be more earth-friendly—and inexpensive—than using natural objects to add beauty and unique textures to your crafting projects? *Paper Crafts* Pro Alisa Bangerter came up with nine beautiful examples of ways to stamp, mask, and add texture using natural items from leaves to salt. Her projects are sure to give you a boost of all-natural inspiration.

Stamp using an apple and dye ink.

Paint a leaf with acrylic paint and stamp.

Spray twigs with dye ink and stamp.

Use fern stem as a mask and spray with dye ink.

Mask dark cardstock with leaves and spray with bleach.

Apply watermark ink and embossing powder around a pine mask and heat emboss.

Wrap a brayer with raffia, ink, and apply.

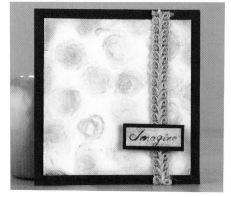

Create natural color and texture by rubbing cardstock with leaves.

Brush on color wash, add salt, and brush off when dry.

Enjoy Card

Designer: Alisa Bangerter

❶ Make card from cardstock.

❷ Cut slightly smaller cardstock piece. Place leaf over fingertip and rub piece, making circles. Stitch piece to card.

❸ Adhere patterned paper and cardstock strips. Adhere ribbon.

❹ Punch circle from cardstock; stitch. Mat with punched cardstock scalloped circle; adhere, ink edges, and adhere.

❺ Spell "Enjoy" with stickers.

❻ Ink brad; emboss. Attach to flower and adhere.

BONUS IDEA

Try rubbing different colors from flowers and other vegetation.

⑤ Thanks Card

Designer: Alisa Bangerter

❶ Make card from cardstock. Tear cardstock strip; distress edges and adhere.

❷ Cut piece of cardstock. Mask with fern stem and spray with Amaretto ink; let dry. Remove mask.

❸ Spray piece with shimmer spray; let dry. Adhere.

❹ Attach brads. Wrap with twine; tie.

❺ Stamp thanks on cardstock; trim. Distress edges and adhere.

DESIGNER TIP

To prepare a fresh fern stem as a mask, place it between the pages of a book, such as a phone book, and place a weight on it for a few days until the stem is flat and dry. Or, place the stem between pieces of plain paper and press with an iron (no steam) until dry.

SUPPLIES: *Cardstock:* (Cajun) Bazzill Basics Paper; (cream) *Rubber stamp:* (thanks from Scripty Words set) Cornish Heritage Farms *Dye ink:* (Amaretto spray) Stewart Superior Corp.; (Close to Cocoa) Stampin' Up! *Specialty ink:* (Golden Terracotta shimmer spray) Tattered Angels *Accent:* (brown button brads) Karen Foster Design *Fibers:* (jute twine) SEI *Other:* (fern stem) **Finished size: 4¼" x 5½"**

SUPPLIES: *Cardstock:* (light green, cream, brown) *Patterned paper:* (Hansel from Gretel collection) Cosmo Cricket *Watermark ink:* Tsukineko *Embossing powder:* (Walnut Stain) Ranger Industries *Accents:* (brown flocked flower) Making Memories; (red brad) Karen Foster Design *Stickers:* (Smokey Joe's alphabet) American Crafts *Fibers:* (green embossed ribbon) Making Memories *Tools:* (2" circle, 2½" scalloped circle punches) Marvy Uchida *Other:* (fresh green leaf) **Finished size: 5½" square**

5 STEPS Teacher Gift Bag

Designer: Alisa Bangerter

❶ Adhere cardstock to bag.

❷ Cut cardstock piece. Cut apple in half; pat dry with paper towel. Apply paint to apple, stamp piece repeatedly, reapplying paint before each image. Let dry. Chalk edges of piece; adhere.

❸ Cut ruler to fit bag. Wrap raffia around ruler and tie through button. Adhere.

❹ Print sentiment on cardstock; trim. Chalk edges and adhere with foam tape.

DESIGNER TIPS

Stamped apple images look better if they don't stamp completely.

Practice stamping on scrap paper several times before stamping the actual project.

Apply several colors of paint to the apple before stamping to create a variegated and blended look.

SUPPLIES: *Cardstock:* (brown, cream) *Color medium:* (brown chalk) Craf-T Products *Paint:* (Meadow) Making Memories *Accent:* (brown button) *Fibers:* (natural raffia) *Font:* (CK Retro Block) www.scrapnfonts.com *Adhesive:* (foam tape) Making Memories *Other:* (cream gift bag) DMD, Inc.; (wood ruler, apple) **Finished size: 5¼" x 8½"**

Lovely Layers

Overlapping or layering paper crafting elements adds interest to any project, whether the style is funky, elegant, or anything in between. Get inspired by Stefanie Hamilton's examples of the many ways to layer paper, fibers, accents, and more.

LAYER TRANSPARENCIES OVER PATTERNED PAPER. Printed transparency sheets look great over plain cardstock, but really make a statement when layered over patterned paper.

PLACE CLEAR BUTTONS OVER PATTERNED PAPER. Use this technique to make a focal point pop.

LAYER FIBERS. Create touchable texture by layering lace trim over ribbon. The color showing through the lace adds interest as well.

COMBINE PATTERNS. Paper with different patterns creates an illusion of depth. Ink the layered edges to add definition.

USE RUB-ONS OVER STAMPED IMAGES. Create a stunning image by adding rub-ons over background stamps.

LAYER TEXTURES. Make embellishments truly unique by stacking similar items with different textures, such as paper flowers layered over felt flowers.

LIVEN UP PUNCHES. Punched accents become more vibrant and interesting when layered over an identical punched accent. Bend edges of the top layer up a bit to create dimension.

CREATE A 3-D EFFECT. Layer and curl several circles, each smaller than the last.

STACK BUTTONS. Adhere different sizes or shapes of buttons together, or tie them together with fibers to pull a project together.

Clever Borders & Boundaries

You may think that "living on the edge" is dangerous, but Wendy Johnson demonstrates that jazzing up the boundaries and edges of our projects is anything but "borderline."

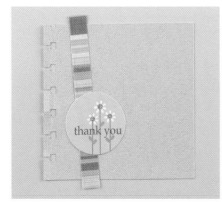

CREATE A NOTEBOOK EDGE. Use a punch to create this trendy decorative edge.

LAYER DIE CUTS TO CREATE A COLORFUL EDGE. Go crazy with your die cut machine and layer multi-colored shapes to create a whimsical, fun edge.

DRY EMBOSS AND CHALK A BORDER. Emboss—then chalk—a border to set off a sentiment.

FRINGE AN EDGE. Add texture to your projects by snipping the edge of cardstock to create fringe.

STAMP AND CUT AN EDGE. Stamp at the perimeter of a project, then cut around the outer lines to create a shaped edge.

PUNCH AND THREAD A BORDER. Thread ribbon through punched holes to create a border with dimension.

CUT A DECORATIVE-EDGE BORDER WITH SCISSORS. Layer cardstock trimmed with decorative-edge scissors for a quick border.

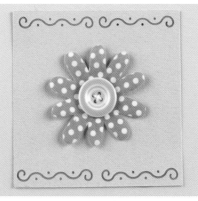

PUNCH AND LAYER A TWO-TONED BORDER. Use a punch repeatedly to create a border, and then layer a contrasting color underneath to make the punched images stand out.

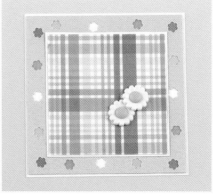

CREATE A MULTI-COLORED BORDER. Layer different colored cardstock underneath a punched frame for a dimensional, colorful effect.

Attention-Grabbing Color Pop

Make the most of your favorite black and white designs by adding a color pop—a bright, exciting spot of color that draws the eye. Kim Kesti shows some of the many different ways this technique can be used to create fabulous focal points on paper crafts.

BLING. To make a splash of color stand out even more, add a little bling. Rhinestones add light to the color, making the contrast really vivid.

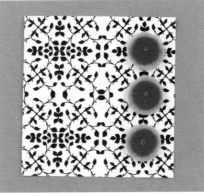

FELT. Felt accents not only draw the eye, they make you want to run your fingers over them, making felt a great attention-getter.

REPLACE WHITE SPACE WITH COLOR. Create additional interest by punching or cutting out part of a black and white pattern, then adhere colored cardstock behind the openings.

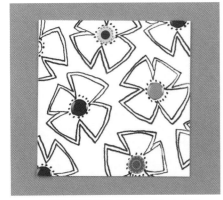

STAMPS AND STICKERS. Make a black and white background with a favorite stamp, and then add shine, dimension, and a dash of color with epoxy stickers.

MARKERS. Get out the markers, pick out a focal point, and start filling in the design for a fresh and vibrant look.

WATERCOLORS. For an artistic and elegant effect, add color pop with watercolors. Don't worry about color bleeding out beyond the design lines—that's part of the artistic charm.

FLOWERS. These accents are perfect for adding color, and it's easy to add a second color with a brad, sticker, or tag in the flower center.

STITCHING. With floss and a needle, any black and white design can be transformed into a rainbow of color.

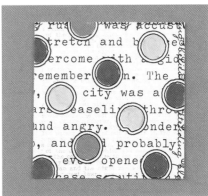

ACRYLIC PAINT. Create pop with acrylic paint for brilliant color, and get a bit of texture by not smoothing out the brush marks.

Monochromatic Magic

Learn how to use different shades and patterns within a single color family for a distinctive look. Celeste Rockwood-Jones demonstrates how easy it can be to create stunning effects when working with a singular color palette.

COMBINE ASSORTED ACCENTS. For an eclectic look, combine accents that are different shades of the same color.

MIX & MATCH PATTERNS. Use scraps of various patterned paper to fill a frame or cover a card. If the colors are similar, the different patterns will provide visual interest without being overwhelming.

STAMP CARDSTOCK WITH COORDINATING INK. Create a beautiful background by using a favorite stamp and inking it in the same tone as the cardstock.

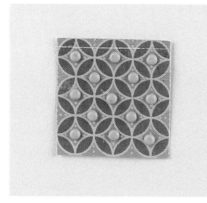

ADD ACCENTS TO ENHANCE DETAIL. Use brads, rhinestones, and other embellishments that are the same color as the underlying paper to draw attention to pattern details.

BRIGHTEN WITH BLING. Make projects sparkle by incorporating glitter, sequins, and other shiny accents.

INCREASE INTEREST WITH MONOCHROMATIC TEXTURES. In single-colored designs, texture adds depth and dimension.

LAYER PAPERS. Layer a patterned paper behind a similarly colored paper and add bling for a fabulous look.

CREATE A MIRROR EFFECT. Go half light-half dark in one color for sharp and stunning results. A ribbon in a similar shade ties both sides of the mirror effect together.

ACCENTUATE WITH A CONTRASTING COLOR. Create a project in a monochromatic scheme, and accent it with a different color.

Aging Beautifully

There's something special about the look of age when it comes to paper crafts. Aging lends depth, texture, and a sense that a project is truly special. Alice Golden explores the many different methods for adding a vintage feel to new paper and embellishments.

DRY-BRUSH WITH PAINT. Dry brushing paint over a textured paper makes the details really stand out.

CURL PAPER EDGES. Curl the edges of paper to make it look older. To enhance the appearance, sand paper edges before curling.

USE WALNUT INK. Sponge or wash paper or accents with walnut ink for instant aging.

EXPERIMENT WITH DISTRESSED EMBOSSING POWDER. Get vintage texture by embossing with this powder, then rubbing lightly to remove some of the crystals.

AGE WITH RUB-ONS. Trendy new rub-ons offer a distressed look with scratched, sponged, or splattered effects, creating age almost effortlessly.

APPLY A CRACKLE FINISH. Use a crackle finish that enables you to apply color and crackle medium simultaneously, achieving an aged effect faster.

CREATE DISTRESS DIGITALLY. Use digital brushes to add an ink-sponged appearance, or drop an aged frame onto a photo.

CRUMPLE PAPER. Crumple paper, and then slightly smooth it out. Lightly sand crumples for additional aging, or add depth by inking or color washing.

MIMIC AGE WITH SANDING. Add instant age by sanding the edges of paper or embellishments. Sand the surface of the accent for heavier aging.

Education is the key to **unlock** the golden door of **freedom.**

—George Washington Carver

The key to wisdom is knowing all the right questions.

—John A. Simone, Sr.

BE
MINE

Be My Valentine

When the heart speaks, the mind finds it indecent to object.

—Milan Kundera

Valentine's Day

Success is not the key to happiness. Happiness is the key to success. If you love what you are doing, you will be successful.

—Herman Cain

One of the keys to happiness is a bad memory

—Rita Mae Brown

LOVE
YA
BE
MINE

If you find it in your heart to care for someone else, you will have succeeded.

—Maya Angelou

Sentiments

Flowers
and butterflies
drift in color,
illuminating spring.

When my kids become
wild and unruly,
I use a nice, safe playpen.
When they're finished,
I climb out.

—Erma Bombeck

Happy Easter

When you meet someone
who can cook
and do housework,
don't hesitate a minute
—marry him.

—Unknown

"How does one become a butterfly?" she asked.
"You must want to fly so much
that you are willing to give up being a caterpillar."

—Trina Paulus

If I had my life to live over,
I would start barefoot
earlier in the spring and
stay that way later in the fall.

—Nadine Stair

Anyone can be passionate,
but it takes real lovers to be silly.

—Rose Franken

Congratulations

Visit our web sites:

www.PaperCraftsMag.com
www.PaperCraftsConnection.com

May peace be your gift at Christmas
and your blessing all year through!
—Unknown

Never worry about
the size of your tree.
In the eyes of children,
they're all 30 feet tall.
—Larry Wilde

Nothing purchased can come close to
the renewed sense of gratitude for
having family and friends.
— Courtland Milloy

May peace be your gift
at Christmas and your
blessing all year through!

MERRY CHRISTMAS

GIVE THANKS

HAPPY HOLIDAYS

Merry Christmas

Sentiments

I love you, not only for what you are, but for what I am when I am with you.
—Roy Croft

"When you are in love you can't sleep because reality is better than your dreams."
—Dr. Seuss

Be Mine

"A kiss is a lovely trick, designed by nature, to stop words when speech becomes superfluous."
—Ingrid Bergman

two lives, two ♥s joined together in friendship, united forever in love. —anonymous ♥

XOXO

Happy Valentine's Day

Visit our web sites:
www.PaperCraftsMag.com
www.PaperCraftsConnection.com

FATHERHOOD is pretending the present you love most is soap-on-a-rope.
—Bill Cosby

A *daughter* is a *little girl* who grows up to be *a friend.*

A man's work is from sun to sun, but a mother's work is never done.

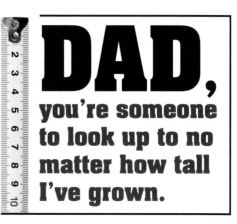

DAD, you're someone to look up to no matter how tall I've grown.

Happy Mother's Day

Happy Father's Day

a good laugh IS SUNSHINE in the house.
-William Makepeace Thackeray

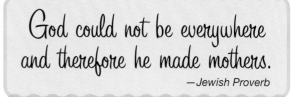

God could not be everywhere and therefore he made mothers.
—Jewish Proverb

Index

Index CONTINUED...

PAPER CRAFTS MAGAZINE®

Visit our social sites and say "Hello".

Find us on **Facebook**   Follow us on **twitter**

Shop online anytime at
www.PaperCraftsMag.com/shop
or visit our websites:
www.PaperCraftsMag.com
www.PaperCraftsConnection.com